Go Tell the Crocodiles

Go Tell the Crocodiles

CHASING PROSPERITY IN MOZAMBIQUE

Rowan Moore Gerety

THE NEW PRESS

25 YEARS

NEW YORK
LONDON

Requests for permission to reproduce selections from this book should be mailed to:
Permissions Department, The New Press, 120 Wall Street, 31st floor, New York,
NY 10005.

Published in the United States by The New Press, New York, 2017
Distributed by Two Rivers Distribution
ISBN 978-1-62097-277-9 (e-book)

LIBRARY OF CONGRESS CATALOGING-IN-PUBLICATION DATA
Names: Gerety, Rowan Moore, author.
Title: Go tell the crocodiles : chasing prosperity in Mozambique / Rowan
    Moore Gerety.
Description: New York : New Press, 2018. | Includes bibliographical
    references.
Identifiers: LCCN 2017042781 | ISBN 9781620972762 (hc : alk. paper)
Subjects: LCSH: Informal sector (Economics)—Mozambique. |
    Mozambique—Economic conditions—21st century. | Mozambique—Social
    conditions—21st century.
Classification: LCC HC890 .G47 2018 | DDC 330.9679053—dc23 LC
    record available at https://lccn.loc.gov/2017042781

The New Press publishes books that promote and enrich public discussion and
understanding of the issues vital to our democracy and to a more equitable
world. These books are made possible by the enthusiasm of our readers; the support
of a committed group of donors, large and small; the collaboration of our many
partners in the independent media and the not-for-profit sector; booksellers, who
often hand-sell New Press books; librarians; and above all by our authors.

www.thenewpress.com

Composition by Westchester Publishing Services
This book was set in ACaslonPro

Printed in the United States of America

2   4   6   8   10   9   7   5   3   1

For Lena

Contents

Introduction
It All Happens on the Margins
MAPUTO/BEIRA

Antes deles quererem partilhar o país, antes deles quererem partilhar os recursos, antes deles quererem partilhar o poder, eles já privatizaram a história . . . já fizeram a partilha da história.

Before they tried to divvy up the country, before they tried to divvy up our natural resources and political power, they had already privatized history, they had already divvied up history itself.

—CARLOS NUNO CASTEL-BRANCO[1]

Dom Jaime Pedro Gonçalves answered the door with a probing squint, peering through horn-rimmed glasses on the other side of a screen. He came outside and invited me to sit down, a tall man bent with age, soft curls of white hair at his temples. "I want to talk with you about peace," I said, first quietly, and then loudly. The seventy-five-year-old bishop cocked his head to hear, smiled slyly, and raised an eyebrow. "The subject of peace in Mozambique is very sensitive," he said. "Very sensitive."

It's true. It was a sensitive moment to be asking about the state of play in Mozambique. The parties in the country's grinding

1

sixteen-year civil war, which ended in 1992, had returned to violence after twenty years of fragile stability. The leader of Renamo,
the opposition party, was holed up in the bush while his men
staged ambushes on convoys of trucks and passenger buses under
military escort, recalling the terrorizing tactics of the 1980s. Thousands of Mozambicans had fled their homes to Malawi, which
once sheltered more than half a million Mozambican refugees
during the civil war.[2] It appeared that troops under the direction
of the party in power, Frelimo, or the Frente de Libertação de
Moçambique, had ransacked villages and burned the homes of
people they accused of supporting the opposition. This renewed
violence had only exacerbated Mozambique's worsening economic
crisis. A steep drop in commodity prices put billion-dollar natural gas and mining projects on hold, while a series of corruption
scandals revealed the rot at the core of large state-owned corporations. Mozambique's currency, the metical, lost a third of its
value in 2015 alone.[3]

Dom Jaime, as people in Beira affectionately called him, was the
retired Catholic archbishop of Mozambique's second most important city. Twenty-five years earlier, Dom Jaime had been a lead
facilitator in the negotiations that brought peace to Mozambique
in the first place. It was Dom Jaime who, in 1988, had boarded a
South African military plane in his clerical vestments and
landed in the bush in the dead of night. There, sitting by a camp-
fire surrounded by men with AK-47s, he'd dared to broach the
subject of peace with Afonso Dhlakama, the leader of the Resis-
tencia Nacional Moçambicana, or Renamo, a group the government often referred to as *bandidos armados*—armed bandits. "When
I went to talk with him," Dom Jaime recalled, he asked, "'So—
can you guys help me end this war?'" Dom Jaime laughed out
loud. "I said, 'Yes: I'm not here for tourism!'"

Surely, if anyone could speak freely, he could. Dom Jaime dis-
agreed adamantly. "You can't speak about [peace] openly, because

Frelimo won't accept it," he said. The problem wasn't uttering the word "peace" so much as suggesting what concessions the ruling party might have to make to achieve it. "Violence is all [Dhlakama] has," Dom Jaime said. "We need to create an environment for democracy, so that his party can be a political party and not an army. But nobody in Frelimo accepts that premise. Who's shouting 'peace' anyway? The president himself goes around saying 'Peace, peace!'" He paused, incredulous. "But then—you're the one who's president!" he said. "You say you want peace and you can't get it? It's a joke."

Fundamentally, Gonçalves saw the simmering conflict as a struggle over what promised to be boundless wealth from recently discovered reservoirs of natural gas in the Rovuma river basin, near the border with Tanzania. As we spoke, he pointed out, Frelimo's powerful Central Committee had just finished a meeting in Maputo. The occasion was billed as a reshuffling of the upper ranks of the party's political operation; Dom Jaime was convinced there were other items on the agenda.[4] "The Comité Central met yesterday all of a sudden," he said. "For what? To plunder the riches of the Rovuma!" His eyes widened sternly. "The resources of this country don't belong to the state, but to the party," he said, referring to Frelimo. "And whoever is the head of the party says how it will be. They say they want peace. What peace?" Both sides had participated in ambushes against civilians, he said, fighting over control of the country's economy while its citizens continued to live in poverty. "They've declared war," he said. "It's a full-on war. You see, Renamo wants some of the riches of the Rovuma, but now Frelimo has said, 'No!'"

For a moment, Gonçalves seemed indignant with the whole line of questioning implicit in the idea of talking about peace. "So, how will it be?" he asked. "A citizen like me, what can I say? It's very hard to get a grasp on politics in Africa. It's the politics of dictatorship," he said. "They do what they want."

His tone shifted. "I've been to the United States," he said. "I've been to Canada—I studied there. And, in fact, I was amazed with American life, Canadian life—that the citizens have real freedom of speech. They choose their leaders freely. . . . How is that? Life is beautiful! Citizens compete for education, for a better livelihood. . . . On weekends, they go out to hear singers. The good life, isn't it? I enjoyed life in a democracy," he said wistfully. "Here, you can't talk."

Dom Jaime Gonçalves died at home exactly two months later. He had allowed me to record our conversation on the condition that I would not share it publicly. "Forgive me," he said. "I know that I have a lot to say about peace, because I've worked for peace. I'm an old man, sitting here now, and my old age has come in the service of peace, of reconciliation between Renamo and the government."

It was moving, frightening even, to hear a man who had shown such courage and leadership in the quest for peace silenced by the threat of violence in the twilight of his life. Privately, Dom Jaime offered a biting rebuke of Mozambique's government and of its backers in the West. It was the United States and Europe, he contended, that allowed the country to turn its back on the promise of the 1992 peace accords he had worked so hard to achieve. And since he need not fear retribution in death, I hope he would approve of my sharing his clarion call here.

Africa's "Success Story"

On my first visit to Mozambique, as a tourist in 2008, I remember being awed at how laid-back it all seemed. Maputo was not the feverish African capital of my imagination, but a sleepy city of Soviet-style apartment buildings and warrens of sheet-metal roofs under a haze of hot sun and Latin-accented *marrabenta* music. Security guards and day laborers greeted me everywhere with an enthusiastic thumbs-up, a gesture to match the universal greeting *Tudo bem?* (Everything good?) Time-rich and cash-poor, people were impossibly polite and unbelievably generous, offering a spare seat, a glass of beer, and unhurried conversation at every turn.

From Maputo, I hitchhiked partway up the coast with a white South African who ran a container-lifting business at the port in Beira. Through vast expanses of coconut palms and thorny acacia trees, we passed village after roadside village where bundles of firewood and neatly packed sacks of charcoal lined the shoulder. The most obvious sign of the war, to my eye, was simply the awful state of the roads. Mozambique's coastline covers an expanse that would stretch from San Diego to well past the Canadian border. Yet when we reached the turnoff at Inchope, a hardscrabble crossroads of container trucks and stalls selling fried food, after eighteen hours of driving, I could scarcely believe how little ground we'd covered. Already, I'd traveled through regions speaking six different languages, yet two-thirds of the country still stretched out before me to the north.

Mozambique's majestic Y-shaped outline, like the maps of so many other African countries, is a consequence of an accommodation between natural boundaries—lakes, rivers, mountains—and colonial ambitions, reached at the end of the nineteenth century without regard for the ethnic and cultural ties the border cleaved in two. Slender Malawi wriggles down into the middle of the country. From South Africa to Tanzania, the coast is a long chain of breathtaking beaches, with the influence of medieval Muslim trade routes felt more and more strongly as you work your way north. Inland, a broad plateau of dry savannah gradually gives way to forests and chains of knobby granite mountains, meeting the highlands of Zambia and Zimbabwe.

For a long time, independent Mozambique seemed to some to be following a period of extraordinarily painful history with an equally remarkable recovery. Until 1975, Mozambique endured a brutal, if uneven, Portuguese presence dating to March of 1498, when Vasco da Gama first sailed up the coast and anchored off Ilha de Moçambique.[5] According to one early Portuguese account, da Gama's cannons had bombarded the town three times over by the time he sailed for India at the end of the month.[6] Today, you can still visit the oldest European building in the Southern Hemisphere, a small Catholic chapel made of coral limestone on the northern tip of the island, built in 1522.

The Portuguese Empire extended its reach in Mozambique over the course of centuries. The sale of slaves, gold, and ivory along the coast and waterways eventually gave way to *prazos*, or plantations. The *prazos* produced cotton, sugar, and peanuts for companies chartered by the Crown but often operating completely outside its influence.[7] From the late nineteenth century, the colonial government acted as a broker in men, earning rents for sending Mozambican men to the gold mines dotting South Africa's Witwatersrand Basin.[8] Those who failed to pay taxes or maintain formal employment had a "moral obligation" to give their labor to the colony, building much of the colonial capital, Lourenço Marques, in forced six-month terms.[9] Another form of forced labor took hold in agriculture, farther north, as colonial enterprises extracted profits by using state-sanctioned violence to boost recruitment and production quotas. Under Portugal's dictatorial "new state," in the mid-twentieth century, the country looked more and more to output from its colonies to propel development at home.

Like Zimbabwe, Namibia, Guinea-Bissau, and Algeria, Mozambique was forged in a violent struggle for independence that culminated in a break from Portugal in 1975. As in Eritrea, the Democratic Republic of the Congo, and Angola, independence in Mozambique was quickly followed by a protracted war fought in part through Cold War proxy, with support from foreign governments.

In the mid-1980s, the devastation of the civil war pushed Frelimo to abandon the hard-line Marxism of its early years and turn to capitalism for relief. Frelimo applied to join the World Bank and the International Monetary Fund, paving the way for rigid economic reforms backed by the Reagan administration. Exxon got independent Mozambique's first oil exploration contract; Lehman Brothers was hired to advise the government in restructuring its debt.[10] But by 1990 Mozambique was officially the poorest country in the world.[11] As then president Joaquim Chissano put it in a speech in Maputo,

> The US said, "Open yourself to . . . the World Bank, and IMF." What happened? . . . We are told now: "Marxism! You are devils. Change this policy." OK. Marxism is gone. Open market economy. OK, Frelimo is trying to create capitalism. . . . We went to Reagan and I said, "I want money for the private sector to boost people who want to develop a bourgeoisie." Answer: $10 million, then $15 million more, then another $15 million. You tell me to do away with Marxism, the Soviet Union and give me [only] $40 million. OK, we have changed. Now they say, "If you don't go to a multiparty system, don't expect help from us."

Mozambique devalued its currency, slowed reconstruction projects, and slashed salaries for civil servants all in the service of meeting the IMF's terms for joining the global economy.[12] Thanks to IMF-backed reforms, a doctor on the government payroll earned $350 a month in 1991, $175 a month in 1993, and less than $100 a month by 1996.[13] For two decades beginning in 1993, Mozambique notched year after year of impressive growth (GDP annual growth averaged 8.6 percent from 1993 to 2012) as the economy clawed its way back from the incalculable damage of back-to-back wars.[14]

By 2004, when Mozambique elected its second president in a decade of multiparty elections, more than twenty African countries essentially had presidents for life.[15] Robert Mugabe, José Eduardo dos Santos, and Isaias Afwerki were all freedom fighters turned despots. Mozambique, however, had democratic elections praised by international observers.[16] Tourism had begun to flourish on the Indian Ocean beaches of the country's meandering two-thousand-mile coastline.[17] Donors funded major health, education, and economic development programs, support that made up more than a quarter of Mozambique's GDP from 1995 to 2010 and, at times, more than half the government budget.[18]

"Success story?" asked the journalist Joseph Hanlon in the title of an article published in 1997, arguing that IMF reforms essentially put the interests of Mozambique's foreign creditors and investors ahead of those of its citizens.[19] Rock-bottom salaries for civil servants, he argued, only encouraged corruption and poor service. Banking restrictions meant that local companies were at a disadvantage in competing with multinationals.

"The newspapers hint at trouble just beneath the surface," Jeremy Weinstein, an American graduate student, wrote in 2002 as donors praised President Chissano for vowing not to run for a third term: "Two major bank failures, the assassination of the country's most respected independent journalist, the continued depreciation of the currency, and stop-and-start talks between [Frelimo] and [Renamo]."[20]

Fifteen years later, you could write the same paragraph almost verbatim. Yet for most of the intervening years, lenders (the IMF, the World Bank) and donors (the U.S. and European governments) have largely stuck to the notion that Mozambique's continued economic growth offset any troubling signs of inequality or political discord.[21] "Following a long civil war, Mozambique has made the transition to peace, stability and sustained economic growth," reads the "About Mozambique" section of the USAID mission's website, "providing an essential link between landlocked neighbors and the global marketplace."[22]

In 2013, the IMF published a study called "Africa's Success: More Than a Resource Story," profiling the high-octane economies of Mozambique and five other African countries. "The main takeaway from the country cases is what my colleagues called a virtuous circle," writes Antoinette Sayeh, director of the IMF's sub-Saharan Africa program, in a blog post announcing the report. "All six countries carried out sensible and medium term–oriented policymaking and important structural reforms, which in turn attracted higher aid flows and made it possible for these countries to receive debt relief, releasing their own resources."[23]

Released indeed, but for whom? The single largest private sector project in Mozambique—responsible for nearly a third of exports—is an aluminum smelter that consumes nearly half the country's electricity but employs just over a thousand people. For every dollar Mozal earns the Mozambican government, its foreign backers earn twenty-one.[24] In the south, Frelimo's Strategic Plan for Agricultural Development includes a large-scale rice-farming project led by the Chinese corporation Wanbao, which stripped thousands of farmers of their land without compensation. Farther north, subsistence farmers have had to make way for South African bananas and Brazilian soybeans, even as the productivity of Mozambique's small farms has declined since the 1990s.

One of the most striking sights in Nampula, the northern provincial capital ringed by some of Mozambique's largest megaprojects, is the massive granite dome just east of the city, where dozens of informal rock quarries operate around the clock. Smoke rises from the rock before dawn and long past dusk as small groups of two to five men stoke fires to heat the granite where it is vulnerable to cracking. They whittle away at the inselberg—a mass of rock some five hundred feet high and a half mile across—with picks, sledgehammers, and crowbars. The mountain is carted away wheelbarrow by wheelbarrow. It's backbreaking work that yields barely enough to live, yet it employs far more men than the $1 billion ilmenite mine on Nampula's coast.

As I write, a stream of crises has stripped the veneer from Mozambique's much-touted success. Donors and international institutions that long acknowledged "challenges" and "short-comings" in their otherwise sunny appraisals have been forced to reckon with the consequences of Mozambique's path to capitalism.[25]

Politically motivated assassinations took the lives of nine Renamo officials in 2016 alone, leading some to suggest the existence of a hit squad linked to Mozambique's secret police. Both judge and prosecutor in a high-profile case targeting a kidnapping ring were murdered two years apart. Police ended an investigation of the judge's death for lack of progress; a suspect in the prosecutor's murder recently broke out of jail.[26] Gilles Cistac, a prominent constitutional lawyer at the leading public university, was gunned down as he drank his customary espresso on a Tuesday morning in downtown Maputo.[27] Cistac had made the mistake of suggesting a legal framework for a power-sharing arrangement between Renamo and Frelimo.

After four years of on-again, off-again fighting, Renamo and Frelimo have entered a delicate cease-fire. It's still unclear how the conflict will ultimately be resolved. International mediators went home at the end of 2016, unable to extract meaningful concessions from either side. Renamo leader Afonso Dhlakama "wants power Frelimo won't give him," Dom Jaime said. As it is, Dhlakama remains in the bush near Renamo's wartime head-quarters, conducting negotiations with President Filipe Nyusi via cell phone.[28] He's said he's fearful of coming out of hiding because he could be assassinated. But if Mozambique's next presidential election is to be held successfully, Dhlakama, who earned 37 percent of the vote and an outright majority in half of

Mozambique's provinces in 2014, will have to campaign in public.

Most damaging of all has been the specter of kleptocracy Dom Jaime raised so starkly on his porch: "The country's wealth doesn't belong to the state, but to the party," he said. Over two decades, many in Frelimo's old guard, along with two presidents and their families, have used their ties to the state to accumulate vast wealth with impunity.[29] At the grassroots, Mozambicans have long bemoaned the *cabritismo*, or "goat-ism," of hospital workers and border guards, from the adage that "a goat eats where it is tied."[30]

It's only recently that *cabritismo* has reached a scale that threatens to bring down the whole economy with it. In 2016, it was revealed that the government had taken out $2.2 billion in secret loans over the past several years to fund three newly formed state companies with ties to Mozambique's security services (SISE).[31] Three hundred fifty million dollars went to buy boats for a failed tuna-fishing venture. Hundreds of millions more bought military hardware from around the world—France, Germany, China, Israel, Sweden, the United States. Many observers speculated that prices on some of the deals had been inflated to line the pockets of Frelimo's elite.

At the outset, Mozambican leaders might have expected that the "wealth of the Rovuma," as Dom Jaime put it, would allow them to repay the secret loans in time without incident. But the new debt coincided with a drop in global commodity prices that put major gas and oil projects on hold, helping to send inflation out of control. Credit rating agencies downgraded Mozambican debt as donors pulled back and the government defaulted on loan repayments. The scandal sparked the biggest confrontation between Mozambique and its Western backers since the end of the civil war. And yet, as noted by Hanlon, now a development scholar and all-around chronicler of Mozambique, "had it not been for the

unexpected drop in oil and gas prices, lenders and donors probably would have allowed it to pass with little comment and a small
slap on the wrist."[32]

Dom Jaime became visibly frustrated when I asked him what
role he thought foreign governments played in Mozambique's ongoing political and economic crises. "They support Frelimo's policies
because they're buying Mozambique's wealth," he sputtered. "What
do you think the Americans are spending so much money on
here? On peace?

"I spoke to the European Union. I told them, 'You're the ones
responsible for the failure of democracy in Mozambique, because
as long as we've had elections in Mozambique, Frelimo has done as
it pleased. Frelimo holds elections all by itself and then imposes the
results on the people. And then the European Union says, "Long
live freedom in Mozambique!"'"

Even when international observers acknowledge that there's been
electoral fraud or misuse of state resources during political campaigns, "even then, Renamo has to accept the results," Dom Jaime
said. "Your government shouldn't be playing this double game," he
said. "Money for Frelimo, and 'peace, peace, peace.'"

Implicit in Dom Jaime's critique is the idea that Mozambique's
embrace of global capitalism has always been more important to
Western backers than issues of corruption and governance.[33] The
secret debt fiasco was made possible, on the one hand, by the
willingness of foreign companies to profit from suspect deals for
military hardware, and, on the other, by the failure of European
banks to perform due diligence on the loans guaranteed by the
government in Maputo. The president of France himself was on
hand for a photo op when Frelimo inked a $300 million deal with
a shipyard on the English Channel; when the first illegal loan
was discovered, the IMF asked only that it be documented in the
national budget.[34]

The Rapper

Five years before I met Dom Jaime, I'd been to a lecture by a rapper called Azagaia that offered my first glimpse of the themes at the center of this book. The venue was a packed auditorium on the campus of Universidade Eduardo Mondlane, in Maputo, named after Mozambique's most famous freedom fighter. Azagaia had studied geology there just a few years earlier, when he was still called Edson da Luz. *Azagaias*, I learned later, were the curved spears warriors in Mozambique's Muenemutapa Empire used in the sixteenth century to fight off the earliest advances of Portuguese colonialism.

Azagaia told the crowd he was growing his hair out in protest. His hair wasn't long yet, perhaps two inches coiled in cloud-like tufts he pulled at for show, but it got a good reaction. "It's a peaceful protest against bad governance," he said, smiling but apparently not joking. Azagaia urged the audience, 150 or so of the country's best students, to join him.

"If you want to know what this country is really like today, talk to your maids and gardeners," he told them. He railed against the country's utter dependence on South African imports at the grocery store, and against under-the-table exports of vast expanses of forest in the form of whole logs. "We won't cut our hair until our demands are met," he said. Azagaia hoped to redefine the priorities of the leaders he held responsible for the sorry state of Mozambican politics.

The theme of the talk was government corruption, and as he connected the dots between bribes at traffic stops and state contracts doled out in secret, Azagaia returned again and again to a single point: "Africa *é informal*," he said. "What we're seeing in this country is the informal being institutionalized: Everything important here happens on the margins."

At the time, I'd been in Mozambique less than two weeks, based at the university's nearby African Studies Center on a Fulbright fellowship. I was there to do research on cell phone use, but Azagaia's observations seemed to follow me wherever I went.

At the building where I stayed in downtown Maputo, apartment owners paid the doorman a small salary, but most of his income came from another, off-the-books source: the job gave him control of an empty hallway in the atrium, along with the space beneath the stairs, which he rented out to dozens of sidewalk merchants who stored their things there overnight. Early every morning a steady stream of vendors came through the lobby with the doorman's blessing to collect huge bundles of women's shoes and clothing tied up in black plastic. In the evenings they returned to drop off their inventory before heading home to far-flung neighborhoods on the outskirts of Maputo.

In Mozambique a side hustle is called a *biscate*. It's Portuguese for "odd job"—literally a beak-full of work. Everyone has one. I met doormen who wove baskets and repaired bicycles or resoled shoes for the families of maids who worked in the apartments above. Outside the city, housekeepers with access to refrigerators sold ice-cold water to construction workers nearby. Security guards in uniform sold cigarettes and phone credit.

In my building, a stark midcentury block of concrete built for Portuguese colonists, the original plumbing system had long since been supplanted by a series of makeshift fixes. The pipes were still there, buried behind the walls, but they'd been dry for years. Water came, instead, through the tangles of exposed PVC that snaked their way up a back stairwell and entered the apartment over the balcony wall.

All these workarounds revealed a society where formal institutions—the police, elections—simply held less sway than I was used to, where the drive to solve problems seldom passed through official channels. Corruption itself is a kind of workaround, but the phenomenon Azagaia described was much broader. There were, of course, standards and rules of engagement for political and economic life, but it often seemed that the most important ones ran counter to what was written down or enshrined in law.

One day, I went with a colleague, Eduardo Jossias, to see a plot of land where he planned to build a house across the river from Maputo. On our way, we stopped by the local store, a bright cube of royal blue on an otherwise empty stretch of road. Behind it were four men sitting in the shade of a mango tree around a bottle of red wine, carrying on gaily. They were not all that old, but they still had barely enough teeth among them for a single mouth, let alone four. The one who seemed to be in charge was a large bald man with a mustache and a pair of Chinese aviator sunglasses perched crookedly on his nose. They were thrilled to see Jossias, greeting him with calls of "Pai!" and laughing until we left.

Jossias described the bald man as the *dono da terra*. I suspect he meant something more than "landowner": he was a big man around Catembe. I asked what his line of business was. "He has a *discoteca*, he has two big stores. He went and lived in Swaziland for twenty years and accumulated some money, and now he's *o rico de aqui*"—the rich man from here, Jossias said. Jossias seemed to be on friendly terms with the lone policeman stationed in the middle of the road to Ponto d'Ouro. The two exchanged small talk on the way out and the officer waved us onward on the way back.

Jossias got great amusement out of telling a story about the cop and the bald man. The cop had stopped a young man from the area for something or other and found him to be insufficiently deferential. The young man spoke impatiently and without apology. Eventually, he shrugged the officer off and simply walked away. What good was it wearing a uniform? Feeling slighted by the encounter, the policeman went to the bald man to complain of a "lack of respect." "Can you see what it's like here?" Jossias asked.

"That a cop will go to a local guy for something like that? He was looking for a solution."

When it came to researching cell phones—the purpose that had brought me to Mozambique—I wasn't getting very far. Phone companies were reluctant to prize open their files and offer any data that would help me understand how and where coverage was growing. Cities and towns were claiming an ever-growing number of young people and strivers from the Mozambican countryside, and I was interested in understanding how cell phones influenced urbanization. The farmers and workers I tried to interview were universally friendly and accommodating, but they often found my questions beside the point. Yes, I have a cell phone, they'd say, earnest and a bit perplexed. It's great; I just don't have enough money to use it.

Occasionally, these interviews did turn up interesting tidbits. In Nampula, I spoke to a young woodcarver, Tino, who came to the city from the Mueda plateau, a storied but dry and isolated corner of Mozambique that had been pivotal in the struggle for independence. Tino and I met one morning in a sleepy café down the hill from where he worked, and he nursed a bottle of Rhino gin while we talked. Asked what he used his cell phone for, Tino repeated an answer I'd heard from many others: "sickness and death."

Tino told me a story from two years before we met. There was no electricity or cell phone service in the part of Mueda where his extended family lived, but an uncle kept a phone. Another relative had given it to him on a visit from the city, and he charged the phone when he could to listen to the radio on it or on the rare occasion when he needed to get in touch with someone in Nampula.

One day, Tino was surprised to get a missed call from his uncle: people in the city call the country, not the other way round. Tino assured me his uncle wouldn't call just to say hello.

With so many people chronically short of minutes, Mozambicans have devised ingenious systems to make the best of the things they are able to do for free on their cell phones. They send promotional text messages with advertisements followed by the words "please call me," or they send "beeps," when the caller hangs up before anyone can answer and start draining the caller's credit. Since only outgoing calls are billed, the question of who calls whom is an important one, intricately tied up with social expectations about wealth.

Seeing his uncle's beep, Tino knew he had only a short window to respond. To make a call at all, you had to walk to the top of a hill an hour away from the village. His uncle would stand there for a few minutes waiting for a call back. But Tino had no credit either. So he did the only thing he could do: he sent a text message, hoping that his uncle had brought along a younger relative who could read: "Uncle: tell us what's going on. Once if sickness, twice if death."

When word came back to Nampula in the form of two *liga me*'s—"please call me" messages—Tino told his grandmother. It took three days to raise money for bus fare and for funeral offerings among friends and relatives in Nampula. Tino's grandmother left for Mueda with a big bag of rice. "She didn't even know who had died when she left," Tino explained, "but she went to see the grave. When the family tells us something that way, they only try to inform us and don't check in again. Money doesn't live in our pockets, so they know we won't be able to come the same day."

This story captured everything I'd heard about cell phones so far: their usefulness, their expense, the ingenuity borne of spotty coverage, the influence of illiteracy. Most of all, though, it highlighted the sheer drive to pragmatism, the search for an improvised solution where an organized system comes up short. It was a theme I'd come to think of as a corollary to Azagaia's talk at the university—the reason, as I saw it, so much happened on the margins. In the government, the dominance of the informal may well represent corruption, but for the rest of the country, the margins were simply wider than the page.

Gradually, I came to see my gleanings about cell phones as part of the larger theme of informality, one that offered a much richer view of Mozambican society when taken whole. Tino and his brother, Beto, were part of a woodcarving cooperative that operated out of the courtyard of the Museu Nacional de Etnografia, turning misshapen logs of ebony and rosewood into ornamental elephants and interlocking columns of human bodies they sold to tourists. On one visit, Beto explained that they also did a decent trade in custom-carved car and machine parts. They made the geared wheels that made CD-ROM drives work, and handles for stoves and soft-serve machines. They made motorcycle brake calipers and parts for film projectors and peanut grinders, a universe of spare parts that the formal economy simply couldn't deliver reliably to northern Mozambique.

In another neighborhood, I spoke with the local headman, Nuanhua, who had watched the countryside where he grew up get swallowed by the city as migrants poured in after Mozambique's long civil war. He told me when the first cell phone tower had gone up and how many families had moved there in the last year.

Then he mentioned casually that his family's ancestral graveyard was now covered with houses, and took me to see it. Owning land is illegal in Mozambique—a holdover from the country's Marxist beginnings—yet here was a place where the workings of an underground real estate market were as plain as day: plot by plot, someone had sold off the Nuanhua family cemetery, and tiny stucco houses had gone up amid the graves. It was an illustration of the chasm between the official world and the reality Mozambicans grappled with on a daily basis. If I wanted to understand the texture of everyday life in Mozambique, cell phones weren't necessarily the best way in.

Life on the Margins

Everywhere in Mozambique, people have devised informal solutions to get by where development has failed: turning to the church for "spiritual cures" where modern health care is unavailable, or digging up rubies and tourmaline by hand after dark to avoid detection by the multinationals that own Mozambique's richest gem fields. This book explores the efforts of ordinary people to provide for themselves where foreign aid, the formal economy, and the government have been unable to. In some cases, these DIY strategies work; in others, they fail completely. In rural areas where the cash economy is tethered to passing cars and buses, you'll find merchants clustered near bad potholes and beside speed bumps— acutely aware that the best chance of making a sale comes where traffic moves slowly. The roadside economy can be especially brutal, though, too. Regular stops draw scores of vendors holding plastic buckets of produce aloft toward open car windows, desperate to make a sale amid a crush of people all selling the very same thing— oranges or bananas, peanuts or avocados. Sales opportunities come sporadically and last a few minutes at best. Prices tumble by the second. City-dwelling passengers roll down a window, demand the last, best offer for a chicken dangling by the legs, and rev their engines, threatening to leave without buying anything at all. Goats go for six or seven dollars, pineapples for a quarter.

In the markets, cardboard boxes are flattened and rolled into tight cylinders, then bound with string to make lightweight stools. Blacksmiths repurpose discarded car radiators to make a more efficient bellows. No effort is spared to extract a day's pay from the resources at hand. On the slopes of Mount Mabu, a mountain in northern Mozambique where British biologists have identified dozens of previously unknown species of birds, plants, and reptiles since 2005, I met a man who had just felled a tree well over a hundred feet tall, its trunk as large as the pylons that support a highway overpass.[35] It had taken two days, but he had extracted several gal-lons of wild honey from a hive high in the canopy, enough to fill a jerrican and make the long trip to town by bicycle. The payoff would be $40. How much, I wondered, would the tree be worth if only he had a means to mill the timber and sell that too? Or else, I thought, what could the man have done with a long ladder or a climbing rope?

I've tried to explore the lives of people in Mozambique to uncover broader challenges to twenty-first-century development through-out Africa: Can you fix a refugee system that abets human traf-ficking? Can you move beyond the specter of violence when a warlord leads the political opposition? Bookended by Ghana in 1957 and Zimbabwe in 1980, more than fifty countries in sub-Saharan Africa gained independence in a period of less than twenty-five years. Now, half a century into the era of African in-dependence, each of these nations is struggling to forge a new path beyond a shared history of colonialism, war, and underdevel-opment, to shore up fragile institutions that have yet to supplant the power of the informal. Along the way, Azagaia's observations still ring true: the see-and-saw of daily life happens on the margins.

The stories in this book were reported primarily over the course of two trips to Mozambique: the first nearly a year, from March 2011 to February 2012, and the second for the month of February 2016. Most interviews were conducted in Portuguese. I have tried to note the exceptions, particularly in instances where I relied on transla-tions from people who are present in the stories themselves.

I regret that this has turned out to be a book that leans heavily toward the voices and experiences of men. In part, that's a feature of the stories I zeroed in on: one chapter focuses on a group of migrants made up almost entirely of men, another focuses on the mostly male entourage of a militia leader turned politician. At times, the slant of my reporting was exacerbated by realities on the ground. Where I have written about people in positions of power, for instance, they are far more likely to be men than women, something that is broadly true across Mozambican society. The few interviews with women that are featured here sometimes arose out of my insistence that men not do all the talking. Nevertheless, as men's voices surfaced in the course of my travels, I wish I had done more to address the imbalance.

The book also bears the marks of my particular experience in other ways: the bulk of the stories here took place in the four of Mozambique's ten provinces where I spent the most time. And, had I set out to write this book again today, I might have included chapters on both climate change and HIV/AIDS, two important social problems that are not much discussed.

Azagaia first came to prominence in 2008, when, during proceedings for World Press Freedom Week, hosted in Maputo, prosecutors from the attorney general's office summoned him to explain the lyrics to a song called "People in Power."

With so many foreign journalists crowded into cafés and conference rooms in the capital, the prosecutors didn't detain Azagaia or formally charge him with a crime. But they did press him with questions about the song for nearly two hours: Did he write it himself? Why? Didn't he think it could provoke people to violence?

The song was written as a response to riots that had swept through Maputo a month earlier, when the government's announcement of fare hikes for public transit became a proxy for a broad array of grievances: corruption, unemployment, the price of flour, the price of rent.

> Senhor presidente, largaste o luxo do teu palácio
> Finalmente te apercebeste que a vida aqui não está fácil . . .
> Se a polícia é violenta
> Respondemos com violência
> Muda a causa pra mudares a consequência . . .

Baixa a tarifa do transporte ou sobe o salário mínimo
Xeeeeeeee . . . isso é o que deves fazer no mínimo
À não ser que queiras fogo nas bombas de gasolina
Assaltos a padarias, ministérios, imagina
Destruir os vossos bancos comerciais, a vossa mina
Governação irracional parece que contamina.

"Mr. President, you've left the luxury of your palace / And finally realized life here isn't easy," Azagaia cries in the second verse.

If the police are violent
We'll respond with violence
If you want to change the consequence, then you should change
*   the cause . . .*
Lower the cost of bus fare or raise the minimum wage
Maaaaaann—That's the least you should do
Unless, of course, you want fire at your gas stations
Riots outside the bakeries and in front of government ministries, just
*   imagine*
We'll destroy your banks and mines
It looks like bad governance is contagious.

Over the course of a few weeks, "People in Power" had become a breakout hit, earning steady radio play around Maputo. It offered a clear moral framework for the chaos that had overtaken the capital with burning tires and barricaded streets, and it made Azagaia a prominent social critic. His interrogation made waves too. The message for disc jockeys, conveyed informally and indirectly, was clear enough: Azagaia has only become more famous in the years since, but you don't hear him on the radio much at all.

A few months after Azagaia's talk at the university, I went to see Ismael Mamudo, director of the archives at Rádio Moçambique, the government radio network, to ask whether Azagaia's music was in fact censored. "We don't prohibit it, but we avoid playing it," he said with a laugh. "No one's going to put a notice on the wall. If you are going to ban something, you have to put up a notice." Instead, it was a more informal arrangement, something like censorship by inference. "The DJs are afraid. They'll never play a thing like that because someone could ask, 'Why did you play that?'"

I asked how it is that people *know* that Azagaia can't be played if it is never declared outright. "We ourselves ask that question. People who work here. I wonder that myself," Mamudo said, leaning back in his chair.

He was at pains to explain how much he liked Azagaia. "There's no musician out there who has more courage," he said. Mamudo had been to Azagaia concerts and said he had copies of his CDs. "Azagaia's message is very strong. I've seen him play, and it's strong. When you hear him in concert, you can see people looking around at one another—" Mamudo mimed uneasy concertgoers looking around incredulously. "Sometimes the truth hurts." He called Azagaia's way of speaking *verdade no ângulo*—the sharp corner of the truth. "Have you ever heard of Fela Kuti?" he asked me, referring to the Nigerian bandleader and political firebrand. "That's more or less what we have on our hands here with this young man."

"Besides," Mamudo said after a while, "there's lots of music we can't play." He gestured at a wall of shelves filled with eight-inch magnetic tape reels. "You know, music from the *luta armada*"— the armed struggle against the Portuguese, when Frelimo was at its most idealistic.

"Our first president, he had a way of speaking," Mamudo went on. "If he said there was no corruption in this country, he didn't tolerate it. And there wasn't: people who were corrupt lost their jobs. Many of those songs are blueprints, plans for the country that didn't come to pass. There are things he wanted to happen for the people—health care, good education, all the land belongs to the people—that is not like the way that things are happening now.

"[Azagaia's] songs contradict a little bit. They are truths from another time. But they're still true."

1

Small-Town Hustle

ZAMBEZIA

*A vida aqui é um jogo de xadrez. . . . O cavalo move assim, o bispo move
assim. . . . Só que a meio do jogo as regras mudam. Comeu-te um peão
porque o cavalo passou a mover-se diferente.*

Life here is like a chess game. . . . The knight moves like this,
the bishop like that. . . . Except that in the middle of the game the
rules change. A peon ate you because the knight started to move
differently.

—MOZAMBICAN DANCER IN MAPUTO[1]

By the time Davane Monteiro started selling cassette tapes, in 1997,
the CD was already king in much of the world. Cassette sales in
the United States peaked at close to 500 million tapes a year in
1988, fell by more than 80 percent in the 1990s, and have only
continued to decline in the years since.[2]

Not so in Mocuba: as Monteiro remembers it, when he bought
his first lot of tapes, the only recorded music to be had there, with
a few exceptions, was on a pair of scratchy radio stations, one of
which played only gospel. Record players had always been rare.

Tape decks were only just making their way into the living rooms of the well-heeled as the economy came back to life after the war. A few people, Monteiro remembers, had Walkmans, but they had to travel a hundred miles to the port of Quelimane to buy new music. So Monteiro went to Quelimane himself and asked the cassette vendors—boys his own age—how to get started. They pointed him to their *tio*, or uncle, the supplier, and Monteiro returned to Mocuba with a lot of twenty tapes, which he sold from a bench at the market. In three days, he had none left. He went and got another twenty. Then fifty, then one hundred. The business went well. When his supplier went out of town for six months, another man approached him, wanting to do the same business. The man went to Malawi, came back with five hundred tapes, and had Monteiro resell them. The next time, Monteiro went with him.

They went to Blantyre for cassette tapes, Tanzania to buy shoes, and Zambia to buy *capulanas*, the printed wrap skirts traditionally worn by women in many African countries. Mozambique's coastline is close to two thousand miles long, yet plenty of imports come by way of its landlocked neighbors. In Mocuba, you can find sugar, cement, and potatoes, as well as fertilizer, used clothing, shoes, and schoolbags that have come from Malawi, often after passing through Mozambican ports. Along the border, there are communities that sell their maize to traders in Malawi, only to see it trucked back into Mozambique as a Malawian "export." Often, the remote portions of Mozambique seem cut off from the rest of the country, their economies tributaries of cities somewhere beyond the national boundaries. Sometimes, this is because of shared language and customs, which are more meaningful, locally, than any concept of national identity. Just as often, it is simply a matter of convenience borne of spotty infrastructure and underdeveloped markets—people go to Malawi to buy things they can't find, or can't find as cheaply, in Mozambique.

Monteiro and his *tio* slept in bus stations and ate in the markets where they bought their merchandise, returning to Mocuba as soon as possible so Monteiro could get back to school. For Monteiro, it was an education in business: what goods packed well, what sold fast, how to negotiate shipping fees with the louts who loaded the buses back toward Mozambique. He picked up snatches of Swahili in Tanzania and learned how to count in English. He describes it now as a "great adventure."

Soon, Monteiro struck out on his own, reselling tapes in twenties and thirties to other kids in Mocuba. Since he was making regular trips to Blantyre—the closest city where you could find something like a full-fledged record store—he began to field special requests. He hunted down songs for Mocuba's restaurant owners and for its nightclubs, the largest of which, the Desportivo, is a colonial athletic club reinvented as a discotheque after the swimming pool was drained in 1975.

Then he unlocked the power of the radio. One day, a song would play on the radio, Monteiro said, "and the next three days, people came to me looking for that song, not knowing that I was the one who had given it to the radio station. Each weekend, I brought back one or two *novidades* and gave them to the radio. The next week, I took those tapes back and gave them others." The radio station began promoting him. Retelling the story, Monteiro wrinkled his nose and put on an announcer's voice: "'And if you like this, you can go see our distributor, the one and only Dany Monteiro.'" He burst out laughing. "We sold a lot of Cape Verdian music, Angolan music, Malawian. It was hard to find Mozambican music in those days."

It's a good measure of Mocuba's distance from the center of the global economy that tape sales there didn't begin to slacken until the mid-2000s and only collapsed altogether in 2009. "Cassettes have been good to me," Monteiro said.

By the time I met Monteiro, two years later, the transition to CDs and MP3s was complete. He was twenty-six and already, it seemed, on his seventh or eighth career. He had sold cigarettes, trucked corn from the country to the city, filmed TV news segments, traded in agricultural equipment, and bought farmland to produce beans and pigeon peas as a cash crop. Monteiro had dabbled in most everything Mocuba's economy had to offer. But Mocuba is a place where you can never have quite enough work; if you want a job, you have to make one. So he continues to multiply his streams of income. He directs music videos, builds houses and rents them out, produces music for local *passado* singers. There's no such thing as too many businesses. It is all simply business.

For a long time, Monteiro's base of operations has been a small room on the first floor of a ramshackle hotel and restaurant across from Mocuba's bus depot. There, midway down a dank hallway, he rents a space the size of walk-in closet that shares a wall with a motorcycle parts stand facing the street. There are no windows and no sign on the door. A Frelimo poster on one wall has been rebranded in support of Monteiro's business: "Preta Dany Studios," it reads in black marker. "Number 1 studio in Mocuba."

"Preta Dany" is a combination of Monteiro's eldest daughter's name, which means "black" in Portuguese, and his own nickname, Dany, but the studio has become so closely associated with the man that most people now simply call him Preta—like his daughter—for short.

There are narrow wooden benches along each wall, and an acoustic guitar hangs from one corner above a jumble of boxes and microphone stands. The centerpiece is a whirring Dell desktop computer loaded with tens of thousands of MP3s and grainy music videos, vaguely categorized by country and by genre. Duplicates abound. Hardly any of the files are coherently labeled with the artist and track title, yet Preta somehow manages to sift through them with precision, distinguishing instantaneously between file names like "Malawi 01" and "!#~0_Malawi."

This is what's become of all the tapes. Preta no longer has to travel to Malawi for music. Nowadays, he goes no farther than his competitors, in the habit of passing around USB keys full of the latest hits from Maputo and Angola. For a while, the local supply chain for all of these MP3 merchants started with TDM, or Telecomunicações de Moçambique, the state phone and internet utility. Employees there used their access to unlimited bandwidth to pipe in music from around the world, spinning it off in bundles to people like Preta.

I first visited Preta's studio well into the evening with a jovial phone credit salesman named Agusto, who referred to Preta admiringly as his "older brother." Agusto is a large, squarely built man whose gap-toothed smile and complete lack of guile sometimes make him seem more like a young boy. Preta, it turned out, had no blood relationship or even close friendship with Agusto, but had gotten him started as a salesman by buying him his first bundle of scratch cards. The longer I spent with Preta, the more of these stories I heard: There was a corn-milling machine he had passed off to a business partner to thank him for his sweat equity after Preta had recouped his investment, and the farmland he bought for cousins on his mother's side to grow beans for market. But Preta also had his own "older brothers," shopkeepers and friends who had come through periodically with loans or advances in a town that had been without a bank branch for most of Preta's life.

Agusto and I left his post together at dark and meandered through the lamplit alleys of Mocuba's open-air market to Preta's studio. The walls still radiated sweltering heat absorbed over the course of the day, like a rock that has been sitting in the sun; a fan hummed feebly in one corner.

Preta was in the middle of editing a music video advertisement for a local phone credit wholesaler called Afro. In the video, a light-skinned singer with short dreadlocks listed all the things you can get from Afro—cheap phone credit, universal chargers— over a gentle reggae beat. These clips were interspersed with footage of Afro himself standing in front of the store, vigorously beckoning at the audience. The singer had recently won a national competition, Preta said, for "best male voice in Mozambique." Afro's hope was that the video would become popular as a song rather than a commercial and go viral, in a sense, on the video CD players of Mocuba's downtown businesses.

A middle-aged man in a gray suit stooped to enter the studio and sat in a white plastic chair adjacent to Preta's desk, wiping his brow with a handkerchief. Preta interrupted his work and swiveled to face him.

"Give me some of that Malawian stuff," the man said. "What's it called? The church music."

Preta looked over from an array of open windows on his desktop. "Gospel," he said.

"Ya, *gospel*! Give me some of that gospel."

"Ya, no problem." Preta trailed off and began clicking through the archives, and the man lit up as Preta played him a sampling, interjecting approvingly. "Ya, ya—that one's goooood." This is the most profitable line of Preta's business. Beginning at eight each morning, the studio receives a steady stream of visitors— overwhelmingly male—who come in to request music à la carte. Songs cost 5 meticais, a little more than 10 cents, videos twice that. Often, customers bring their own cell phones or USB keys to make the transfer. A burned CD is $2.

A boy in his school uniform hums a song from Angola. It's the one about a party, he says, a fast one, with a girl singing. Preta frowns at the screen, wipes his forehead with a clean white rag. Double-clicking steadily, he seems to pull files at random. Two seconds of one song, then another. The boy looks on quizzically. Miraculously, the song in question is found inside of a minute.

The boy gives Preta Dany his SIM card and 5 meticais and leaves a few seconds later, with his favorite song buzzing from his cell phone. The efficiency is almost hard to believe. In a place without running water or piped sewage, where crops are grown without animal traction or fertilizer, the intellectual property of an entire planet is at his fingertips.

Mocuba is a gritty crossroads of a town known, according to Lonely Planet, for "dirty water and for being nobody's favorite Mozambican town. Do what you can to avoid overnighting here," the guidebook advises—more, I suspect, out of concern for the possibility of boredom and discomfort than for any risk to visitors' safety.[3] The most traveled intersection in town, the strip by the bus depot, is a riot of activity. Mototaxi drivers come and go on $300 Lifan bikes to form a buzzing scrum of metal and young men at the entrance to the municipal market. Piles of coconuts, pineapples, and mushrooms spill onto the sidewalk in front of dark storerooms. Small girls bearing baskets of overripe cucumbers on their heads dodge traffic and ward off catcalls with blank faces. Phone chargers and electric fans hang from the rafters in the converted shipping container shops that line the street. Preta seems to know everyone.

Most of the work that animates this scene would fit under the banner of the ballooning unemployment figures often featured in the news. Beneath an *Al Jazeera* headline bemoaning Mozambique's "dire youth unemployment crisis," for instance, you'll read that 70 percent of Mozambicans under thirty-five "cannot find stable employment."[4] The World Bank puts the total unemployed for ages fifteen to twenty-four around 40 percent.[5] And while those numbers do a fair job of describing the problem—most people don't have jobs, per se—they can also be a bit misleading. Most people considered unemployed in the United States or the United Kingdom don't spend twelve hours a day carrying a bucket of frozen water bottles back and forth through traffic, or rise at five each morning to weed their cassava fields. Yet that, too, is a fair description of unemployment.

It was a debate over the meaning of "unemployment" in the developing world that first gave rise to the concept of an "informal sector" of the economy. The term was introduced by the anthropologist Keith Hart, who was trying to account for all the messy work arrangements that defined life in the ramshackle market neighborhood where he lived in Accra, Ghana, in the late 1960s.[6] People there were certainly not "unemployed," and yet, they weren't exactly employed, either. They were in between, toiling long hours for low returns and without job protections, or cobbling together streams of "informal income opportunities."

A half century later, economists are still wrestling with how best to describe the size or shape of the workforce in the developing world. No matter how you parcel out the economy, "formal" and "informal" are mixed, sometimes contradictory categories.[7] There are formally licensed construction firms that hire day laborers under the table, and big-time timber brokers who organize their businesses on the margins of legal industry; unlicensed beauty salons that pay steady wages and have set hours of operation, and self-employed porters or market sellers who pay municipal taxes.[8] A phone credit salesman is, in a way, like a franchise operator. Agusto, whom Preta had gotten started selling phone credit in Mocuba, had no ties to MCel or Vodacom, yet here were the terms of the deal: he contributed sweat equity and start-up costs, and the corporation provided the materials, pricing, and back-end system that constituted his business.

One day, at a bus stop outside Nampula, I made a note of everything vendors carrying their shops on their persons tried to sell me and my fellow passengers in an open-back truck during the ninety minutes we waited to get on the road:

- New and used shoes
- Bottles of water, refilled at home and frozen solid
- Fluorescent SunnyD-like bottles of "juice"
- Backpacks
- Bags of bread—rolls and loaves
- Dragon energy drink
- Peanut candy
- Hard-boiled eggs
- Perfume
- Body lotion
- Belts
- Sunglasses
- Clothespins
- Long, tan bars of laundry soap
- Beauty soap
- Leather wallets
- Thermoses
- Cream crackers and assorted cookies
- Fried dough balls
- Toy cars, police and civilian
- Scrub brushes
- Plastic beads
- *Capulanas*
- Angola brand toothpaste
- Phone credit

Each of these has its place in the hierarchy of buying and selling that forms a career path of sorts in markets all over Mozambique. Gender and age are often dividing lines, along with the amount of cash required to get started. Fried dough balls call for nothing more than a dollar or two of ingredients—oil, flour, sugar, water—and a place to put them together, along with enough charcoal to cook. For

cold drinks you need some kind of access to a refrigerator, at someone's store or at home. Cell phones, shoes, and textiles require more
capital.

This is the world where Preta has made his living all along,
straddling the fence between survival and entrepreneurship. With
luck and more than a little grit, this kind of selling gradually opens
the door to expanded inventory, more expensive goods, higher
volume, or an entirely new line of business—but not, in all likeli-
hood, a job with fixed hours or fixed pay.[9]

One way to divvy up the workforce is based on who buys the
service of your labor. In that scenario, the economists Sam Jones
and Finn Tarp suggest, the "informal sector" might be considered
everything other than wage work—both self-employment and
unpaid household or farm employment—which actually constitutes
the vast majority of work done in Mozambique.[10] As such, they
write, "In rural areas only 5% of jobs are plausibly located in the
formal sector; this rises to a little over 30% in urban areas. . . .
Only 12% of all workers report receiving a wage, of which almost
80% are men."[11]

With so much work taking place outside formal hourly or salaried
jobs, the most useful distinction is not employment versus unemployment but full employment versus underemployment: essentially,
full-time versus part-time work.[12] In urban areas, the rate of
formal employment has stagnated even as Mozambique's growth
has soared. Jones and Tarp put the urban unemployment rate at
6 percent, but they estimate another 26 percent of people can't get
enough work. Just one out of three is fully employed.[13] Mozambique's farms, which employ some 80 percent of the country's
workforce, represent a staggering amount of labor for very little
income. In rural areas, Jones and Tarp find that fewer than one in
two hundred people is unemployed, but close to half are underem-
ployed. There is only so much work family farmers can do without
access to credit, fertilizer, irrigation, or animals to help them plow.

* * *

Preta spent his early years in the provincial capital, Quelimane, part of the exodus from the countryside that took place across Mozambique during the civil war. When the peace was signed, he and his mother went to live with his stepfather in the country-side. Davane chafed at the change. The local school, held under a tree, stopped after third grade, and Davane, who'd had the benefit of actual desks and chairs in Quelimane, wanted badly to continue to study.

He barely knew his father, but he'd been told he had an older sister and an uncle in Mocuba, some fifty miles away. When visitors came from out of town, Preta says he would tell them, "I'm going to go back to Mocuba with you." The first person to take him seriously was the husband of one of his mother's relatives, who came to visit periodically on his bicycle. Around his ninth birthday, Davane left home while the man was still in town. He told his mother he was going to pick beans for a neighbor. Instead, he walked the few miles to a church along the main road and found a group of kids playing out front.

"Which way to Mocuba?" he asked.

"It's very far," they said, pointing out the way. "What will you eat?"

"I remember, I was carrying three pieces of boiled cassava," Preta told me. He held up his hands to mime the exchange, an irresistible grin spreading in anticipation of a punch line.

"'If Jesus could survive for more than a month without even cassava, then I will be able to make it to Mocuba,'" he said. It was another forty miles or so to the city. He set out under a light rain until the man overtook him that afternoon and brought him to live with his uncle in town. Davane began to sell things as soon as he could manage. He bought his fourth-grade pencils and note-books by selling corn and okra he picked for a neighbor. When his uncle gave him 50 meticais to buy a pair of sandals, he used the money to buy peanuts instead, which he roasted and shelled and turned into 70. At school, a teacher took the money, saying he hadn't paid his school fees. Davane returned home with no sandals and no money. "You see?" his uncle said. "That's exactly why I can't have you staying with me." But he didn't go home. Preta remembers being so impatient to be a grown-up that he glued hair clippings to his upper lip and went around town with a fake mustache. He sold cashews and gasoline measured out in glass soda bottles. Once, a transit policeman gave him 10 meticais, which he used to buy cigarettes he resold one by one, until he had multiplied the money fivefold. When he saw the cop again, Preta recalled with a laugh, he practically taunted him: "Do you see what your 10 meticais has become?" he cried out. Cassette tapes would come soon after.

Preta is slight but well fed, with skin the color of dark chocolate. He wears a thin mustache and scraggly goatee and has big, persistent eyes that give him a look of concentration whether he is frowning or showing all his teeth in a wide grin. He speaks softly, doesn't drink, and tips his hat to the grace of God in the way that some people say "you know?," as in "By the grace of God I had a good breakfast," or "By the grace of God business is good today." By his own accounting, Preta sleeps just four hours a night. Under the spell of hot weather, beer, and the fatigue of speaking a foreign language, I've always found it hard to carry on a conversation in Mocuba much past ten p.m., but Preta likes to sit up at night in a plastic chair outside his house, reading or simply looking at the stars. This, he says, is when ideas come to him.

There are two businesses, both now well established, that Preta takes credit for pioneering in Mocuba: burning CDs and running motorcycle taxis. Neither involves any particular original insight other than the notion that Mocuba was ready for something new. But the same could be said of every hardware store, restaurant, and movie theater launched in a small town that previously went without. "Someone once asked me," Dany told me, " 'How do you think of all this stuff?' I told him, 'Whenever I see something nice they're doing in big cities, I just try and figure out if there's a way to bring it to my town.' " He let out a long, full-throated laugh.

The problem, of course, is that Preta's main advantage was simply being months, or perhaps a year, ahead of the curve. The "prevalence of perfect, or rather . . . near-perfect competition" is one of the key features economists have used to describe informal work.[14]

Writing in 1954, the St. Lucian economist Arthur Lewis described the dynamics of work in developing economies with what he called an "unlimited supply of labor." "The workers on the docks, the young men who rush forward asking to carry your bag as you appear, the jobbing gardener. . . . These occupations usually have a multiple of the number they need, each of them earning very small sums from occasional employment; frequently their number could be halved without reducing output in this sector. Petty retail trading is . . . exactly of this type . . . each trader makes only a few sales; markets are crowded with stalls, and if the number of stalls were greatly reduced the consumers would be no whit worse off."[15] Mozambique's workforce is set to double by 2050, with more and more restless young people moving into cities and towns like Mocuba all the time.[16] The supply of people continues to outstrip the supply of jobs.

Chinese-made motorcycles started arriving in Mocuba in large numbers shortly after Preta began renting his Honda out by the day to a friend who took paying passengers. The good times lasted only long enough to pay for a second motorcycle. The business's margins soon collapsed under the weight of its popularity. Soon, there were fifteen mototaxis working in downtown Mocuba; today, there seem to be hundreds, mostly sitting idle while their teenage and twenty-something—universally male—drivers backslap and wait for the next ride. Now the town has once again reached an inflection point: *xapas*, or minibuses, have begun to ply a couple of main routes in Mocuba, thanks to another entrepreneur who saw something in the big city and found a way to bring it home.

Over the years, Preta has tried to move into businesses that aren't so easily disrupted or replicated. His forays into shooting videos and recording local musicians have been steps in this direction—there are even a couple of Preta Dany–penned ballads making the rounds—but there are only so many singers in Mocuba whose ambitions justify the expense. In 2009, on a trip to Maputo, Preta signed up for a computer and photocopier repair course and brought the trade back home. Now, he says, his late nights are often spent peering into the bowels of scanners and trying to coax Dell desktops back to life.

Opportunity in Mocuba had always seemed circumscribed, even compared to Quelimane's or Maputo's relative development. The reason Preta had moved to Mocuba from his childhood home was so that he could continue his education. But when he finished high school, he'd gone as far as he could go in Mocuba. In 2010, when the Universidade Mussa Bin Bique opened a branch there, Preta jumped at the chance to go to school without leaving home. Mussa Bin Bique is a private college christened for a precolonial ruler of Mozambique Island whose name Vasco da Gama reportedly garbled into "Moçambique," giving the region, and later the country, its name.[17]

Preta enrolled to study business as part of the first cohort and spent more than $1,000 on tuition in his first year. A few months into his second, the campuses in Mocuba and another Zambezia town, Pebane, closed without warning. After weeks of protests over unfinished classes and lost tuition, it ultimately took nearly a year for students to learn that the college had been operating with unlicensed faculty and without approval from the Ministry of Education.[18] The next closest place to earn a bachelor's degree was an hour and a half away, in Quelimane, so Preta rented an apartment there and made the trip every weekend. Finally, he became a *doutor*, as people with BAs are often called in Mozambique, with a thesis on internal audits. All that stood between him and a diploma when we last spoke was $2,000 in assorted fees.

On my most recent visit, the street-facing side of Preta's music business—a tiny wooden stall cut into the front wall of the building where he keeps his studio—had been reinvented as an ice cream shop. The booth itself has just enough room for a man to stand and turn freely, so the new tenant stood with a soft-serve machine plugged into the wall in the building behind him, pivoting carefully to hand out cones over the counter.

"Deixei, deixei," Preta said. "I left it." For years, this booth had provided a soundtrack for the intersection, with a VCD player and a tiny TV pumping out Malawian music twelve hours a day under the eye of an associate. But after almost twenty years of scrimping and selling to boost his buying power and diversify his lines of business, Preta had finally gotten what most everyone in Mocuba wants: a job. In 2014, he was hired as a teller at the local branch of Barclays Bank, and he put his businesses aside. He liked the regular hours, the pay. Dealing with the customers came naturally to him. Then, just over a year later, the bank was badly damaged in an electrical fire and closed for several months. When it reopened with a new manager, most of the staff was replaced as well.

Preta returned to the small-town hustle. Two thousand fifteen had been a rough year, he told me. After years of mounting discord with his in-laws, he had separated from his wife and moved out. His brother had been badly injured in a motorcycle accident, drawing the whole family into paying what they could for his treatment. The music business, meanwhile, had slowed considerably while Preta's focus was elsewhere. "I'm restructuring," he said. "I'm in a rebuilding phase."

The first order of business is a house. Preta now lives in a tiny unfinished apartment with soccer posters nailed to the walls, next door to the construction site where his house is going up. There's a high school across the street. Originally, Preta says, he bought the lot hoping to build a computer school, but he'd had to scale back his ambitions.

The location continues to serve him well. When he moved in, Preta arranged to put a photocopier behind the counter at the soda, soap, and crackers store his landlord keeps in the front room of his house. Many classes are taught without the benefit of text-books, so teachers compensate by drawing up twenty- or thirty-page booklets the students must then find a way to copy. Preta approached teachers with the promise of a reliable copy machine just steps from the schoolhouse door and keeps the originals of each packet on file. At 2 meticais a page, each booklet brings in about a dollar. On days when he has nothing else to do, Preta sits in his front yard and sells ice pops—*fruta gelo*—branded with a line drawing of Snap, Crackle, and Pop lifted straight from the Rice Krispies box. Photocopies, burned CDs, and ice pops are gradually building Preta's house.

The day after I arrived, we spent the morning checking up on Preta's various plans and ventures in a car he'd borrowed from a friend who owed him a favor—Preta had been the go-between who allowed the owner to buy a new car battery on credit. "This is my town," he said proudly. "I never have trouble getting things in Zambezia."

You could see how eager he was to keep it that way: Preta drove the car like it was made of glass, rolling gingerly over speed bumps and through the ruts and trenches of the sandy roads in his neigh-borhood, then cruising at a jogging pace through the swarm of pedestrians in the center of town.

At the market, Preta took over for his cousin briefly to help a customer with a USB key full of music that had inexplicably turned to digital mush, all crackle and hiss. A woman in a bright pink blouse came in with her son and sat on the bench across from me. She was looking for a new song by a *pandza* artist from Maputo—a sort of fusion of hip-hop and *marrabenta*, the playful dance music popular in the last years of the colonial era. Preta started clicking through a list of files marked "Mr. Boss," playing snippets of music that seemed far too short to allow anyone to ID a song. The woman held up her phone. "I have it here if you don't have it on your computer," she said.

Preta glared back at her skeptically. "Is that possible? Is there anything this computer doesn't have?" he retorted, only half joking.

"Well, sometimes that computer doesn't have *new music.*"

The internet, I thought, has finally arrived in Mocuba. At last, smartphones were bringing music piracy to the masses, and at least part of Preta's business might not be able to withstand it. Cell phones had seemed from my first visit to Mozambique to be washing over society in a wave, just as they had and would continue to do around the world. In 2006, I spent a couple of months in a tiny roadside town in the Himalayas, Tapovan, with a single, erratic pay phone next to the barbershop. Ten years later, that seems inconceivable in India, Mozambique, or much of anywhere else.

Mozambique has about one landline for every three hundred people.[19] For businesses, families, entire towns, the arrival of cell phones was synonymous with the arrival of any kind of telephone at all. I spoke to a sociologist in Maputo who said his maid, accustomed to traveling home to see her parents in the countryside every six months, hadn't been since she got a cell phone, but now spoke to her parents more often. Mkesh and M-Pesa have just recently added the possibility of transferring money instantaneously. Minutes are still too expensive for most people to use much, but there are close to eight cell phone numbers for every ten Mozambicans.

And we are only at the beginning of the curve—internet users still represent just 6.4 percent of the population.[20]

Across from the district government office, three men standing in the shade of a large acacia tree called out a hello as we got out, and Preta went over to greet them. As he walked away, one of them shouted after him: "If you have any projects," he said, "I'm here."

"I'm a bit *desprojectado* right now," Preta countered. He'd joked to me that morning that he was an entrepreneur, but an entrepreneur without money, an *empreendedor sem dinheiro*. Next door, we entered an airy, wood-floored office that held what was left of Preta's second attempt to get a computer school off the ground. There was a photocopier, half a dozen desktops, and a laptop where a young man was teaching a single student Microsoft Word in a whisper. Preta said hello and left quickly. This was supposed to have been a kind of cooperative: Preta provided the equipment and enlisted two friends to man the copy machine and teach basic skills. The three of them were supposed to pool revenue to cover basic costs.

Instead, Preta says he started to notice that the toner got depleted, or big stacks of copies had been made with no money coming back in. He had already taken another batch of his computers and put them into storage, but he hadn't said a word to his partners about closing the place, and he didn't necessarily plan to. To do so would run counter to the reputation Preta had painstakingly earned over the years. Preta, after all, had spent a long time studiously avoiding bad blood of any kind. When you do business in a town as small as Mocuba, he said, it's not prudent to make anyone angry. What, I once asked him, would he credit with his success? "I'm very patient with my friends, and I'm never greedy."

*   *   *

Each time I've been to Mocuba, I've stayed in the home of a friend and college classmate of Preta's, Hortência Pililão, who teaches at an elementary school in town. It's a tidy, humble stucco affair on a gently sloping triangular lot. The road is a ways off in either direction, with clusters of small houses in between. Hortência's is two bedrooms with a corrugated metal roof, a freezer, a small television, and a VCD player. Two cases of empty soda bottles in the corner. A plastic table and four plastic chairs, none of which sees much use unless there are guests. Her bed is by far the nicest piece of furniture. In a corner of the living room, a small cement shelf covered in cloth holds a stapler, aloe cream, and a vase of pastel plastic roses.

The walls are decorated with bits of lace hanging under pictures she received at a training years ago. The theme was "development

Hortência Pililão and Davane Monteiro met as classmates when the first four-year university opened in Mocuba; it closed amid allegations of fraud before they had time to finish their degrees, so they commuted together to take their last classes in the provincial capital, Quelimane, an hour and a half away.

Hortência Pililão's simple house passed for middle class in Mocuba: a sheet-metal roof, a television, and a chest freezer she used to sell cold soda to supplement her income as a primary schoolteacher.

in mountainous areas," she said; the intent of the pictures was to show the Mozambicans "that you don't have it bad." One shows a landscape of Swiss apartment blocks on a snappy, clear day after a blizzard, the whole landscape sagging under mounds of snow. Another shows a lone nomad driving a line of yaks through a snowy mountain pass.

Outside, Hortência had used a month's salary to put in a forty-foot well in 2009, then almost as much again the next year to cover it with a cement slab. The well had water six months a year for a few years, then dried up altogether, so that she had to walk a few minutes each morning to fill buckets at her pastor's house. Electricity comes over a cable stretched to a twenty-foot section of railroad steel stuck into the sand beyond the porch, where we'd sit after dinner with Hortência's teenage twins, Dolman and Amilcar, doing their schoolwork by the light of a single bulb. At night, Hortência takes the lightbulb in from the porch to keep it from being stolen. By daybreak, she and dozens of other women in the neighborhood have already been out sweeping, leaving each dirt courtyard cross-hatched with brush marks and free of loose sand and debris.

Hortência grew up in a remote, mountainous area of Zambezia called Namarroi and had her twin sons as a fourteen-year-old with a father who never gave them a second thought. She sent them to live with an aunt when they were one, then took them back at three and continued to go to school. She wouldn't finish high school until they were eight years old. She beat steep odds to get a teaching position and build a middle-class home, yet it seems hard to imagine a middle-class existence more precarious than hers.

When I first visited in 2011, the Universidade Mussa Bin Bique was moving to charge 3,600 meticais in monthly tuition ten months out of the year, which amounted to 100 percent of her salary as a primary schoolteacher. At the time, Hortência supplemented her income by selling chilled sodas out of her chest freezer and occasionally got help from Preta or an aunt who worked as a school principal. When her freezer broke, she took it to get repaired and never heard from the repairman again.

When I returned to Mocuba in 2016, Hortência still hadn't been able to hold on to enough money at one time to buy a replacement freezer. She had poured most of what she made into traveling to Quelimane to finish her degree on weekends after the Mocuba campus closed. As a public schoolteacher, a bachelor's degree would mean an automatic raise. Like Preta, outstanding fees were all that stood between Hortência and a diploma. But Hortência was much less sure she'd find a way to pay. Besides, there were other things she was focused on: getting the freezer replaced and seeing her sons through the end of their education. While I was there in February 2016, one of the twins, Amilcar, was home on a break from medical school in Tete. He was going back to finish his first year, as long as they could get together the bus fare.

2

What Can You Do with an Aging Warlord?

ZAMBEZIA

On the northern edge of Maputo, the Benfica market stretches seaward from the main road in a warren of tiny wooden stalls broken into vague sections like those in a department store. Aisles of electronics, tools, and motorcycle parts are followed by stacks of canned tomato paste and mounds of dried fish. Carts of oranges, great piles of coconuts. It was one of the first places I explored when I arrived in Maputo. At the end of an hour's wandering, the maze of market gave way to a residential neighborhood, with a string of women selling Coca-Cola and bottles of frozen tap water from coolers forming a kind of half-empty buffer zone.

Rosa, sitting on an empty rice sack in the sand, waved a pillowcase and shouted "Cinco, cinco"—5 meticais, about 20 cents at the time—drawing customers to a heap of secondhand bedclothes on the ground.

"You don't want to marry me?" she asked, laughing, as I passed.

Rosa was from Inhambane, and she'd come to Maputo in 1982. "War," she said when I asked why. She was born in 1966, in the second year of Mozambique's war for independence; she turned twenty-six before the country was at peace for longer than a year.

When she arrived in Maputo, Mozambique was six years into a marathon civil war between the government of Frelimo, the Marxist party that won Mozambique's independence from Portugal, and Renamo, an insurgency with backing from the apartheid regime in South Africa. At the time, Rosa explained, things in her part of Inhambane stayed quiet until the day Renamo came out of the bush in her hometown to eat. The rebels looked for houses with metal roofs and multiple rooms. These were houses with "conditions," she said—running water and the prospect of a good meal. Her father fled as soon as he saw them approaching, a gaggle of teenagers toting AK-47s. Rosa stayed, because, well, "What do you do if they come to your house and sit down?"

"When my father came out of the bush again," she went on, "Frelimo blamed him for hosting Renamo, and they killed him." She sighed. "Frelimo killed; Renamo killed; there isn't anyone who didn't kill. Today, I vote Frelimo. I know that Frelimo killed my father, but I vote Frelimo. They say you need to go vote, so what do you expect?"

Rosa gave me my first glimpse of a perspective I encountered again and again in Mozambique, an incisive view of politics coupled with the feeling that there were no choices to be had for the average citizen. Frelimo has been in power since 1975, as long as Mozambique has been its own country, and long enough, for many people, to seem like the only plausible option. Indeed, in the early years, this was simple fact. Frelimo ran a one-party state until 1992, when the Catholic Church helped mediate a truce to the grueling sixteen-year conflict that killed more than 1 million people and forced 4 million more from their homes, Rosa among them. When the war ended, the UN gave stipends to demobilized soldiers, or *desmobilisados,* who agreed to hand in their weapons. Mozambique became a multiparty democracy, and Renamo's troops became part of the political opposition.

Even after twenty-five years, it's a role Renamo's leader, Afonso Dhlakama, is yet to fully embrace. Dhlakama the politician has never managed to match his exploits as a warlord. In four consecutive presidential elections, his share of the popular vote eroded from 48 percent, in 1994, to 16 percent, in 2009, while Frelimo consolidated its power in public institutions.

Today, though, Dhlakama is newly resurgent. In the most recent elections, in 2014, he managed a 37 percent showing even as Frelimo campaigned using fleets of government vehicles.[1] Frelimo sympathizers stuffed ballot boxes and altered vote totals at a number of polling stations, yet the ruling party, which looked invincible with more than three-quarters of the vote in 2009, won with its narrowest margin in fifteen years.[2] A second opposition party, meanwhile, the Movimento Democrático de Moçambique (MDM), which split from Renamo in 2009, crumpled in its first national campaign.

But even now, it seems far-fetched to think Dhlakama will ever be elected president. Instead, the bulk of his political leverage continues to derive from the threat, real or imagined, of a return to full-fledged armed conflict. Violence has turned out to be a powerful political tool.

As his caucus in the legislature dwindled following Mozambique's long-fought peace, in 1992, Dhlakama engaged in escalating bouts of political theater, calling for boycotts, demonstrations, revolution, and finally war. In October 2012, just days after Mozambique's *Dia de Paz*, the twentieth anniversary of the truce, Dhlakama announced he was returning to the bush. "I am training up my men," he told the papers, "and if necessary, we will destroy Mozambique."[3] He would not attack of his own accord, he promised, but he and his men stood at the ready to defend their positions in a dusty grove of mango trees beneath Mount Gorongosa.

The next three and a half years brought bursts of ambushes on civilians and skirmishes with the army. At the peak of the conflict, in 2015–16, Renamo carried out 107 attacks in a nine-month period, killing forty people and seriously injuring seventy-nine more.[4] Both sides reportedly worked to minimize casualties by warning each other of attacks in advance so as to avoid direct confrontations, and yet, warfare is warfare. Schools closed.[5] Police commanders sent officers home with their guns to avoid losing them to Renamo raids.[6] Traffic on parts of the main national highway traveled in convoys under military escort.

The larger impact, by far, has been psychological. Many of the attacks aped Renamo's tactics during the 1980s—burning buses, raiding health posts, and digging trenches in the roads to force trucks to stop—stoking fears around the country that Mozambique was slipping back into war. Renamo reoccupied many of its old bases. In the first few months of 2016, twelve thousand people abandoned their homes and fled to Malawi following clashes between guerrillas and the police.[7]

Observers suggested that Renamo's army had fewer than a thousand men, without the resources to wage a full-fledged war. Joseph Hanlon, who covered Mozambique for *The Guardian* during the war, pointed out that Dhlakama's ex-fighters are "old men" who have been out of the bush for more than twenty years.[8] Dhlakama himself was already over sixty. Whatever arms caches Renamo may have buried in the woods, they had no new source of weapons or ammunition, not to mention cash. As such, it was tempting to see Dhlakama's return to arms as one more tragic bluff in a quixotic political career. He seemed desperate. As his guerrillas continued to spread terror throughout Mozambique, Dhlakama announced plans to run for president once again, and he dispatched negotiators to hammer out a deal with Frelimo. In Maputo, Renamo's deputies in parliament continued to debate and vote on legislation as though nothing was amiss.

As negotiations wore on, Frelimo began to seem desperate too, increasingly captive to Dhlakama's appetite for mayhem. Frelimo made a series of important concessions on electoral reform and eventually signed a renewed peace agreement that did not require Renamo to lay down arms.[9]

Foreign investment in Mozambican mining and energy alone could reach tens of billions of dollars over the next decade.[10] For Frelimo, there was a lot to be lost from the fear of instability; for Dhlakama, much to be gained. "[Renamo] does not understand why," he wrote President Armando Guebuza after six months of renewed fighting, "we continue to be excluded from enjoying the wealth brought by the peace we helped to achieve and maintain during the past 20 years." Renamo, the letter went on, needs more money "to remain a political party."[11]

Luís de Brito, a Mozambican sociologist I spoke to in Maputo, says Dhlakama never managed to transform Renamo from a guerrilla army into a viable political party in the first place.[12] With his return to the bush, Dhlakama seemed to concede the point: Mozambique's largest opposition party was not a party at all, but a militia.

Yet Renamo remains Mozambique's leading opposition party, and Dhlakama remains its leader. "Far from being Renamo's death knell, its resumption of hostilities was a political masterstroke," wrote the Institute for Security Studies, a South African think tank, in its analysis of the elections, under the headline "Renamo's Renaissance, and Civil War as Election Strategy."[13] "Oddly enough," the report read, "by pulling out of the democratic process, Renamo was able to demonstrate its commitment to it; at least as far as its constituency is concerned."

Again and again, Dhlakama has rung the same old bell, threatening to split the country in two. He has called president-elect Filipe Nyusi a "thief" (Frelimo's spokesman called Dhlakama a "baby"), opened new guerrilla bases, and marched his troops toward the capital, warning the government army to stay ten to twenty kilometers away from Renamo's men.

All this, writes Hanlon, who has been a scholar of Mozambique since the early years of the civil war, "would surely be considered unacceptable in most other countries." In Mozambique, it simply underscores the bizarre symbiosis of the two main political parties. Much of Frelimo's popularity depends on the absence of a credible opposition: for voters like Rosa, the option to vote Frelimo or Renamo is a false choice. Frelimo may govern incompetently, they may govern corruptly, but at some basic level, they do govern. Whether they like Frelimo or not, a great many people in Mozambique doubt whether Renamo could match even that.

Dhlakama, for his part, is relevant mainly as a foil to the ruling party. Without forty years of Frelimo rule, there is no entrenched cabal for Dhlakama to decry, no Goliath that could plausibly turn him into a David, nothing that might justify his extremism.

As it is, Dhlakama's political position is as strong as it's been since the 1990s. Young people—perhaps too young to remember the carnage of the war—have been quoted in the press supporting Dhlakama's hard line. Dhlakama's all-or-nothing negotiating strategy is gradually eroding the wall surrounding Frelimo's political power. To voters, it seems, a vigorous opposition, even one led by Dhlakama, is better than the alternative.

There has always been a core of truth in Dhlakama's assaults on Frelimo. Though Western governments have tended to look on postwar Mozambique as a success story, Frelimo supporters acknowledge that peace has not delivered all they'd hoped. Corruption and patronage are widespread, and the fruits of Mozambique's development thus far have gone mainly to a tiny political elite. Former president Armando Guebuza, who stepped down at the end of 2014, is thought to be the country's richest man. A recent World Bank study concluded that while Mozambique had the world's sixth-fastest-growing economy between 2000 and 2010, indicators of rural poverty remained unchanged since the end of the war.[14] Poor Mozambicans are awaiting a more credible politician to take up Dhlakama's rallying cry: "We want to say to Guebuza, you are eating well; we want to eat well too."[15]

I spent a week following Afonso Dhlakama through the Mozambican countryside in July 2011, after a long, halting dance by phone with the minions in Renamo party headquarters, who referred to him only as "His Excellency the President." For nearly a month, Dhlakama had been clamoring through remote hamlets in the North, preaching revolution and flirting, in the spaces his speeches left unfilled, with a return to civil war.

There was no discernible logic behind the timing of Dhlakama's tour. It had been two years since his loss in the last presidential election, and he had been in a sort of political hibernation ever since. In fact, Dhlakama seemed to be breaking a promise. On the campaign trail in 2009, he vowed never to run for president again if he lost. And he did lose, badly. When Renamo's fifty-one deputies took their seats in the national assembly after the 2009 elections, Dhlakama called them traitors and said they had no connection to the party. He moved away from Maputo and took up residence in a lavish home in Nampula, in the North, calling for the dissolution of parliament. One of the deputies granted an anonymous interview to a weekly paper in Maputo: "What is Dhlakama doing in Nampula that is useful for the party?" the deputy asked.

In time, Dhlakama softened his position and the deputies remained in office. But under his leadership, Renamo has only drifted further and further from the actual practice of politics. If we take him at his word, Dhlakama is holding out for the creation of a transitional council to rule the country until free and fair elections can be held, though—in spite of documented pockets of fraud—international observers have repeatedly called

Mozambique's elections "free and fair" already.[16] At the time, I wondered why Dhlakama was on tour at all.

With the exception of intermittent coverage by local radio and one independent television network, Televisão Independente de Moçambique, or TIM, Dhlakama's tour was largely ignored on radio and television. But he did make himself heard: for weeks on end, while he rabble-roused in the north, an unattributed advertisement ran repeatedly on the state-run network TVM, or Televisão de Moçambique, with no title and no introduction. A voice brimming with urgency described images of devastation as they flashed across the screen over ominous orchestral music. Famine. Destruction. Schools and hospitals bombed. Roads destroyed. "If you support that program, then you need only look to Somalia," the voice said. The stills showed emaciated refugees and UN food trucks in an arid landscape. Viewers were reminded to preserve the peace, and then the commercial ended abruptly: an attack had been made on a nameless antagonist, but one whom no Mozambican would fail to identify. It seemed somehow that Frelimo bought into Dhlakama's own propaganda, as though saying his name would only add to his power. Frelimo and Renamo seemed to face off with dueling paradoxes: Dhlakama crusaded for reform of a political system he refused to engage, while Frelimo agitated for peace by playing up the possibility of renewed war. I hoped that meeting Dhlakama would help me understand the future of democracy in Mozambique.

The people on the phone in Maputo were exceedingly polite. Renamo has long been marginalized in the Mozambican press, and the phrase "American journalist" seemed to flatter them endlessly. Yes, yes, I would have an audience with His Excellency, but it was difficult to work out his schedule. They would call me again tomorrow. Each time we spoke, Dhlakama was headed to a rally in a different city and they gave a different date of return.

While we played phone tag for three weeks, I had time to consider what it would be like to interview someone with a long list of war crimes to his name. What I'd read about Dhlakama before visiting Mozambique inspired terror. During the war, Renamo was notorious for its coercive recruitment of child soldiers, kidnapping boys as young as six or seven, and for its uniquely gruesome brand of violence against civilians, which often included public mutilation: cutting off limbs, breasts, and facial features, castration, and even crucifixion.

At times, Renamo combined these terrible specialties—mutilation and forced recruitment of children—by making young recruits murder their own neighbors and relatives, as a way of cementing their bond with the rebel army.[17] To instill a fear of traveling in the population, Renamo burned whole buses full of passengers. When they conquered a town or village, Renamo set fire to houses, torched fields, and, as one war reporter put it, "destroyed whatever could not be carried away."[18] Renamo even published figures on the number of villages it claimed to have destroyed: nearly fifteen hundred in 1981 and 1982 alone.[19]

Journalists reported excesses among Frelimo's soldiers too, but Renamo's reputation for destruction was unique. It was rumored that Dhlakama and his fighters, called *matsangas*, had supernatural powers, that they were bulletproof, even immortal, and that they could cast spells of confusion on their adversaries, making the *matsangas* invincible.

What could you ask of a man like that? Would he own up to any of the war's excesses? Did he stand for anything more concrete than revolution?

As a rule, buses in Mozambique leave early. After a five a.m. departure from Mocuba, I arrived in Milange before nine a.m., cramped and mildly disoriented from the minibus's constant seesawing over the badly rutted road. To the giggling disbelief of my fellow passengers, I was dropped off directly in front of the Renamo office, where I'd arranged to meet Dhlakama's convoy. In Mocuba, Frelimo's local headquarters is a brilliant candy-cane-colored building two stories high, with a first-floor shop that sells blenders and refrigerators. Renamo's office in Milange was striking for its humility: a two-room stucco house without electricity, bare of paint and nearly so of furniture: inside, there was a single desk, two chairs, and two small benches. The bathroom was a tattered tarp enclosure out back—no hole, simply a patio of urine-stained bricks. The courtyard was already full of supporters there to welcome His Excellency. While they waited in the mottled shade of the office yard, old women wearing wraps printed with Dhlakama's face sat on the ground with outstretched legs. They fanned themselves in the heat and tended a dwindling fire where they were boiling cassava whole. There were men with drums and a marimba, and a woman with a whistle who led a circle of frail dancers in song:

> *Renamo, Renamo, that's who brought democracy to Mozambique.*
> *Dhlakama, Dhlakama, that's who brought democracy to Mozambique.*

And,

> *Angry, angry, we are dying angry because our president never wins.*

Lieutenant Lemos Buelekue Ofece, a *desmobilisado* with a birdlike torso and a rattling voice, took me around party headquarters to meet his former comrades, who introduced themselves by military rank and full name. All of the veterans still carried ID cards issued by the UN in the early 1990s, as part of a hefty and largely successful program of cash grants for soldiers returning to civilian life. These IDs were their only formal proof of their status as veterans, and it seemed as though they had been waiting for years to show them to someone who might report their grievances more widely.

Not long before, Frelimo had drafted new pension legislation limiting government benefits to those who fought in the war for three years or more, and which counted a soldier's service beginning only at age fifteen.[20] Though Renamo has never publicly admitted to recruiting child soldiers, this last provision made a sizable portion of Renamo's army, which had done most of its fighting before they turned sixteen, ineligible. The men brandished their UN IDs like badges, surefire proof of their eligibility for benefits and of the injustice of their situation. But the legislation had already passed.

Afonso Dhlakama was born on January 1, 1953, in Mangunde, a village of scrubby veldt and baobab trees in southern Sofala Province, where his father was the *régulo*, or traditional chief. *Régulos* in the colonial era were typically aligned with the Portuguese government, which sanctioned traditional authority as a means of subordinating it. Dhlakama was educated in the local Catholic mission, and as a young man, he worked as a schoolteacher.[21] He fought in the Portuguese army against Frelimo. He defected in 1972, joining Frelimo's guerrillas less than three years before they won independence in 1975.[22]

Nowadays, Dhlakama speaks of his time in Frelimo with pure derision: "I've already been in Frelimo," he'll say to supporters who accuse him of "eating with Guebuza," the president of Mozambique from 2004 to 2014. "I was a commander in Frelimo, and I left Frelimo thirty-five years ago. Why? Because they are communists!"

It was as a soldier with Frelimo that Dhlakama first met André Matsangaissa, Renamo's commander in the early years of the civil war. After independence, Matsangaissa was expelled from the army for theft and imprisoned at a Frelimo reeducation camp in

Gorongosa. Curiously, he was freed in 1977 by forces from the white-ruled government of Mozambique's neighbor to the west—Rhodesia, or present-day Zimbabwe. At the time, Mozambique's new government was following the example of Tanzania, which had sheltered Frelimo in its independence struggle against the Portuguese. In turn, independent Mozambique offered a refuge to the African National Congress, which fought apartheid rule in South Africa, and ZANU-PF, a guerrilla army led by Robert Mugabe fighting for black rule in Rhodesia.[23] When Mozambique closed its borders to Rhodesian trade in 1976, Rhodesia retaliated with its own campaign to disrupt the Mozambican economy and force Frelimo to withdraw support from black rebels across the border. It was Rhodesia's Central Intelligence Organisation that created MNR (later Renamo) in 1975, and which brought Matsangaissa back to Rhodesia.[24]

Matsangaissa was killed in 1979 in a Renamo raid on the town of Gorongosa, and it was Dhlakama who took his place. Rhodesian backing of Renamo dissolved following Zimbabwean independence, but the apartheid government in South Africa took over where the Rhodesians left off. The Frelimo government was sheltering South African rebels as well, and the apartheid government began providing training, arms, and logistical support to Renamo: anything it could to undermine the Mozambican state.

Dhlakama's popularity in Milange was startling. Here was a politician who had delivered nothing to speak of in twenty years, yet who could nevertheless count on hundreds of subsistence farmers to give up a day's work or more and wait to greet him on the side of the road. Dhlakama seemed like the patron saint of dashed hopes, the people's best chance to voice their frustrations with a system that did little to improve life in Milange from day to day. All afternoon, it was rumored that he'd be arriving any minute, so the local party chief encouraged the crowd to keep up their chants and percussion: "Today is an important day to show ourselves!" he cried. "Let's make enough noise so people from Frelimo come and join us." It was important for His Excellency's convoy to roll up in the midst of a feverish rally. But Dhlakama was waylaid in Morrumbala, a good three hours off. During a break in the middle of the afternoon, a group of his bodyguards had encountered an off-duty police officer in a restaurant, seized his weapon, and held him captive in a hotel room.[25] The delegation couldn't leave for Milange until they negotiated the policeman's release.

When Dhlakama did show up at nightfall, it was at the head of a line of seven gleaming Ford Ranger pickups flying the Renamo flag. Traveling along with His Excellency were seven of Renamo's deputies in Mozambique's parliament, who received the pickups as part of their official compensation, a dozen bodyguards and their cook, a handful of Dhlakama's political aides, a cameraman and newscaster from TIM, and a local reporter from the government radio network, Rádio Moçambique.

Dhlakama stepped eagerly from the lead pickup with a smile, one hand raised to the crowd. Short and stout at age fifty-nine, Dhlakama had gently sloping features and a dense cap of gray hair.[26] He wore the same uniform throughout my visit: penny loafers, a blue blazer, and a starched white dress shirt with French cuffs. Within seconds, Dhlakama picked me out as the lone white face in the crowd and extended a hand over a group of eager supporters. "*Você é o americano?*" "You're the American?" he guessed. "Welcome!" Flanked by the local party chief, Dhlakama strode to the center of the courtyard and awaited his introduction. "Hurray for Dhlakama!" the party chief prompted the crowd over a megaphone. "Hurray for Dhlakama!" the people echoed him. "Hurray for Dhlakama! Long live Dhlakama!"

Dhlakama was in no mood for a rally. He apologized for his tardiness and pled fatigue from the road, then strolled leisurely past a line of military police to his rooms at the Tumbine Lodge. I trailed behind him, hoping to ask an aide what time the convoy would take off in the morning, but no one knew. Instead, Dhlakama himself interrupted his conversation with a deputy from the national assembly and turned to me: "Which state do you live in?" he asked in Portuguese.

"California," I told him.

"Ahhh, California," Dhlakama said longingly. "Isn't that where Jimmy Carter is from?"

"I think Carter is from Georgia," I said. It was unclear whether he heard me.

"Yeah," he mused. "[Carter] invited me there a long time ago. His NGO was monitoring elections here. I went to California and he showed me where his parents are buried and the place where he was born." Dhlakama seemed deeply satisfied.

"Jimmy Carter is a friend, in spite of being a Democrat," he said. "My party's friendlier with the Republicans, as part of the family of the Right, but the Republicans are *complicados*."

Complicado is a Mozambican catchall for all things negative that are better left unexplained. Variously, *complicado* can mean complicated, demanding, devastating, impossible, deceitful, unreasonable, indiscreet, angry, unsettling, dangerous. As a single adjective, it can occasionally take on outsized or absurd powers of description, as when, in the reporter William Finnegan's narrative of the Mozambican civil war, *A Complicated War*, Mozambicans described their country's tragic situation as, simply, *complicado*.

Dhlakama paused for a beat. Then he said, "I want you to be my English teacher."

By seven thirty the next morning, the lodge was buzzing. It was a clear, sparkling day. Behind a row of motel-style rooms, jack pines and stark green meadows crept up the flanks of Mount Tumbine to a brilliant, white-flecked sky. The aides were up and dressed in pressed slacks and button-downs, moving purposefully about the parking lot. His Excellency was nowhere to be seen.

In a meadow beyond the lodge, Dhlakama's security detail was eating breakfast in shifts, bivouac-style. A half dozen men in olive-green uniforms and berets sat by a canvas lean-to and scooped cornmeal and stewed dried fish from pots over a charcoal fire. They ate with their AK-47s lying across their laps. An equal number stood at attention, guarding the perimeter of the lodge. Again, no one knew what the day's schedule was or where the group was headed: "Yes, yes," the aides begged off when I asked them, "we are just waiting for the president."

Before His Excellency emerged, I sat on the lodge's small restaurant terrace drinking instant coffee. An operative named Torres said the lodge was the fourth place they had sought out a bed for Dhlakama, and he had been worried about the quality of the accommodation. When he was not on tour, Dhlakama split his time between lavish homes in Nampula and Nacala, on the coast. In Milange, other arrangements had been made, only to fall through at the last minute, for what Torres suspected were political reasons.

Renamo's convoys always draw a heftier police escort than they ask for. As a condition of the peace signed in 1992, Dhlakama retained a force of several hundred Renamo fighters as his "Presidential Guard," or personal security retinue. When he travels on land, he is never with fewer than a dozen of them, and the police like to follow behind in equal numbers. The Mozambican government now maintains that Dhlakama's Presidential Guard is illegal, though it has not tried to disband them. Throughout Dhlakama's itinerary in Zambezia, a pickup truck carrying eight military police trailed the convoy at a discreet distance, reliably visible in the rearview mirror. Ostensibly, both the police and Renamo's own guards were there for Dhlakama's security and that of the lesser politicians traveling with him. But the primary threat

to public safety always seemed to me to come from the antago-
nism that arose between the two groups. Each had members who
fought on opposite sides of the civil war. Any contact between
them was like flint on steel.

Now Dhlakama's strong men were facing off with a group of
helmeted military police officers clustered around the lodge's
entrance, preparing to hand over the gun they'd confiscated in
Morrumbala. The journalists from Rádio Moçambique and TIM,
the television network, were standing by. One of Renamo's collared
security personnel began to taunt the government cops: "While
we were making war, you were still in primary school."

A half hour later, Dhlakama's security chief, a tall man with a
hint of a mustache and neatly styled hair, came onto the terrace
for a juice box and explained the exchange with the police. "That's
just provocation! In Morrumbala, we found a plainclothes police
officer with a gun. . . . He had three foreign passports with him
too. 'Where are the owners of these passports?' we asked. He said
nothing. So we said, 'Then you must be a bandit,' and we seized his
weapon. Then he went running to the police station. When we got
here, those police officers came down and asked for the weapon,
and we told them to send the police chief."

Maria Inês Martíns is one of the seven Renamo *deputados* in the
national legislature who lent her government-issue truck to
Dhlakama's tour through the north. At nine thirty, she arrived
from another, less luxurious guesthouse on the other end of town
and wiped the sweat from her brow. *"O Velho ainda não pareceu?"*
she asked. *O Velho*—the Elder, or the Old Man—is how Dhlakama's inner circle refer to him in the third person: "The Old Man
hasn't showed up yet?"

He had not. Even when he is on tour, Dhlakama keeps the pace
of a politician contemplating retirement. Martíns took a seat on
the terrace, facing the mountain. Over her shoulder, I saw His

Excellency's door open for the first time all morning. Two aides stood outside in suits. Through the doorway, I could see Dhlakama, wearing a towel, doing push-ups on the floor.

Martíns has been in the assembly since 1999. She chairs the legislature's External Relations Committee as well as Renamo's own women's organization. Martíns became a deputy at the most optimistic moment the Mozambican opposition has seen since the end of the civil war. President Joaquim Chissano had discredited both himself and Frelimo through a series of corruption scandals that trailed the country's shift from Marxism to a free market economy. He barely beat Dhlakama in the presidential elections of 1999, giving Renamo 117 seats in the Assembly of the Republic, just nine shy of a majority.

By 2009, Renamo's contingent in the assembly had dwindled by more than half. While we spoke at the Tumbine, waiting for O Velho (pronounced *O VAIL-yo*) to get dressed, Martíns seemed worn down by the ordeal of being a lawmaker in the permanent minority. She complained of what she called Frelimo's "dictatorship by vote"—the party's practice of voting in a unified bloc, comprising, at the time, nearly 80 percent of the seats in the assembly. The practice allows Frelimo to set and enact its own legislative agenda, essentially without input from lawmakers outside the party. Martíns gave the example of the *Cesta Básica*, or Goods Basket, a monthly food subsidy that would be given, in kind, to needy families around the country. The measure was introduced in April 2011 over strenuous objections by the opposition, who argued that the logistics involved made the initiative impractical. "We said, 'This will not work. How are you going to get this program to function?'" Martíns recalled. "'How can you apply it?' But they insisted, 'It will work.' This country is vast—'How will you distribute these baskets?'"

Thanks to Frelimo's sweeping majority, the $10 million measure was passed without pause. Within three months, Prime Minister

Aires Ali was already calling the program into question: "We're going to analyze the situation as a function of the [global financial] crisis," he said in June.[27] "And the budget that was approved for the *cesta*, where will that be spent?" Martíns demanded rhetorically. "That's what the opposition is asking." Ultimately, the program was called off; its budget allocation was never explained.

It is hard to fault Renamo for frustration at the stalemate they face in the legislature. But the party seems past any productive engagement with Frelimo and, often, even with the government as a whole. Renamo's answer to the failures of Frelimo rule has been to hoot and holler and cry foul, not to organize or scheme. Writing in 2004, Hanlon captures Renamo's legislative style neatly:

> Renamo has never become an opposition in a European or US sense, where the party out of power proposes alternative policies, suggests legislation, and tries to amend government bills in ways that would benefit its constituency. . . . Renamo makes no effort to, for example, challenge spending priorities or amend IMF-imposed policies in ways that would benefit the poorest. Renamo limits itself to speeches, often vague and confused, criticising Frelimo, and to disruption. In some cases Renamo creates a cacophony with horns, kazoos and whistles to disrupt proceedings; in December 2000, President Chissano's state of the nation speech was simply drowned out.[28]

Both Hanlon and Luís de Brito, the Maputo sociologist, would blame part of Mozambique's stalling democracy on the fact that each of the main parties—Frelimo and Renamo—thinks of itself as the only legitimate political party in the country. Carlos Nuno Castel-Branco, an economist who works with de Brito at the

Institute for Social and Economic Studies, calls this the "privatization of history," with each side laying claim to its own narrative of Mozambique's national identity—"Frelimo, because it fought against Portuguese colonialism, and Renamo, because it fought for democracy."[29]

When Frelimo won independence for Mozambique, the guerrilla movement became the government, and that government became a one-party state. Renamo, meanwhile, was founded to overthrow Frelimo, not to compete with it. "Not only was Frelimo historically a singular party, which still considers itself a singular party, but Renamo has always had exactly the same position," de Brito told me. "In the first years after the war, it wasn't so obvious," he went on. "But after '99, it became clear that Renamo was not a political party, except in the formal sense. It is a movement which has a single leader in whom all powers are concentrated. [He has no] political clarity nor any actual political program, but simply the ambition to be in power."

"You know," the lodge's proprietor told me glumly, "politically, everything revolves around money. So I have heard—I have *heard*," he repeated—"that Frelimo sometimes gives him a lollipop for him to shut up. This is the way it works."

When Dhlakama came out for breakfast, he was in a mood to reminisce. It was past eleven, and he was dressed in the same uniform as the night before: khakis, navy blue blazer, starched white shirt, and horn-rimmed glasses. In conversation, Dhlakama has the unhurried cadence of a man who is used to being waited upon. His sentences unfold in a warm, husky baritone, punctuated by frequent full-throated laughs. You get the sense that he is not often interrupted.

His Excellency took a seat across from Martíns at the table next to mine and smiled broadly. "Will you buy me breakfast?"

he asked the deputy. Martíns laughed and rolled her eyes, and Dhlakama ordered Nestlé *Ricoffy,* a powdered blend of coffee and chicory root, whipped to a froth with condensed milk, and *prego no pão,* tenderized steak in a bun. A fondly nostalgic look came across Dhlakama's face as he perused a mental catalogue of American politicians. "Dahn Burrr-tone," he said, chewing each syllable studiously. "Jeh-see Ellms." These two, Senators Jesse Helms and Dan Burton, were Dhlakama's *grandes amigos.* "They didn't know me, but because I was fighting for democracy, they supported me," he said.

At the start of the Mozambican civil war, in spite of U.S. backing for anticommunist rebels in Angola and Nicaragua, both the Carter and (later) Reagan administrations officially supported Frelimo's Marxist government. As the Cold War grew more intense in the early 1980s, the U.S. State Department met with a rising chorus of opposition from a cohort of right-wing politicians, led by Jesse Helms. In the early years after independence, Frelimo was ardently secular, and some of its most repressive policies were reserved for religious groups: it nationalized the property of the Catholic Church (which included churches and schools that became state institutions), while thousands of Jehovah's Witnesses were deported or sent to reeducation camps.[30] As a result, it fit neatly into the religious Right's conception of communism as a worldwide foe of Christianity.

Evangelical missionaries in Rhodesia and South Africa helped paint Renamo as a force for God in Frelimo's Marxist stronghold. By the mid-1980s, Renamo was getting sympathetic coverage on outlets like Pat Robertson's TV show, *The 700 Club,* and financial support from Christian groups based in the United States—Christ for the Nations, Don Ormand Ministries, and the End-Time Handmaidens, among others.[31] One letter circulated on behalf of Rhodesian missionaries in the United States sought funds to "outfit the entire [Renamo] army with Bibles."[32]

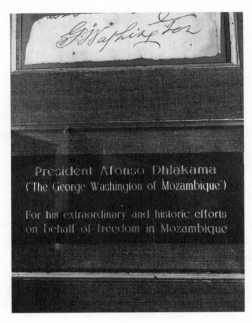

A plaque bearing a scrap of paper with George Washington's original signature, given to Afonso Dhlakama by one of his right-wing backers in the United States. "President Afonso Dhlakama ('The George Washington of Mozambique')," the inscription reads. "For his extraordinary and historic efforts on behalf of freedom in Mozambique." (Photograph courtesy Afonso Dhlakama Jr.)

Renamo received an additional boost in stateside PR with the publication of *The Mozambique Report: Eyewitness Testimonies of Persecution and Atrocities*, a booklet by a South African missionary named Peter Hammond. Hammond was a veteran of the South African Army who considered the apartheid-era military to be a "missionary force." *The Mozambique Report* described Renamo as "freedom fighters" and detailed numerous instances of mutilation and violence against Mozambican civilians, inflicted—Hammond claimed—by government troops.

Later, he would allege that Mozambique's first president engaged in cannibalism and "pledged his soul to Satan."[33] But at the time, Hammond's credibility was not yet in doubt in Washington, D.C. Senator Helms read *The Mozambique Report* into the congressional record and stirred support for Renamo among his conservative colleagues in Congress.[34] When Melissa Wells, Reagan's nominee for ambassador to Mozambique, denounced Renamo's attacks on civilians, Helms rallied twenty-eight Republican senators to sign a letter of rebuttal and blocked Wells's nomination for nearly a year.[35] When she was finally confirmed, Wells made a series of fact-finding missions throughout Mozambique and found that Hammond had simply attributed to Frelimo the very atrocities that had actually been committed by Renamo.

"She insulted Renamo and called us *bandidos*," Dhlakama scoffed, telling his side of the story. "We've had bad luck with American ambassadors." He turned to Martíns: "Who was that black woman that I went around insulting? The one who said 'Frelimo! Frelimo?'" Martíns didn't remember; it turned out to be Condoleezza Rice.

Though he is short on specifics, Dhlakama still considers Renamo a "right-wing" political party. Even at a time of unprecedented cooperation between the Mozambican government and multinational corporations, he railed against Frelimo's "communism" and lamented the lack of incentives given to investors in Mozambique. In his speeches, Dhlakama continues to get a lot of mileage out of the unpopular Frelimo policies that gave Renamo support during the war—travel permits called *Guias de Marcha*, the forcible creation of communal villages, and, especially, the persecution of churches: "Frelimo are communists," he said at one rally. "Now, they say they aren't communists anymore, and we're supposed to believe them? Twenty-five years ago, you weren't allowed to pray, but now they say they believe in God?"

"The world is false," he said earnestly. "When I write my book, whomever reads it will cry, because I've suffered a lot."

At last, after noon, an aide appeared at the steps to the terrace. "*Sua excelência?*" The party had been waiting for hours.

"Everything's ready?" Dhlakama asked, mildly indignant. "Why didn't anyone tell me? I've been waiting for you all. I just want to drink one more cup of coffee."

The largest crowds I saw in support of Dhlakama were in the place we visited that afternoon, Majaua, a tiny hamlet deep in Zambezia, Mozambique's poorest and most populous province. The road that leads to Majaua is a packed dirt track skirting the Malawian border. Along it, you pass great yellow fields of wild grass and clusters of thatched mud huts whose color changes gradually from red to brown with the makeup of the soil. I was riding in the back seat of the third of seven pickups, next to Torres, who was in charge of Dhlakama's PA system.

Like most of the people Dhlakama surrounds himself with, Torres was a great nostalgic. For all the Mozambicans I'd spoken to outside of Dhlakama's cortège, the war seemed to be a terrible, and now, after two decades, mercifully distant memory. It hardly ever came up directly, except to explain some contingent circumstance— why someone was only just now completing high school in their thirties, or why they'd grown up living with a distant relative. Torres seemed to look on the civil war as his heyday, although he'd never been a fighter. For a group whose base had always been in the countryside, Torres was one of Renamo's rare urban organizers. He recalled carrying Bibles under his arm to secret gatherings disguised as prayer meetings, and making arrangements with an underground member who worked for the electric utility to create a blackout while Renamo plastered Nampula with their posters.

We stopped in a series of villages along the way where support-ers had nailed campaign posters from the 2004 election, seven years earlier, to mango trees along the road. At each of them, men on bicycles would race along behind the convoy until they were submerged in a cloud of dust. Some of the campaign stops were in-voluntary. Banging away in the middle of the road, one group barred our path with drums until Dhlakama stepped down from his pickup and said a few words through a translator.

The people he was speaking to are so isolated from the rest of Mozambique that they might as well live in neighboring Malawi. They share a language, Chichewa, with the folks on the other side of the border, and speak next to no Portuguese. They count in English. Their tiny brick churches bear plaques branding them as Seventh-Day Adventists and Jehovah's Witnesses, both mission-ary groups that entered Mozambique from Malawi when it was still the British colony of Nyasaland. The rest are not Catholics, like the Portuguese, but Anglicans. They buy and sell their goods across the border and spend Malawian *kwacha* rather than meticais. There are no Mozambican radio stations that reach Majaua. Cell phone service in the area is from Zain, a Malawian provider. Maputo must seem to them impossibly remote, abstract. Yet they are Mozambicans, and they support Renamo by the thousands.

When we reached Majaua, His Excellency stepped down into an adoring scrum on an unbounded soccer field marked only by wooden goalposts. A few local old-timers kept up a fierce form of crowd control, yanking children by the arm and admonishing them sternly, preserving a buzzing circle of open space where Dhlakama walked. His entourage followed along, buffeted by the crowd, and a group of former Renamo soldiers sang chants where Dhlakama's name was a prominent refrain: "Our father, Dhlakama, our father, Dhlakama, lead us to victory, father Dhlakama." At one end of the field, two pickup trucks backed up so their beds stuck out under the crossbar of the goal. Torres clipped speakers to

In Majaua, a tiny hamlet along the Malawian border in Zambezia, it seemed as though the entire district had come and waited for hours to hear Dhlakama speak. A banner on the road read "Welcome His Excellency, the Source of Democracy."

the goalposts, wedging them in place with the aid of lengths of sugarcane.

Dhlakama danced and laughed with his ex-guerrillas and listened to a song composed by a young man named Dias Francisco Guilhermo, who was three years old when the war ended. Guilhermo played a homemade three-string guitar and sang in a charming nasal voice. The chorus went like this: "No, no, no, I haven't forgotten the time of war. No, no, no, I won't forget the time of war, the time of war, the time of war." The rest of the song recounted the struggle of life during the war—the hunger, the exhaustion, the heavy burdens that people carried over long distances. Afterward, I went and talked to him. Why are you a Renamo supporter? I asked. "Because my father was a part of Renamo itself," he said. There you have it.

It's tempting to look at local support for Renamo as the stuff of cultural legacy, carried forward by men like Ofece and Guilhermo because they've never believed in anything different. And yet, to people in Majaua, the idea of Renamo rule is also the counterfactual of a lifetime. It is the opportunity to imagine their district with roads, with electricity, with a high school—with any of the things you might take for granted if your interactions with government weren't confined to altercations with armed border guards.

As it was, the dominant political issue in Majaua seemed to be the matter of border crossing. Majaua is a prosperous farming community, in terms of yields, but it is too remote and the roads are too muddy for merchants on the Mozambican side to come to the area to buy the corn and beans they produce. People in Majaua don't simply live off less than a dollar a day, as the statistic has it. Mostly, they don't live off dollars at all. They eat what they grow and exist on the margins of the cash economy, scrounging soap, salt, and cell phone credit as they are able. Guilhermo complained that when they cross the border to sell their corn, the border guards confiscate it. "I don't know why they don't let us cross," he said. "All I know is that they are robbers and thieves." They solicit bribes—in Malawian currency, no less, he complained— "and if you refuse, they will beat you as they please." What Guilhermo wanted above all, he said, was *democracia*. What is that? I asked. "Democracy would be something where I can walk from here to anywhere." Life in Majaua is certainly better than it was twenty years ago, but not better enough for people like Guilhermo to give up the idea that there is an alternative more promising than Frelimo rule.

Western scholars often refer to Mozambique as a darling of the donor community, receiving consistently high aid flows since the end of the civil war. In 2006, aid to Mozambique was nearly $80 per capita, or almost twice as much as its neighbors Tanzania and

Malawi.[36] Only a handful of African countries received more foreign aid than Mozambique in 2015; all five of them—Ethiopia, the Democratic Republic of the Congo, Tanzania, Kenya, and Nigeria—have at least twice as many people.[37] Mozambique is known, in travel guides and investors' briefs around the internet, for abandoning Marxism in favor of structural adjustment, pulling itself up from the devastation of the war, and becoming a "fledgling democracy," with free elections and peaceful transfers of power.

All of this is true enough. But the space, or at least the perceived space, for meaningful dissent in Mozambique is minimal. Corruption has worsened steadily in recent years, and there is a crushing sense, in conversations with ordinary Mozambicans, that there is no avenue of recourse against the abuses of the ruling party.[38] People are afraid to speak their minds, and a Renamo rally is one of the only opportunities they have to come out, en masse, in a joyous show of dissent. It doesn't matter that Dhlakama speaks unconvincingly of revolution. No one else in Majaua is speaking out at all.

Although more than 1 million Mozambicans (out of 15 million total) died in the fighting between Renamo and Frelimo, some scholars still disagree as to whether the conflict can truly be called a civil war.[39] In its early years, in particular, it was often called a war of aggression, or a war of destabilization, because of the apparent incoherence of Renamo's attacks against Mozambique. "Don't invest any money," Renamo's U.S. spokesman once told a group of American businessmen. "We will blow up anything you build."[40] It was thought obvious that Renamo's interests were simply those of the Rhodesians and, after 1980, the apartheid government in Pretoria.

Yet Renamo's cruel tactics toward Mozambican civilians seemed counterproductive for an insurgency that relied on peasant labor and intelligence to feed themselves, to plan their movements, and to transport their gear. How was it that they could stage ambushes over such vast swaths of the countryside without alienating the people who lived there?

By the mid-1980s, it was clear that Renamo had taken on life independent of its backers in South Africa. Out of the international gamesmanship of white supremacy, the rebels crafted local rationales for the war. Renamo found a rallying force in widespread opposition to some of Frelimo's core policies: the government forced resettlement in communal villages; it required peasants to contribute precious crops and work hours to state-run cooperatives and farms; it sidelined tribal authorities in the name of Marxist liberation. Renamo proposed to destroy all that and more. In the words of the political scientist Carrie Manning, "Renamo's defining feature during the war was that it was whatever Frelimo was not."[41]

Stephen Lubkemann, an American anthropologist who worked in southern Mozambique in the 1990s, has described the conflict as a "fragmented war," for the lack of a coherent national agenda among supporters of either side. He argues that it was common for the political stakes of the war to be subordinated to the village-level spats in any area where fighting took place.[42] This makes the appeal of each side seem rather like a mafia's: warring factions provide protection and personalized violence in exchange for political support. But the analogy helps to explain how the everyday disputes Lubkemann presents as examples—a man's jealousy of his brother's prosperity, mutual mistrust by two wives of the same husband—could escalate to lethal proportions during a war. A Human Rights Watch study estimated that more than 6 million AK-47s entered Mozambique during the war, not to mention handguns, grenades, and land mines.[43] To make his case, Lubkemann retells the story of neighbors who had a long-standing dispute over a wild honeycomb in the bush near their village. One neighbor, he writes, "actually managed to obtain a landmine through a family member who was a part of the government militia, and planted it near the honeycomb. The other man and his wife were both hit by the landmine when they visited the honeycomb. The man died instantly and the woman was fatally injured. She died later the same day after crawling back to the village."[44]

Renamo and Frelimo became the vehicles for the escalation of any conflict, the airing of any grievance. And for Renamo, that principle remains valid today.

For four days, the party slept in Milange, making half-day outings to communities in the surrounding bush, never setting out before eleven a.m. Dhlakama was adamant that we avoid showing up too early, before his supporters had come back from the fields for the day, or had the chance to pour in from the surrounding countryside. In the evenings, Dhlakama grilled local party officials about outreach, making sure they'd sent *enchentes*, or "filler-uppers," to each stop in advance. The day we left, Dhlakama was more prompt than usual. Torres called at eight thirty and told me to meet the convoy at the gas station. Filling seven trucks took about an hour, so I sat on a stone wall eating banana bread with B, a young cameraman from the independent TV network TIM. Dhlakama was perched a few yards away in the open door of his pickup. Holding a calculator on his knee, His Excellency peeled bills from a Bible-sized stack of meticais to pay for gas. "You see that?" B asked me. "Dhlakama takes the money out of *his* pocket. No one else touches it." Is it always like that? I wondered. "Every time!" he said. "Dhlakama? *Porra!*"—Fuck!

B had already been covering Renamo for three weeks as they toured through Nampula and Cabo Delgado. He explained that fieldwork by television reporters in Mozambique is financed largely by the institutions and people being covered. The best gig, he said, is covering the Millennium Challenge Corporation, an aid and development organization that pays a $50 per diem for

Everywhere Dhlakama spoke, dozens of well-worn Hero-brand bicycles were stacked against trees and buildings, testament to the distances his supporters had come to hear him preach revolution.

food alone. There were only so many stories to squeeze from an erratic stump speech, so B made time on the road with Dhlakama to film quick spots on working conditions in Milange's tobacco warehouses, or crop prices in the market. "The guy won't let you go," B confided over beers one night. "You tell him, I can stay for four days, and he says okay, but then he changes his mind. That guy? *Shheeeeee*! He loves to be on television." Dhlakama was fond of making himself scarce or unapproachable as B's departures neared, sending stern messages through intermediaries to get the camera to stay an extra day. "Don't you see there are journalists here filming?" he asked the population of Morrumbo, a tiny hamlet we reached after three hours on dry dirt roads interspersed with wheat and onion fields. "Our friend came all the way from America to be here," he said, waving a hand in my direction. "I'm not whispering this stuff like this," he said in a stage whisper. "Everyone is hearing it. [President] Guebuza himself is hearing it!"

In Gurué, Dhlakama spoke in the middle of a soccer field at the tip of a nose-shaped ridge the town's sprawl covers like a bandanna. With a wide panorama of steep inselbergs and rolling tea plantations bathed in late afternoon sun, he could not have asked for a grander setting. I found myself on the sidelines standing next to a man in his forties who wore a baseball cap and threadbare, baggy khakis. "Do you support Dhlakama?" I asked him. He paused. "What he is saying—his voice—you can understand it. You can accept it. You can hear it. But Frelimo has ideas too—" he said. "We children are here in the middle between Renamo and Frelimo. We're like a plant that is in the water. When the wind starts blowing to the left, the plant will follow. When the wind starts blowing to the right, the plant will follow there, too. When the wind stops, the water is still, and so is the plant. You know, when a child is beaten, it runs to its mother. We're fleeing. The world is tearing itself apart from one end to the other. Whatever words we hear, we'll follow."

He was pleased to hear Dhlakama speak of a revolution; he thought there was a chance a revolution would bring more jobs. The man declined to give his name, so I asked if I could identify him by his profession. "That's the problem," he said. "I don't do anything. I only work in my garden; I sell charcoal."

I was scheduled to interview His Excellency at nine o'clock the next morning. Aides were coming and going from Dhlakama's front door, waiting, just as I was. The military guards were packing and unpacking their bags, doing laundry, taking catnaps with their guns positioned under their mats like pillows. I asked a group of three how long they'd been with Renamo.

Crowds lined the road for the better part of a mile to see Dhlakama roll into Gurué at sunset.

"*Eeeeeeeeee*," came the reply, as if to count the years in vowels. One joined in 1981 at age thirteen, another in 1982 at age eleven. "I grew up in the war; I got married in the war; I had my kids in the war." He laughed. The third couldn't remember. He considered this for a moment and then pointed to his waist and said, "I joined when I was this tall."[45]

Over the previous week, I'd been struck at the commitment of these guards to their peculiar cause, serving as the personal army of a retired warlord and sometimes politician. To continue to camp and clean their guns daily twenty years after their war had ended, to live the lives of child soldiers well into adulthood, even after they had families. Most of the men are now over forty, but they've known little else. They joined Renamo as boys and have a fierce, quasi-religious devotion to Dhlakama. "A lot of people support our president, right?" one of them asked me in Majaua,

A pair of soldiers from Dhlakama's Presidential Guard, coated with dust from head to toe, show off roasted field rats—a dry-season delicacy—at a roadside stop on the way to Gurué. Many of the men in the Presidential Guard joined Renamo as children and traveled everywhere with Dhlakama, riding in the bed of each pickup in the seven-car convoy.

grinning as he looked over the crowd. By dint of habit, belief, manipulation, or charisma, somehow, Dhlakama managed to make them stick around.

The megalomania of the whole enterprise was striking. In a week of public appearances in Zambezia, Dhlakama did not once mention the name of any of the legislators traveling with him—local, provincial, or national. Seven members of the national assembly had taken weeks away from work simply to watch their president perform. When they appeared onstage, it was only to lead the crowd in cries of "Dhlakama O Ye! O Ye!" or to translate. Dhlakama didn't hold meetings with local officials or residents or outline any program more specific than revolution. He made threats and sketched derisive caricatures of the government: his only policy prescriptions were taunts at Frelimo.

But these are not the effects of old age or senility. The French anthropologist Michel Cahen noted Dhlakama's narcissism even in 1994, while traveling with His Excellency during his first presidential campaign. "Although Renamo's membership may be overwhelmingly civilian now," he wrote just a few years after the war, "the organization still continues to function with an exclusively military mentality. With the exception of some of the few competent provincial or national leaders, no one takes even the slightest initiative and everyone remains waiting for orders, even concerning such trivial details as what kind of drinks and sandwiches to provide for reporters. The consequences are disastrous and affect all levels of the organisation. Renamo may be a civilian party, but it is not an exaggeration to say that the political department . . . does not function at all."[46]

Still, B and the two other reporters I met on the Dhlakama beat were actually receptive to a good share of Dhlakama's criticism of Frelimo. They agreed that state institutions had been politicized, that electoral fraud was a problem, that the ballooning exports of unprocessed wood and minerals were not benefiting most Mozambicans. But they saw something fundamentally hollow and ineffective in the way Dhlakama ran his operation on the road. "Dhlakama is right," B told me over beer and chicken in Gurué. "What he says is true. But what kind of government would they have?" This was one of B's refrains throughout our itinerary, when Dhlakama heaped slurs on Frelimo or tallied up his own gas bill. "He couldn't govern," he'd say of Dhlakama. "He just couldn't."

Dhlakama's whimsy and micromanagement often seemed to interfere with any political organizing that Renamo might have accomplished on their sweep through the country. When the journalists were given money for meals, B told me, they went to Dhlakama's room and watched him take the cash directly from his wallet. For dinner, then again for breakfast, and again for lunch. "The party's money *stays* with him," B said.

Partly, I imagine, this is so because Dhlakama doesn't see the money as being the party's money at all. While he maintains that he receives only a small stipend from the party, Dhlakama has never disclosed how much he is paid. The majority of Renamo's funding comes from Mozambique's state budget, which, with the support of Western donors, funds political parties in proportion with their representation in the assembly.[47] Renamo's funding fell dramatically after the election in 2004, along with its shrinking minority in parliament. But since seats in the assembly were awarded according to votes cast in the presidential election until recently, there is a sense in which Renamo still owes all its funding to Dhlakama's personal appeal. After thirty years with Dhlakama at the helm, no one in his inner circle seemed to question this.

In the mornings, before he stepped outside, Dhlakama could usually be found in his room, manually entering sheets of prepaid scratch cards in a small collection of cell phones. He used $15 cards in batches of $100 or $200 for each of the major cell phone providers—MCel (owned by the Mozambican government) and Vodacom (part-owned by Armando Guebuza, president of Mozambique from 2005 to 2015).[48] The man spent a lot of time on the phone. B said he never called twice from the same number. Understandably, Dhlakama felt he was at risk of having his phones tapped, so he bought SIM cards on the street and changed numbers as often as possible. What is harder to understand is why Dhlakama felt the need to personally scratch off the little foil film on each card and punch in the lengthy codes himself. During all of this, it was generally understood that Dhlakama was not to be bothered. So it was that, at one thirty, though I'd been waiting half the day, Martíns emerged from Dhlakama's bungalow at the Catholic mission and told me that O Velho had too much work to see me.

His inner circle treated him more like butlers than like campaign operatives: they didn't manage O Velho; they simply gave him his space.

At times, it was as though all distinction below His Excellency had dissolved. Renamo's deputies in the national assembly were simply old military buddies of the Presidential Guard who had decided to put on button-downs. On our way to Gurué, pickup number five nearly lost a wheel. All six lugs came loose and rattled off into the brush by the side of the road. The convoy stopped when the problem became apparent, and a small committee—deputies, aides, and soldiers—went to work while the rest of us crouched in the sun and chewed knots of sugarcane.

While we waited, it came to light that a member of the Presidential Guard had taken the liberty of having sex inside a deputy's truck the night before and been caught in the act—like a member of the Secret Service having sex in a congressman's car. A colleague went to tell the truck's owner, and the deputy went out to see for himself. He knocked on the window, but the offender refused to open the door. Now he was sheepishly dodging guilt without comment while his comrades had at him. The mocking exchange kept nine of Dhlakama's entourage going at a good clip for about twenty minutes, with frequent bouts of laughter that climaxed with the following line: "You know, maybe we're having car trouble because you had sex in the car. People who have sex in their houses don't usually have this problem."

Even in their critiques of Frelimo, B and his colleagues took pains to highlight the ruling party's competence. On our last night in Gurué, I sat on B's bed as he and a radio reporter traded half-scared, half-admiring exclamations about the party's work ethic and ruthless efficiency. "Frelimo is a machine; those guys can work," B said. "You see them in the office at one, two a.m.," the radio reporter countered. Junior cadres stayed up all night to plan their rallies and conferences—whatever it took to get things done.

Frelimo's capacity for organizing and political discipline verged on the sinister. Yet each of them lamented the fact that colleagues from the capital would likely be sent to the Tenth Frelimo Party Congress, later in the year. "Luxury hotel, $100 daily stipend," B said. "*Poooooorrra*," the radio reporter exclaimed. Fuuuuuck! "Frelimo?" B said in his characteristic tone of challenge. "*Shheeeeee*! Frelimo is a machine."

One hallmark of Frelimo's political skill has been the party's ability to pass the baton from one leader to the next: Frelimo itself has never become personified by a single head of state, and it has repeatedly resisted splintering at times of internal strife. While Dhlakama alone has faced off against four successive Frelimo heads of state, there have been no splits, resignations, or expulsions of high-level Frelimo officials since independence.[49]

In December 2011, interim elections were held in three cities where unpopular Frelimo mayors had resigned within days of one another. Ostensibly, each one stepped down for personal reasons, though it was widely presumed that the party had leaned on them, so that more popular Frelimo candidates might take their place before the general elections two years later. Renamo did not take part in the elections, and Frelimo's candidates faced only MDM, the newest party in the opposition. Unexpectedly, the MDM candidate in Quelimane—by far the largest of the three cities—won in a landslide, hinting that the balance of political power in Mozambique was shifting.

On December 8, 2011, the day after the by-elections and two weeks from Dhlakama's self-imposed deadline for revolution, the president granted him an audience in Nampula, the first time the two men had met since Guebuza took office in 2005. It lasted less than an hour; only Dhlakama spoke with the press afterward, suggesting that Guebuza did not take the meeting all too seriously. The conversation turned on "matters that affect the country at the political, economic, social and democratic levels, and national reconciliation in this country," Dhlakama told reporters. Guebuza "listened and took note of all the questions dealt with." The meeting did not necessarily preclude Renamo from holding demonstrations, Dhlakama said, but it signaled "consensus" and a return to dialogue between Renamo and Frelimo.[50] In other words, no revolution was necessary.

I had dinner with B a few weeks later. With Christmas past and no revolution in the works, I'd stopped trying to keep abreast of Dhlakama's antics. "*Sheeeeeeee*," B said, predictably, when we sat down. "I didn't know you were in town. You missed it." What? I asked. That afternoon, B had filmed the provincial conference of *desmobilisados* in the hangar-like prayer hall of the Community of Sant'Egidio, the Catholic lay charity that mediated the peace accords that ended the civil war. This was an internal meeting of the party, held, Dhlakama announced, at the request of his former soldiers. The first part of it was open to the press. While cameras were rolling before an audience of several hundred Renamo rank and file, the *desmobilisados* began to speak out against O Velho, accusing him of "protecting" Frelimo while he repeatedly put off protests to unseat the ruling party.

"Gentlemen, Dhlakama is compromised," one said, standing up.[51] "We want our weapons so that we ourselves can start a new war," announced a soldier from Mogincual. "We've reached the conclusion that Dhlakama is wrapped up with Frelimo."

Maurício Silvano introduced himself as a veteran of the "war for democracy." Silvano thought Guebuza had cut Dhlakama a generous check when they met in December. "If Mr. Dhlakama is eating out of the same plate as Guebuza, that's his business," he said. "But we want to start with the demonstrations, and if possible, this very day," he added, to loud applause.[52]

In all, nine former soldiers stood up to point their fingers at Dhlakama, B said. Several approached the stage as they spoke, but

Dhlakama's bodyguards held fast, and the man himself remained seated with an indulgent smile, waiting for the protests to pass.

"My brothers," Dhlakama replied when the hubbub settled, "you are right to say that you are tired of waiting, and you are right to accuse me of eating with Guebuza. But I want to tell you to stay calm."[53] He was supposed to have a second meeting with Guebuza, he said, but it hadn't taken place because Guebuza's mother fell ill. In fact, Guebuza had been away in South Africa at an international conference. "If I were compromised," Dhlakama said, "I wouldn't be here. . . . I was already in Frelimo: I left Frelimo in 1977," he continued. "The protests will begin next week, and whomever opens fire on the protesters will be killed on the spot."[54] A state news service reported the event as a hoax: "Men who claim they once fought for Renamo on Saturday insulted and threatened Renamo leader Afonso Dhlakama at a public meeting in the northern city of Nampula—but left journalists covering the event wondering whether it had been staged to give the impression that Dhlakama is a moderate, under siege from extremists in its own party."[55]

Over the next few weeks, a group of several hundred *desmobilisados* set up camp outside Renamo's Nampula offices, awaiting Dhlakama's orders to begin their long-postponed protests.[56] As usual, a large police detail was assigned to keep watch over the gathering. As they had in Milange, the police and the *desmobilisados* exchanged taunts periodically, but things came to a head only early one morning in March. Police and Renamo *desmobilisados* (no one admitted to shooting first) opened fire on one another, killing one man on either side.[57] It was the first time in twelve years, and only the second time since the war ended, that Dhlakama's men had exchanged fire directly with the police.[58] Police reinforcements moved in swiftly, arresting thirty-four Renamo members and restoring something like order, but as you'd expect, ordinary people in Nampula were terrified.

Afterward, each side hastened to spin the event as it suited them. Dhlakama did not step outside his house, but Renamo officials claimed, variously, that Guebuza had called Dhlakama to ask him to maintain the peace, that Dhlakama had called Guebuza, that the police had attacked "defenseless *desmobilisados*," that seven police officers had been killed, and that a group of one thousand soldiers was being summoned from Sofala.[59] The police, meanwhile, maintained that Dhlakama's Presidential Guard had fired first and attacked a police vehicle and that the *desmobilisados* were in Nampula not to protest Frelimo rule, but rather to claim backpay from O Velho.[60] To me, both possibilities are still convincing even after four years of sporadic violence. Dhlakama's own motives are transparent enough, but I'm not so sure what's driving Renamo's guerrillas to stay in the bush. Is it devotion to their father, to the warped ideals of grown-up child soldiers? Or perhaps a stubborn promise from Dhlakama that a steady paycheck awaits them when peace returns.

"He has his version, and I have a different vision of reality," Guebuza explained to the press after meeting Dhlakama in Nampula.[61] Guebuza's successor, Filipe Nyusi, has taken a decidedly different tack. After months and months of deadlock between Dhlakama and Guebuza over a meeting location, O Velho and Nyusi quickly reached a compromise. They met twice at the Maputo hotel where Dhlakama stayed following the presidential election in 2014, emerging from their second meeting "wreathed in smiles," according to the state wire service.[62]

Conflict and reconciliation seemed to be moving forward along parallel tracks. Negotiations over the makeup of Mozambique's army went through 104 fruitless rounds before collapsing in May 2015. Dhlakama wanted to see his men reinstated, with equal power in the armed forces for Frelimo and Renamo. Frelimo had kept the army deliberately small for twenty-five years, largely to avoid the threat of a coup, doing much of the recent fighting with Renamo through special police units called the Rapid Intervention Forces, or Forças de Intervenção Rápida. A few weeks later, Dhlakama signed an agreement with the government to rid the civil service of undue Frelimo influence, but he ordered an attack on government troops in Tete the very same day.[63]

By the end of September, Dhlakama had returned to the bush, saying he feared for his life: "If I am not dead, it is because God is still with me," he explained later.[64] This rhetoric had been a staple of Dhlakama's repertoire for more than twenty years, but for the first time since the end of the war, it finally seemed credible. There had been two separate attacks on Dhlakama's convoys as he traveled in Sofala in September.[65] Assassins seemed comfortable picking off more and more important figures in Dhlakama's entourage. There were whispers that Frelimo hard-liners were pursuing the "Savimbi option," a reference to the Angolan opposition leader who was assassinated in the midst of a political impasse in 2002.[66]

When this second, shadow war began, some of the men I'd met as part of Dhlakama's political entourage began to show up in newspaper photographs with guns in Gorongosa, having traded their loafers and button-downs for green fatigues and black berets. I read that Armindo Milaco, a child soldier who had risen to become a Renamo deputy in parliament by the time we met in 2011, had been killed in a government raid near Dhlakama's base.[67] A lawmaker one day, a guerrilla the next. That, I thought, was the Renamo way.

But by 2016, it no longer seemed to matter whether Renamo's top brass were in the bush or in the city, whether they thought of themselves as guerrillas or politicians. Manuel Bissopo, a sitting deputy in parliament and Renamo's secretary-general, was shot across the street from Beira city hall after a Wednesday morning press conference.[68] Later in the year, as Dhlakama continued to threaten to split the country by force, a member of Renamo's negotiating team was killed on a jog along the Maputo waterfront.[69]

This seesaw of attacks and negotiations continued through much of 2016. President Nyusi and Dhlakama finally agreed to a cease-fire during a phone call the day after Christmas.[70] As of this writing, that peace has held for nine months, although Dhlakama remains holed up in an encampment under the stars.[71] "The war is over," he told reporters recently, speaking by cell phone from Gorongosa—this, for now, is how he is holding press conferences in Maputo.[72]

With presidential elections on the horizon in 2019, and with them the need for both sides to campaign safely, three groups of negotiators are hashing out the elements of a more durable peace: leadership roles for Renamo in the army, a more decentralized national government, and—unmentioned but perhaps just as important—the innkeeper's "lollipop," or some kind of payout for Dhlakama.[73]

Government troops have withdrawn from Renamo bases (some, though not all), schools have reopened, and the convoys have stopped on the main national highways.[74] Even Dhlakama has softened his stump speech, speaking of a "truce without deadlines." He wants to reassure the world, he says, "that Mozambique now has another image, an image of peace, tranquility and of a country that has all the conditions for investment."

It remains to be seen what peace deal could satisfy a man who earned 37 percent of the vote. If history is any guide, Dhlakama will cling to the ability to put up armed resistance as long as he possibly can, with no guarantee his demands won't shift again. Mozambicans, meanwhile, are caught between two parties who think democracy means they always win.

3

Branco é Branco

ZAMBEZIA

A terra não se vende, mas compras.

The land isn't for sale, but you can buy it.[1]

Late one night in November 2014, a large tractor pierced the whir of crickets as it came to life beside a soybean field some forty miles outside the town of Alto Molócue. It was planting time, and the field was covered in the scraggly beard of weeds, roots, and dry stems left from the last soybean harvest. Dragging a massive plow, the tractor made its way from end to end and through several turns, bright-white headlights guiding the way.

Anselmo João, a soybean grower from the area, was one of the first people to stir in the ruckus. Namilepe is not the kind of place where people are accustomed to hearing heavy machinery as they sleep. No one there had ever used a tractor to till a field at one a.m.

João got dressed and went outside with two neighbors. Through the starlight, he could make out enough of the scene—the thrum of a large motor tracking behind a wedge-shaped beam of light—to know that someone was plowing a field that didn't belong to them.

In fact, the field was João's, or at least partly his. For the last eight years, João has been part of a collective that grows soybeans for seed, working on contract for a company in Maputo, Lozan Farms, through a system called *machambas em bloco*, or "block fields." Members of the group store seed together, time their plantings and sell their crops collectively, and share equipment and labor. Small commercial cooperatives like these have been a bright spot in Mozambican agriculture. They are not common, but in pockets they've managed to work around some of the basic obstacles to scaling farms by sharing assets and working together to gain access to markets.

Farmers in the Associação Lozan Farms are a prosperous bunch. In the space of a few years, members have rerooofed, then rebuilt their houses in brick and corrugated steel, sent children to college, purchased tractors, and gradually expanded the footprint of their farms. In a country where most farms are tiny—the median a single hectare (two and a half acres)—several members of the Associação Lozan Farms farm eight times as much land or more.[2]

"We went straight out to see the truth, and we found the machines there working," João recalled in disbelief. They stood by the field and yelled to the driver, then waved their arms as they crossed his headlight beams, but there was no reaction. "Three of us walked out in the middle of the night to try to get the tractor to stop, and he wouldn't even slow down."

By the time the tractor stopped, more than thirty acres—an area equivalent to some twenty-five football fields—had already been prepared for planting. Nova Algodoeira, a Portuguese cotton company with an operation based in Alto Molócue, was doing the work.

The next day, members of the association watched from afar as Nova Algodoeira's workers returned with a seeder and planted the whole area with cotton, taking over in a day what might have taken them weeks to plant, about 20 percent of the land they farmed as a group. Then they decided to take the land back. The day after Nova Algodoeira finished seeding the parcel, João's group gathered nearby.

As Marques Dias recalls, it took some convincing to get everyone to follow through. "There wasn't a single person who had the courage, or the conviction, I had," Dias told me. Dias is an activist. He chairs the advocacy committee for the provincial chapter of a national smallholders group, União Nacional de Camponeses, or UNAC. He'd heard other stories of land disputes between agribusinesses and locals who occupied desirable farmland, some on a much grander scale, and he was convinced that as long as they could keep a united front, the problem wouldn't last.

"So I got everyone together and said, 'Hey, we can't be afraid,'" Dias recounted. "'We have to sow our soybeans—all of us—no one can sit out. No one can hold back. If one of us doesn't take part, that will be another problem.'"

This was their land, wasn't it? Who begins planting in the middle of the night? Where was the piece of paper that gave the cotton company the right to come in? But even with backing from Maputo—Lozan Farms held the legal certificate that gave the association rights to that particular stretch of land—it was a slow start.

"All of us will sow, whether you have one hectare or more," Dias urged, "and when the cotton sprouts, we have to cut it. We can't leave it. These were our ancestors' fields!" Dias and his fellow farmers were born in Alto Molócue. They were cousins, sisters, in-laws. Their kin had lived and farmed chunks of land along the Namilepe for generations.

While Dias and his neighbors were sowing, António Regalo, the Portuguese director of Nova Algodoeira's operations in the

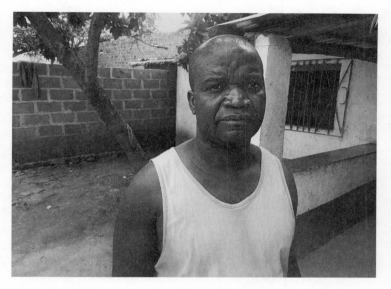

Marques Dias is part of a soybean-farming cooperative in Namilepe, Zambezia, that has repeatedly had to fend off incursions from a Portuguese-owned cotton company that claimed rights to the land.

area, drove his pickup truck out to Namilepe and came as far as the edge of the field, only to stand and watch, then leave without saying a word.

Once the cotton and soy both sprouted, though, Regalo proposed leaving both crops in the ground until harvest. João, smiling, seemed to see this as pure trickery. "They knew the soja doesn't have much strength," he said. "The cotton would choke it out."

When it came to pulling out the cotton, members, again, approached the work with hesitation, hanging back to see who would go first. There were rumors that Regalo was going to try to make the association pay 25,000 meticais in damages for every hectare of cotton they pulled out.

The end result was just the opposite: Regalo's tractor had saved the association weeks of work, clearing fields for planting in a fraction of the time it would have taken them with smaller equipment. All members had to do was sow their seed. It seems like Regalo even helped you, I said to Dias, tentatively, and he began to laugh. "Yes, yes," he said. "We made good profits that year."

A year later, though, members of the Associação Lozan Farms again found a tractor and two excavators working in broad daylight to clear land on another parcel that belonged to them, just below the first. The routine repeated itself: unanswered pleas for the drivers to stop, a hurried meeting of the members, and a phone call to Lozan Farms' headquarters in Maputo.

This time, they took their complaint to the *posto administrativo*— the nearest government office—and received official blessing to send Nova Algodoeira packing. Again, they planted soybeans where the cotton company had tilled the land, and again, the association was spared the expense of tilling a large field.

Dias's group has something most rural farmers do not: a title, or DUAT—Direito de Uso e Aproveitamento da Terra—the legal document confirming their right to the use and improvement of the land.

DUATs are still the exception to the rule of land tenure in Mozambique: according to the World Bank, of a total of 3 to 4 million parcels in the country, fewer than 5 percent have been formalized with a DUAT.[3]

Land disputes, or *conflitos de terra*, have become a hallmark of development and investment throughout Mozambique. What makes Anselmo João and Marques Dias's experience with the cotton company noteworthy is not that there was a dispute in the first place, but the fact that they won out so easily.

Mozambique's land law stipulates that land cannot be sold. Land belongs to the state, and anyone who occupies it gets the right to do so in one of two ways: occupying a parcel continuously in "good faith" for ten years or more, or submitting a proposal to the government to use it for a set period and a specific purpose.[4]

Most of the land in rural areas like Namilepe falls under the rubric of "customary use," which allows parcels passed down from generation to generation within a local community to be grandfathered into the legal system without a DUAT.[5]

In practice, though, rights stemming from customary, or traditional, use have proved devilishly difficult to uphold, sometimes even when they are formalized.

By 2009–10, "community" land rights had been mapped out across 12 percent of Mozambique's total landmass. But a study of these "delimited" communities by Mozambique's Judicial Training Center (Centro de Formação Jurídica e Judiciária), a branch of the Ministry of Justice, found one out of every six they surveyed in "open conflict with a private investor or the state."[6]

Some contend that conflict has been a feature of every major land deal during Mozambique's boom years. Examples abound: not far from Namilepe, in Lioma district, hundreds of soybean farmers cried foul soon after a Portuguese holding company was awarded a concession that included land they'd farmed in cooperatives for years. When it came time for planting, the company, Quifel, targeted rich land that had already been cleared—regardless of whether it was included in the original concession.

In Chikweti, Niassa, in Mozambique's far north, a huge forestry project powered with money from a Dutch government pension fund and managed by the Lutheran Church made front-page news in the Netherlands after Mozambicans resorted to vandalizing equipment and burning pine and eucalyptus plantations to make their frustrations heard. Chikweti Forests of Niassa is the subsidiary of an investment fund founded to promote "forest-based investments with high potential returns and a strong ethical, environmental and socio-economical profile, including community development." But the company had ended up seizing twice as much land as the Mozambican government had originally awarded it, and reneging on promises to compensate those who had been displaced.[7]

Farther east, on a dry plateau not far from the border with Tanzania, the multinational mining company Gemfields—among the world's largest suppliers of sapphires and emeralds—became interested in a ruby deposit discovered by a local farmer in 2009.[8] By the time Gemfields got involved, the land was controlled by Raimundo Pachinuapa, a Frelimo general and the former governor of the province, Cabo Delgado. As the journalist Estacio Valoi has reported, locals dispute Pachinuapa's claims that he compensated them for the land, but he was nonetheless able to secure a prospecting license and Gemfields's backing to dig rubies out from 81,000 hectares of red clay. Once mining got under way, farmers and small-scale local miners clashed with the company and complained of violence at the hands of the security subcontractors and plainclothes vigilantes. In 2014, units from the Forças de Intervenção Rápida, Mozambique's equivalent of a SWAT team, responded to the unrest by burning more than three hundred homes.[9]

Both the Chikweti forestry project and the Hoyo Hoyo soybean-growing operation in Lioma undoubtedly suffered setbacks as a result of land protests. In Lioma, the local administrator prolonged the standoff by siding with the smallholders. UNAC's Niassa chapter appealed to the stated mission of Chikweti's investors in a petition: "We do not understand why church institutions and other investment funds invest their members' money in projects that exploit the poorest of the poor."

But both projects were ultimately undone by the underlying economics. The commodities they wanted to produce became too cheap; the costs of doing business in a remote country with poor roads and unreliable power were too great to make either scheme viable. Demand for rubies is apparently not as sensitive to price fluctuations as it is for wood pulp and soybeans. Both a sitting president and an attorney general made visits to Montepuez in the wake of strife between Gemfields and local people, and yet today, mining continues in what observers now believe to be the largest field of rubies in the world.

Over time, scenarios like these have given rise to a deep skepticism that the basic protections the land law prescribes will actually be upheld. Investors, after all, are supposed to have access only to "unused land," or to enter into negotiations with the communities their projects will displace. However incrementally, the growing record of overreach has prompted a reevaluation of Mozambique's long-held development strategy, which has often pushed large-scale investor-driven projects above all else.

In 2009, Mozambique signed a partnership with Japan and Brazil to transform millions of acres of "unproductive" land in the north of the country into a showcase for development.[10] The project, dubbed ProSAVANA, was predicated on the idea that the economies of scale unleashed by foreign capital and expertise would accelerate development across northern Mozambique.

ProSAVANA was to be modeled after the 1980s boom that transformed the vast, dry Brazilian Cerrado into a feeding trough for the global meat industry: together, Brazilian corporations and Japanese know-how would harness a North Carolina–sized stretch of Mozambican land to grow soybeans for the world.

Locals and Mozambican civil society organizations questioned the project's basic premise: what, exactly, did Mozambicans stand to gain from ceding control of vast tracts of productive land to Brazilian agribusiness? Why not boost technical assistance and financial support for the farmers who were already there? Fierce opposition from groups like UNAC was buoyed by international advocacy campaigns highlighting "the largest landgrab in Africa."[11] Activists and academics alike lambasted the lack of community participation in drafting ProSAVANA's master plan, which leaked out in bits and pieces and appeared to exclude small farmers altogether.

As Brazilian executives arranged trips to Mozambique to scope out land, press accounts confirmed the smallholders' worst fears—that Brazilian companies expected to secure vast tracts of uninterrupted land in one of the highest-density agricultural regions in Mozambique.

"Mozambique is a Mato Grosso in the middle of Africa," Carlos Ernesto Augustin, president of the Mato Grosso cotton producers association, told *Folha de São Paulo* in 2011, referring to his home province in Brazil, a commodity farming powerhouse.[12] "The price of land there is too good to ignore."[13]

"Mozambique has enormous areas available for agriculture," Charles Hefner, head of GV Agro, the group coordinating Brazilian investments, told a São Paulo weekly when he returned from a trip to the Nacala corridor. Hefner said investors planned to target "abandoned areas," where no agriculture was practiced. "There's space for mega-projects of 30 or 40,000 hectares without major social impacts," he said.[14] But Brazilian investors do not appear to be interested in ProSAVANA: a fund set up to raise $2 billion to promote agribusiness in Nampula's Nacala corridor closed in 2015, as low commodity prices and Brazil's own economic crisis made it a riskier bet.

Local opposition and international campaigns branding ProSAVANA a "landgrab," meanwhile, pushed the Japan International Cooperation Agency, JICA, to send its team back to the drawing board. "We have changed the concept, so it is now not for big farmers but for small farmers," a JICA spokesperson said in 2016.[15]

Today, ProSAVANA continues to limp along through successive planning phases as local opposition smolders. Some observers see the project's halting fate as a major victory for the land rights movement and a sign of Frelimo's evolving development policy. As Joseph Hanlon has noted, not a single large-scale plantation project has succeeded in Mozambique in the forty years since independence—from Frelimo's cooperative farms in the 1980s to a litany of biofuel and feed projects promoted by international boosters and local politicians.

José Pacheco, a former governor of Cabo Delgado who became agriculture minister in 2010, began his tenure by saying "we want to do here what they did in the [Brazilian] Cerrado thirty years ago." But the work plan Pacheco ultimately drafted for the Ministry of Agriculture called for prioritizing small and medium farms and reversing 1990s-era World Bank restrictions on locally grown seed and government support for domestic agriculture.[16] Some of these measures would undoubtedly help, if only they can make it out of the ministry and into the *machambas* intact.

Government land ownership has been a hallmark of many of Mozambique's peers and neighbors—one strand of the "African socialism" that took root in the early years of independence in Mozambique, Tanzania, Senegal, and many other countries.[17] In a sense, nationalizing land offered a powerful way to throw off the yoke of the colonial era: to curb the wealth and influence of groups that had benefited under empire and to restore the rights of people long denied the ability to create wealth for themselves.

Less than two weeks before independence, Samora Machel, the fiery Frelimo commander who became Mozambique's first president, made a speech in the concrete stands of a soccer field outside Beira.[18]

"We want to create a new Mozambique. New type of relations between people," he said to a crowd who stood on the grass before him, calling Beira "the center of white racism."

Beira, the port city near the crook in Mozambique's Y-shaped map, had been a center of colonial resistance to Frelimo's gradual march south until a cease-fire was signed less than a year earlier. With the war now won, Machel was on a monthlong victory tour, holding rallies from the "Rovuma to Maputo"—tip to tip of Mozambique.

"We know that our country is in ruins. We don't have hospitals," Machel boomed. "Yes or no?"[19]

"*Yes*!!" the crowd roared.

"We don't have schools. We don't have factories. We live without blankets in our huts. Yes or no?" he asked.

"*Yes!*"

> But we have a chance to grow cotton. Yes or no? (Yes). We live on drinking hot water all the time, to avoid stomach ache and stomach disturbances because we have no rice, because we have no corn at home. The fields are occupied. Yes or no? (Yes). They are properties. Here in Mozambique, there is no land for so-and-so, there is no land for the people, here! . . .
>
> So, it's only FRELIMO that will indicate where each one of us will produce. We didn't die to create private farms, private properties here in Mozambique. Above all, the land, the land belongs to mankind, to the people. It isn't anybody's. Do you hear? (We hear).

To read Mozambique's 1997 land law is to see some of this revolutionary spirit on paper. It asserts the right of equal access to land for men and women, and the authority of rural communities to participate in awarding land titles, resolving disputes, and managing natural resources.[20]

It places a "community consultation" at the center of the process for awarding title to investors. But the concept of community consultations is squishy, and the process for allocating land is often comically lopsided. Like anything with the potential to constrain profit, the noblest parts of the law—the requirement for community input, say—can be difficult to enforce and tempting to ignore.

One of the law's primary goals has been to insulate land distribution from the pressures of the market. In practice, the law hasn't removed market forces so much as distorted them, placing the levers of supply and demand in the hands of a powerful set of gatekeepers. The result is a kind of paradox: land cannot be bought or sold, yet profit remains the driving force behind a huge share of land transactions.

This is true even where money is not directly involved. As in ruby-rich Montepuez, or in Catembe, a suburb that will soon be connected to Maputo by a bridge, the prospect of a return on investment is what drives interest in a given slice of the map. Yet the prohibition on buying or selling means that even with a clearly valuable piece of land, the people with the most to lose often don't get a full seat at the negotiating table. The transaction is not between the people who want the land and the people who already live there, but between the people who want the land and the public officials who can deliver it to them. Far from Machel's message of liberation, the net effect of Frelimo's land policies has often been to carry forward some of the very injustices the party aimed to upend.

Nova Algodoeira's land forms a gentle slope on the south side of the Rio Namilepe, an undulating, shallow river that gives the community its name and forms the boundary between Nampula and Zambezia—Mozambique's most populous and most agriculturally productive provinces.

When I visited, in February 2016, the whole tract was planted in a single massive field, with rows hundreds of yards long, and pink and white cotton blossoms beginning to unfurl in a sea of green.

Until 2013, some thirty families kept their homes and raised corn and vegetables in the parcel where Nova Algodoeira now grows cotton. The land is some of the best around, nearly seven hundred acres of dark, loamy earth, loose to the touch and free of stones.

To the north, across the river, half-bald inselbergs covered with tufts of forest rise from a landscape of gentle hills and shallow valleys. To the west, the county seat is a full day's bicycle ride—or, more commonly today, a couple of hours' motorcycle ride—away.

I made my way to Namilepe with Damião Caixão, a fiery, barrel-chested farmer and organizer with massive hands and a silky baritone laugh. Caixão splits his time between the UNAC office in the county seat of Alto Molócue and a farm in Namilepe just downhill from Nova Algodoeira.

We left at six a.m. on what would become a scorching-hot Sunday. Caixão wore a fully zipped fisherman's vest and jeans over a button-down and a long-sleeve T-shirt, even as he complained about the heat. *"Esse calor, pa,"* he said, repositioning his hat and wiping his face with a handkerchief.

Along the way, houses advertise single-item stores of sorts with front yard displays—a pile of beans and an empty tin can set out on a rice sack, or an upside-down wrapper for Safari cigarettes planted on a stick stuck in the ground. A curtain of corn and cassava gradually narrowed the roadway as we got farther from the city.

Caixão's complaints about Nova Algodoeira began at the tail end of the trip. First, the road—he blamed the constant back-and-forth of heavy equipment for deep ruts and channels worsened by the rain—and then everything else.

People on their way home from church crisscrossed the field every which way, trampling plants underfoot without seeming to notice. Caixão laughed and explained that the company had eliminated the footpaths people used to rely on.

Late in the afternoon, Caixão and I went up the hill from his house to look for Lucas Arturo Kutula, the *líder da zona*, or local headman, of the community that had been displaced. Caixão pulled his tiny blue Geo Tracker to a stop on the road that cuts Nova Algodoeira's field in two. Nearby, a woman with a baby on her back was plodding through the furrows as though she were walking on deep sand. This was Kutula's wife, Joaquina António. Caixão called out to her in Lomué, and she disappeared beyond the field's edge for a few minutes before returning with her husband.

"I was born here, and raised here too," he proclaimed plaintively, "in this very field. I've been living here for sixty-five years, but now I've been kicked out."

"They surprised us," António added, speaking of Nova Algodoeira.

"They just came, and we didn't know a thing about them," the *chefe* said, breaking into Portuguese, as Caixão translated. "They didn't even do a *consulta comunitária!*" said António.

Even in the more remote areas of Mozambique, people seem to be familiar with the basic quid pro quo of the land law: companies are required to conduct meetings, or community consultations, to tell locals about a proposal, vet conflicts, and agree on compensation or community benefits that will flow from the project.

In Namilepe, as it turned out, there had been a community consultation for that parcel of land. Back in 2008, residents had agreed to move when a school and a health clinic were promised in exchange. But that agreement was made six years before Nova Algodoeira's arrival. In fact, it involved a different entity altogether: the Associação Acção Rural Contra a Pobreza Absoluta, or ARCOPA, an association of veterans of Mozambique's war for independence who planned to grow corn with farming equipment donated by the government.

On the three-page agreement noting community approval for the project in Namilepe, the stretched-out cursive of a technician from the local office of economic development records the names of eight people present for the *consulta comunitária*, though another blank says "15" members of the community were present.

Locals placed high hopes in ARCOPA: "We hope the new investor creates a good partnership with us, as members of an association counting on more support," one farmer said, according to the form. Damião Caixão was there, it notes, representing Lozan Farms. "We would like to see lots of initiatives like this one. We are ready to welcome you, and hope for a better partnership so that we can fight absolute poverty together," he said.

There's no mention of the promises ARCOPA made to people in Namilepe, and no term sheet or suggestion of what might happen if the project failed.

ARCOPA went through the process of getting a land title only to sputter and fold within the first couple of years. "They were lazy," is how Caixão described it. Here and there, ARCOPA farmers stripped the brush from bits of their 250-hectare parcel to open new fields, but they never managed to clear and plant enough land to make the effort viable. So Kutula and his neighbors stayed on, undisturbed.

For years, locals wondered what had happened to ARCOPA and to the promised school and clinic that had never materialized. Then, much as it would happen downhill with the Associação Lozan Farms, one day in June 2013, António Regalo showed up with his tractors.

As it turned out, Nova Algodoeira hadn't even pretended to go through the motions of obtaining a DUAT legally. Instead of approaching the government to initiate a new investment proposal, the company simply paid ARCOPA to take the reins of its failed project. Regalo freely admitted as much. "We got the land, started working it, and 'pronto!'" he'd told me.

Regalo and his employees began at the high end of the parcel, using an excavator to remove trees and set them in piles to burn,

The *líder da zona*, or headman, Lucas Arturo Kutula, right, stands in Nova Algodoeira's six-hundred-acre cotton field in Namilepe with some of his neighbors, who say the company forced them out and bulldozed their homes.

grading the area with a tractor as it was cleared, stopping work only when he reached a garden or a house.

As Caixão and I spoke with Kutula and António, our conversation gradually drew a peanut gallery of fifteen or twenty people who seemed to materialize out of nowhere into the deserted expanse of cotton all around us. Women walking with canes or with children strapped to their chests, men with sacks slung over their shoulders, people who might have been on their way to a relative's house or simply strolling in the shade of mango trees on the edge of the field. One by one, the curious set down their things and squinted in the sun, listening, until the school director, Castelo Xavier Mutupa, who stood leaning against his bicycle, broke in to help the couple tell the story.

It turned out that these were the *líder*'s former neighbors, some of the many who had lived in the cotton field where we now stood.

"He came with his machine ready," the school director broke in, in rapid-fire Lomué.

"And there you were working your land. He'd say, 'Senhor, you have to leave here' . . . with his *máquina* behind him," the school director said, switching for a moment to Portuguese.

"'*Voce, sai daí!*'" You, get out of there.

"This is the basis of our complaint," he said, as though he were facing António Regalo directly. "Look, you're standing there at home thinking, 'This is too much. You're going to destroy my house; you're going to destroy my orange tree; you're going to destroy my cassava plants. And where will I end up? At least give us something!' And that's when he'd pull out 1,000 meticais, maybe two, hand it over, and say, 'Okay, now get out.'"

"They didn't calculate what to pay based on what people actually possessed there, whether there was a house or an orange tree. Everything was destroyed"—he paused here to mime the sweep of heavy machinery with one arm—"whether people were satisfied or not. They just handed out money and the person had to leave."

Earlier in the day, Anselmo João had given me a similar version of events, and at first, I was taken aback. A string of questions rattled out: Did anyone show them documents? How did they agree on an amount for each house? How much advance notice was there? How much time did he give them to move once they got paid?

"He didn't give them any time," João said of Regalo, while we sat beneath the thatch roof sheltering the tractor Caixão rents out to other members of the association. "It was only, 'We bought this field, mister, get out!' He had the tractor running there behind him. And, pronto, the person in question left."

With more clarification, it seemed Regalo had gone about clearing the parcel over the course of a few days, paying families to leave more or less on the spot as tractors reached their homes.

"That day, all you heard was loud complaints," João said. "'We're homeless, *desalojados*, where are we going to live?'"

"Since *branco é branco*," João continued, a faint grin softening his resignation, "*não havia de discutir.*" Since a white man is a white man, there was no discussing it.

Delicate flowers were just starting to unfurl from tens of thousands of Nova Algodoeira's cotton plants, filling a fertile belt of black soil above the river. João's neighbors, meanwhile, had been reduced to coaxing cassava from hard, sandy ground just beyond it, to the north. "Everyone was lamenting the sand there where they're trying to figure out a way to live now," he said.

Branco é branco is a phrase I've heard again and again in talking to Mozambicans about land. Essentially, it means there's no stopping them.

"Where did the phrase come from?" I asked João. We were sitting in white plastic patio chairs just yards from the edge of the cotton field. João and Caixão laughed out loud. "Is that how they talked when you were a kid too, '*branco é branco*'?" I asked João, now in his seventies.

"*Simmmm!*" he said insistently. Yessss! There was more laughter.

"Because white people have what they need in life—they have means."

"Do you remember hearing it for the first time?" I asked.

"My story is this: when a white person came around . . . he'd get to the *régulo*'s house, the *régulo* would invite the people to gather round, and say, '*Ja recebemos um branco.*'" We have a white guest. *Régulo* is the Portuguese word for Mozambique's hereditary chiefs. Historically, *régulos* had authority over local land and community disputes, based partly on their role mediating a community's connections with ancestral spirits.[21] During the colonial era, the Portuguese worked to consolidate control over rural Mozambique by making *régulos* represent state interests at the local level—extracting labor and taxes, or upholding colonial laws.[22]

"This white man came to deal with such and such—either a field, or he was starting a store, or something else," João went on. "So, if the spot in question, if there was someone who already lived there, he was informed, 'Sir, get out of here; this white man is going to do some work here.' And from there, you had to clean up and get out of there. And they'd give you a bit of change, and then you had to get out of there. You had to be grateful for whatever you got."

João threw up his hands with finality.

"And you'd say . . . ?" I asked.

"And you'd say, '*branco é branco.*'"

At times, foreigners' interest and influence on the Mozambican economy can seem inescapably modern—the mining of minerals used to make white paint and toothpaste, the cell phone–enabled chatter of the Chinese logging industry, the harnessing of farmland not to grow food for export, but to grow biofuels. And yet the land conflict in Namilepe is an example that reaches straight into the past, through several generations of displacement.

In the colonial era, Anselmo João explained, Namilepe was home to a farm where he worked from the time he was a boy, weeding cabbage and potato fields and harvesting melons in the lowland flats by the river. Hundreds of acres more—from the river up to the *régulo*'s house, about a thirty-minute walk, João recalled—were planted with corn. The whole plantation was owned by a Portuguese family.

A few of the buildings still stand: a store gradually being conquered by vines, an eroding clay-brick warehouse without a roof, neat rows of cotton planted right up to their foundations.

Anselmo João stands by the crumbling outbuildings of the colonial farm where he worked as a boy, weeding cabbage and potato fields and harvesting melons in the lowland flats by the river.

A handful of families, João recalled, had had to abandon their homes to make way for the farm. When the operation shuttered after independence, they were quick to reclaim the land: colonists had taken the most productive areas for themselves. Soon afterward, the Mozambican government started a plantation of its own.

"Those of us who lived within the *machamba* started to work with the *empresa*," he said, referring to the state-owned company. "It was a choice: those who left here chose their land somewhere else. And the people who got to stay and work for the company, the company arranged houses for them, and left them there."

It was a pattern seen throughout the country. In an effort to salvage some of the engine of the colonial economy, Frelimo took up the same plantation approach to agriculture the Portuguese had, dusting off equipment that, in many cases, had been deliberately sabotaged by colonists who abandoned their holdings amid the war for independence.

Frelimo envisioned a kind of cooperative utopia, using modern practices and collective labor to multiply the bounty of each acre. But there was another lesson this approach impressed on Namilepe, too. "When it came to the land," as João put it, "the population had no rights left to defend."

Civil war ultimately undid the government's farming ambitions in Namilepe as well. By the late 1980s, rural Zambezia had been ravaged by nearly a decade of Renamo ambushes on anything associated with government. Counterassaults laid waste to communities deemed sympathetic to the guerrillas. A generation after the war, the most palpable evidence of its devastation are hundreds of hollowed-out buildings and half-standing walls, like the ones that mark the former plantation in Namilepe, abandoned to the elements after an attack, or actively burned to the ground.

In the center of Alto Molócue, seat of the county that includes Namilepe, there's a large concrete office building built in the austere midcentury style of the colonial government, divided neatly in two. On the right, a fresh coat of yellow paint and neat lettering welcome visitors to a recently renovated tax collection office. On the left, it appears nothing has been touched since the building was shelled in the 1980s: a massive concrete wall on one end looks as though it might fall at any moment, hanging in permanent half-collapse.

After the state farm in Namilepe planted its last crop, brush and trees slowly began to grow up in what had been a vast expanse of corn. People who had been displaced returned to the plantation again, building houses and carving out parcels of pigeon peas, cassava, and squash.

The first hint of renewed outside interest in Namilepe didn't come until ARCOPA's arrival in 2008, starting the cycle anew.

A fascist colonial government, a black Marxist government, and a multiparty capitalist democracy: over the course of several generations, people in Namilepe have had their most fertile land seized under all three, with little given in return. What can we make of this?

The law, of course, has become much friendlier to ordinary Mozambicans today than it was under the colonial regime, or even under the stricter impulses of Frelimo's early Marxism. Yet for all the changes that have swept through Mozambique since independence, the distance between the law and its application can sometimes seem insurmountable.

To reach Namilepe, enforcement and empowerment both must cross barriers of education and literacy, climb over broken motorcycles, nepotism, and the unpaid salaries of government workers, and break through the entrenched entitlement of the rich over the poor. On the other side of all those obstacles is the peasant experience, changed in critical ways, yet somehow marked by a fundamental continuity with respect to the powerful. No matter what else has changed, it seems, *branco é branco* still remains.

For his part, António Trebouco Regalo, director of Nova Algodoeira's operations in Alto Molócue, still seems much the same man he might have been in 1968, when he arrived from Portugal at twenty-one to serve in the colonial army.

Regalo works out of a low-slung stucco building on the outskirts of Alto Molócue. Rows of cotton seedlings run from behind the office right up to the service road wrapping around the company's warehouses, nearly to the edge of the street, as though the company sees each square foot of grass as a hit on profits.

When I visited, at seven a.m. on a cloudy Monday morning, more than forty women festooned with brightly colored *capulanas* were seated along a low wall beside the building and gathered around the entrance, waiting, they said, to be paid.

Inside, I passed through two well-kept offices manned by Mozambican clerks looking through longhand account books, and into a disorderly back room with the lights off and a large safe in one corner. Regalo shuffled about in the baggy dress clothes of a man more at home in the field than in the office. He's a small, rotund man with dark eyes and mussed hair, his face at rest in a soft grimace. Regalo looked up from an array of motorcycle parts, padlocks, and stacks of paper laid out on the desk before him, flashed a weak smile, and motioned for me to sit down.

At age twenty-eight, Regalo left military service, settled on a stretch of rich land in Nampula Province, not far north of Namilepe, and started planting cotton. "I had more than a thousand hectares of cotton when I ran my business," he said wistfully. "I was a young man. I was young, very young." He began his farm just before Mozambique won independence from Portugal. Many colonial settlers left rather than accept the new terms of existence under Frelimo. Regalo stuck it out for another decade, until the disruptions of the civil war meant he could no longer import fertilizer or replacement parts for his tractor. "It was a communist country," he said. "We didn't see a future, didn't see a way to earn anything for ourselves, for our old age."

After the war was over, though, Regalo returned and stayed. "I like to be here." He shrugged. "I earn a good salary, I have a good job, and I've been here until now."

The operation Regalo runs today is in many ways an heir to the colonial enterprises that dominated Mozambique in the early to mid-twentieth century. Nova Algodoeira's offices and blue-and-white warehouses were built in the 1950s by Companhia dos Algodões de Moçambique, whose concessions once covered half of Moçambique and Zambezia Provinces, an area the size of New York State.[23]

Today, the company both plants its own fields, Regalo told me, and engages local farmers as sharecroppers, providing fertilizer, pesticides, and equipment in exchange for a share of the yield. That side of the business, Regalo said, "doesn't work very well, because the people aren't very motivated to grow cotton." After years of trying to expand its footprint in Zambezia, the company grows its own cotton on close to fifteen thousand acres, and it sharecrops just a fraction of that amount.

Regalo wasn't sure how to explain this. "The way I see it, before independence, people here weren't motivated to grow cotton on their own because there were a lot of weeds and they didn't get good results," he reasoned.

"The only work some people do today is strolling around town," he said, raising an eyebrow. "There's no interest in picking up a hoe and starting to work."

What this dim view of Mozambican smallholders leaves out is the system of forced labor that allowed the Portuguese to build a cotton industry in Mozambique in the first place. In the 1930s, after a period of tumultuous government that left Portugal nearly bankrupt and helped lead to a military coup, the regime of a right-wing António Salazar resolved to get more out of Portugal's colonies. Mozambique would be the engine that made Portugal's domestic textile industry flourish by providing a steady supply of cotton to replace the imports that fed the looms in Lisbon factories.

By the end of the 1930s, huge swaths of Mozambique were divvied into concessions for a small number of state-sanctioned cotton companies. The firms enjoyed monopolies as buyers in the areas where they operated, and the assurance that they could rely on the colonial government to enforce cotton-growing quotas imposed on every adult living within the bounds of their territory.[24]

In Nyasa Province,[25] local administrators imposed a quota of four hundred kilos of cotton per year; in other areas, Mozambicans were forbidden from tending the crops they grew for food except after five p.m. and on some Sundays. Colonial administrators enforced such provisions with whips and clubs and the threat that those who refused would be sent to work on government railroads and tea or sugar plantations with no pay at all.

"If we refused to grow cotton they arrested us, put us in chains, beat us, then sent us to a place from where we didn't come back," an old woman in Niassa told Frelimo militants in an interview recounted by Eduardo Mondlane, the founding father of Mozambique's independence struggle.[26]

Peasants resisted mightily: they fled cotton-growing zones, burned the crop and scattered its ashes through the woods, filled cotton sacks with pebbles to make weight, and robbed colonial warehouses in order to resell the cotton elsewhere to meet their quotas. A Cabo Delgado man interviewed by the historian Allen Isaacman in 1979 recalled living on a mountain where a group of refugees hid in caves and rolled boulders down on top of Portuguese soldiers trying to drive them out by force.[27]

In one successful ploy practiced throughout the country, Isaacman writes, whole villages of farmers fooled colonial officials into thinking cotton wouldn't grow on their land at all, by agreeing collectively—and in secret—to cook their cottonseeds before planting them. "Once this collective decision had been made, those involved went through all the motions of clearing, sowing, and weeding, but few or no plants germinated. Cotton officials and the colonial authorities were naturally surprised at the low yield, which they attributed to the poor quality of the soil or other natural deficiencies. By repeating the subterfuge over a two- or three-year period, many peasants freed themselves from the tyranny of the cotton regime."

"The Africans in this part continually fabricate excuses why they have not seeded any cotton yet," complained an agriculture official in Nampula Province in 1947. "This year it is the lack of rain."[28] Farmers refused to accept cottonseed distributed by the colonial government and skipped rounds of required weeding as it grew.

To colonial administrators, all these were evidence of Mozambicans' "laziness and bad will"—not, as Isaacman points out, "conscious efforts to maximize food production."

By some measures, resistance worked: official figures from the early 1940s show that across the northern part of the country, Mozambicans cultivated an average of only two-thirds of the minimum area colonial law required.[29]

Yet cotton was extracted in ever greater quantities, often at the price of widespread hunger, as the forced labor system gobbled up both the space and the free time people needed to grow things they could eat. In 1927, Isaacman reports, Portugal's colonies contributed only 5 percent of the cotton needed to sustain its textile industry. By 1953, just twenty-five years later, Mozambique alone produced all the cotton required for Portuguese industry and a surplus for export besides.[30]

A sour look spread over Regalo's face as I relayed the peasants' side of the story. "It's not true! We're here to do things in a consensual way," he protested. "This followed negotiations; it was voluntary," he said. "People presented themselves to move and get compensated."

Regalo didn't dispute that these "negotiations" happened with a tractor running in the background, clearing away the neighbors' houses, or that the amount of compensation was determined with a tape measure—based solely on the square footage of people's plots, rather than the value of the crops and homes within them.

The group I'd spoken with in Namilepe seemed most worked up by the costs and time required to replace what they'd lost.

Metal roofs and wooden rafters had been damaged as the houses were dismantled in a hurry, or simply knocked down and left for salvage. Rosa Paolo, an old woman in a purple shawl, had rattled off a list of the trees Nova Algodoeira's tractors had uprooted when she lost her home. "*Banana, mangueiras, laranjeiras, pera abacate,*" she said. Banana, mango trees, orange trees, avocado. "And they only gave me 3,000." At the time, 3,000 meticais would have been about $100.

"They got 10,000!" Regalo objected. "Some got 12,000!"

I ceded the point: let's say they did get 10,000 or 12,000 meticais. Did $300 or $400 really seem like enough for people to give up houses, mature fruit trees, and some of the most desirable farmland in the area?

"In America, $300 might be just enough to find a place to sleep, right?" Regalo ventured. "Here, the quality of life is very different. I'm not saying you become rich with $300, you stay poor, but you can organize something to help yourself. And besides, that *machamba*, people may have had small little plots with houses there, but they had houses in other places too. If someone owns a little bit of land, he'll treat it well, plant trees, he'll do things well because it belongs to him," Regalo said.

"But here in the bush, a person can change *palhotas*, he starts growing somewhere else, his trees are abandoned, his trees are burned, because it doesn't belong to him: his land isn't limited."

Regalo's gripe goes to the heart of a central question of land tenure in Mozambique (and anywhere else where land is held in common, or without title): what does it mean for land to be "available"?

The dominant form of farming in Mozambique uses no tractors, no animals, no fertilizer, no pesticides, and no irrigation—nothing Regalo might recognize as farming. The vast majority of farmers have no access to credit to buy seed or inputs ahead of time. They grow food with a machete, a hoe, and very little else. Accordingly, a large chunk of small farms in Mozambique don't grow enough food for the families who run them.[31]

Most small farmers shift their growing areas periodically, letting fields go fallow for years at a time to restore the soil. And while the average size of these subsistence farms is small—about the size of two football fields—keeping the farm productive year after year often requires alternating with an equivalent area of fallow land.

Should that fallow land be considered "free and unoccupied," as the land law requires for it to be leased to outside investors?[32] What about the vast hillsides and tracts of scrubby savannah used for grazing goats and cattle? Or the miombo woods and ironwood and mahogany forests where people hunt and collect plants for construction, medicine, food, and handicrafts?

There's a wide range of opinion on just how big a pie investors and rural Mozambicans have to share in the country's fields, grassland, and forests not part of national parks or other government lands. Estimates run from 12 to 19 million hectares, or, roughly, from an area a little bigger than Maine to one that would cover all of New England.[33]

But for a time, at the peak of Mozambique's economic expansion in the 2000s, land deals seemed to track with Regalo's view of a resource that "isn't limited." In a six-year period starting in 2004, the government granted investors concessions covering close to 2.5 million hectares.[34] That's nearly half the area used by Mozambique's smallholders—some two out of every three families in the country.[35]

Land deals made at that breakneck pace laid bare the weak process in place to safeguard community rights, along with incoherent aspects of the land law itself. Concessions given to investors overlapped with parcels already delimited as "community" land.[36]

Conflicts sprouted by the hundreds.[37] Eventually, in 2009, the government imposed a moratorium on concessions over a thousand hectares, which lasted until 2011.[38]

Yet government officials have continued to appear in many transactions not as impartial arbiters or advocates, but as the cheerleaders and even bedfellows of powerful people seeking land. In spite of its progressive roots, the land law offers only vague answers on key questions of process. The fragility of the Mozambican state and the lack of education in the countryside have often combined with tragic consequences for communities that rely on the land for their livelihoods.[39]

The District Directorate of Agriculture in Alto Molócue is on the west side of town. When I visited in February 2016, a bad flood had washed out a bridge over the Molócue River the year before, separating half the city and a number of government buildings from the main highway and commercial downtown.[40] Cars had to take a several-mile detour to meet their passengers on the other side. Motorcycles made their way over an improvised plank crossing just inches above the water level.

Just twenty feet downstream, the open jaws of the original bridge framed a cascade of muddy water as construction workers stood on the banks.

I crossed over the bridge's unfinished replacement in a stream of pedestrians who casually ignored logs placed at either end to prevent anyone crossing.

Leandro Marcos, a UNAC colleague of Caixão's who had come with us to Namilepe, was waiting on the other side. Marcos, a lanky, moon-faced agronomist with a nasal voice, had arranged a meeting for me with the district director of agriculture, Argenio Candua, and he spent much of the bumpy ride home eagerly coaching me on how to approach the interview.

"'Senhor Director, I just want to talk about the agricultural economy here, the level of development,'" he suggested. "Start with general questions.

"There's not a question he won't answer," Marcos continued, smiling. "He'll answer every single thing you have to ask him— he'll just lie." Marcos urged me, for his own sake, not to let the director know I'd been with UNAC to Namilepe already. "He'll say, 'I'm the boss, how could you bring visitors around my district without coming to see me first?'"

"I don't need to tell him everything," I countered, "but I can't lie to him." It wouldn't be worthwhile, I thought, to recount much of what the director had to say about land conflicts in his district if I couldn't ask questions or write about the visit to Namilepe.

"*Não, não, não, não!*" Marcos protested gamely. "In the book, say everything. *Everything,*" he insisted. "Don't hold back. Just *tomorrow* . . ."

When we got up the hill, we were told the director hadn't come in yet. Marcos ran out to cash a check at the bank, and I took a seat on the concrete wall that bordered the property. Forty-five minutes later, an assistant ushered us into a mint-green office that felt, as the rest of Alto Molócue climbed into the nineties, like a walk-in refrigerator. Once upon a time, this building had been part of the colonial administration, and it was obvious that it was being gradually reclaimed from the decay of the war years.

Trails of delicate rosettes swooped and curled up the walls and across the ceiling, showing where vines that once grew inside the building had been pulled down. Cabinets on one end, battered and missing fixtures, had received a new coat of brown paint.

Yawning, the director waved us in and scolded Marcos for leaving to run an errand while I waited for the meeting to start. "We agreed on eight thirty," he said sharply. "You came and then you left your guest here. You can't do things that way."

("He's a boss," Leandro said with a shrug when I asked him about the reprimand later. "He has to talk that way, to show he's a boss.")

Candua spoke in a low monotone and yawned throughout our meeting, but I found him more candid than I'd expected after Marcos's disclaimer.

Frelimo's stated land policies have taken a turn in recent years. Low commodity prices, popular pressure, and the evolving views of donor organizations have hastened a shift away from megaprojects and toward a development agenda that puts more emphasis on small and midsized commercial farms. For the time being, these farms number well under a hundred thousand, out of close to 4 million nationwide.[41] The vast majority of Mozambican farmers aren't able to grow enough food to support their families throughout the year; to bridge the gap, they toil at the margins of the cash economy selling firewood and charcoal, or doing day labor known as *ganho ganho*.[42]

"Many producers in the family sector participate in the market in a highly unfavourable way: selling quickly after harvest for very low prices, then returning to buy the same products during the hunger period, but at very high prices," reports the Strategic Plan for Development of the Agriculture Sector, a government plan meant to guide farming policy for 2011–20.[43]

"More than 90 percent of Alto Molócue's producers grow crops primarily for their own consumption," Candua said. "We're trying to help more producers participate in the whole supply chain—not just production, but getting things to market, and if possible, processing."

For this strategy to succeed, the land law will need to work better than it has in the past. Investors, naturally, are most interested in land with the same characteristics that make it desirable to Mozambican farmers: soil quality, access to water and roads. Enticed by pitches promising rapid expansion and a slice of future profits, the government has not often been willing to say no to foreigners in order to support what the researchers Teresa Smart and Joseph Hanlon call "emergent" farmers.[44] But the gains from closer management of these family-owned commercial farms—familiarity with the land, close relationships with the people providing the labor, mixed cropping, and willingness to experiment—can actually outweigh the economies of scale of a giant farm and leave much more of the profit to filter into the local economy.[45]

"The land law isn't finished," Candua said. "It's not a perfect document: it's evolving." Candua thought people were working on "corrections" in the legislature and in the Ministry of Agriculture. The most significant change in recent years has been to require two meetings, rather than one, for community consultations—one to map out the land in question and another to seek community approval.

As the national director of agriculture, Rafik Valá, told the sociologist João Feijó in a recent book of interviews, the problem with the way resettlement has often been done is that "there was no vision of what we wanted for the [affected] population."[46]

"You can't compensate someone by saying 'how much did you produce last year?' 'This many hectares.' 'Okay, take this, look, you can have 7,000 meticais,'" Valá said. "You have to consider his whole life." The government had had some missed opportunities to level the scales between communities and investors, he acknowledged. But he also bristled at criticism of community consultations by groups like UNAC. When you hear an old farmer speak out, he said, "You can see he's being used. He doesn't know what he's saying, because he's been convinced to say certain things."[47] Of course, that description also sounds a lot like the community consultation held in Namilepe.

An imperfect land law—even one marred by poor record keeping, power imbalances, and, sometimes, unseemly arrangements with local officials, as the sociologist Madeleine Fairbairn has

pointed out—is probably better than none at all. Without it, Fairbairn reasons, Mozambique's postwar boom years might have
brought "an unbridled scramble for land" with little to stand in
its way.[48]

But there are still glaring omissions. "There's no legal mechanism, as it stands, for someone to advocate for the *camponês*"—or
peasant, Candua, Alto Molócue's district director of agriculture,
said. "Only the local government."

"District administrators retain a central role," writes Joseph
Hanlon, "and are often caught in the middle."[49] "On one hand, many
want to support their local communities, and would like to defend
communities in conflict with would-be investors. On the other
hand, district administrations often receive mobile telephone calls
from senior party people, at the provincial or national level, saying 'find land for X,' who may simply be the relative of someone
important in Frelimo, or who may be a serious investor."

There is also no specific standard for what constitutes community
approval. Five people? Ten people? Five hundred people? Which
people? On what conditions?

On these questions, "The law isn't clear," Candua said. In spite
of the requirement for two or more meetings, community consultations for an area the size Regalo occupied often take place in a
single, brief encounter, with no opportunity for communities to
engage in meaningful deliberation or inform people who are not
present before they sign off.[50]

Typically, Candua said, advance notice is sent through the *chefe da
localidade* or *posto administrativo*—the most local levels of government. Representatives for the business seeking land arrive alongside officials from the district or provincial government and pass out
a "goodwill" payment of 300 or 500 meticais (depending on the project) to be shared among community members in attendance.[51]

"It's natural to say the community, which has far less experience and knowledge in these things, is influenced to give answers in favor of the business," Candua said. "They don't get a period to analyze, how exactly is this going to be? And there's no one there, no documents to tell them, 'Okay, this is what's possible,' so they could look and say, 'This is how this program is going to benefit us.' That doesn't exist, so most of the time, it culminates in this kind of sudden, improvised answer, which is, 'No, we can! We want the business here.' But our current framework looks at that as a legally binding contract," he said, whether or not community representatives seem to understand it.[52]

After Candua and I were done speaking, Afonso João Colaço, a gracious, cheerful technician who oversees survey work for land deals in Alto Molócue, walked me down the hallway to the office where he maintains copies of hundreds of DUATs and completed community consultation forms arranged in chronological order.

Colaço lifted a thick white binder onto the counter and took his seat on the other side. The paperwork for each consultation ran to only a couple of pages, leaving much of the process to the imagination. As has been noted in other parts of the country, participants are given a half dozen handwritten lines to outline any objections or concerns over a proposed project.[53]

In many cases, the signatures of people listed as "*camponês*"—peasants or smallholders—are scratched out in the tentative scrawl of someone who barely knows how to write. Some lists of community signatures are all spelled out in the same hand, presumably because some of the people "signing" can't read or write at all.

Concessions covering thousands of hectares were approved by tiny minorities of the people living within them: in one case, investors secured a timber concession nearly twice the size of Manhattan with the presence of twenty-five people from the surrounding communities.

One section of the form reads: "At the end of the meeting, this consultation contract was read in Portuguese and translated into _____ (local language)."

There is no space to lay out a project's scope or requirements beyond simple acreage, and there's nowhere to record what investors promise in return for cooperation from the locals, so that they might be held accountable for it later.

In theory, communities have the option to decline projects on their land for any reason at all. DUATs awarded to foreign investors can also be revoked after two years if they don't follow through on their development plan for the parcel. But neither Colaço nor Candua could recall an instance of either happening in Alto Molócue.

"They didn't even do a *consulta comunitária*," Joaquina António had complained, standing beside her husband in the cotton field. But the unfairness of their situation didn't necessarily strike them as being illegal. They'd never lived in a system where their land rights could be reliably asserted over those of outsiders.

"If you go there and ask people, 'Who do these fields belong to?' they'll say 'ARCOPA, Nova Algodoeira,'" Colaço said. "But if you come here, there's nothing that shows that's true."

Colaço said he'd visited Namilepe recently on other business—the most common disputes he's called to resolve are between family members after the death of a relative—and stopped to take stock of the situation with Nova Algodoeira.

He'd heard the company was going through a process with the provincial government to put ARCOPA's parcel into its name, but even that didn't match up with the reality. "The land that was measured out" for ARCOPA, Colaço said, "is not the parcel that's being cultivated."

Even so, the people in Namilepe seemed at a loss for how to resolve their situation. They said no one from the district government had been out to see them in more than two years, long enough that the top official in the area, the district administrator, had been transferred elsewhere.

Marques Dias, one of the UNAC activists who'd stopped Nova Algodoeira's incursions on his own fields, explained it this way: "[The administrator's] approach was always to boost morale for the population. He didn't say anything bad. Just 'I'm going to resolve your problem.' Then, when he left, nothing happened. He never said anything bad. He didn't speak very much. But they were always waiting for a favorable answer that didn't come."

"And people never went to town to follow up?" I asked.

Dias shook his head emphatically. "Nooooooooo—now, the person who could have accompanied them to do that is the *régulo* himself," he explained—the traditional headman. "But the *régulo* was eating his piece too. And when he's eating his share, there's no way."

For people who are accustomed to walking into the DMV or the county assessor's office in a tank top and sandals, say, and demanding prompt and responsive service, this scenario is difficult to imagine. How could it be that people would allow their homes to be usurped without making a thirty-mile trip to protest or demand answers from their government?

Dias laughed. "People here, the first thing they do is respect the *proprio régulo*. I don't know. I don't know how to say it. You can't do it." He paused. "For us, to contradict the *régulo*?" He trailed off. It was simply inconceivable.

I'd tried to ask the same question of the people in Namilepe, prompting Caixão to launch into an animated exchange that sent ripples of laughter through the group until I interjected to ask for translation.

"We were talking about the story of some monkeys," he said. "Two monkeys were together and they went to a third, saying, we want to divvy up our cake. The [third monkey] had a scale so you could weigh out equal parts. So he said, 'Fine, cut your cake in half and put it on the scale.' When it was heavier on one side, he'd cut a little bit off that side and put it in his mouth. Then the other side would be heavier, so he'd cut a bit from that side and put that in his mouth. By the time the scale was balanced, the cake was gone, and the two monkeys didn't get to eat their cake. That's the way it is here: the *régulo* said, '*Calma, calma, calma—a gente vai resolver a vossa problema.*' But when Mr. Regalo comes [with his cotton company] and says, 'Look, Régulo, here's a bit of wine,' he takes it. . . . Then, the time passes and the people are the ones who lose out."

Here, Castelo Mutupa, the short, wiry principal of the school in Nova Algodoeira's fields—now conducted, he said, under a mango tree—broke in. "Once the *régulo* says, 'Wait for me to resolve this problem,' there's not much thought of going around him."

"I didn't know that a race like yours felt the suffering of others," he said earnestly. "Now that I see that you are, in fact, understanding what we are going through . . . that gives us the idea that you can't just limit yourself to the *régulo*."

The *régulo* himself wasn't home when I visited Namilepe. But regardless of his motivations, the tragedy in all this is that it's up to the *régulo* to conduct negotiations on behalf of the community in the first place. Put aside the allegations of self-dealing and petty corruption and consider this example reported by Nicholas Hess, an American student doing dissertation research in Gaza Province, in southern Mozambique. Hess's fieldwork took him to a community on the Limpopo River where a consortium of international investors had recently launched a project to produce ethanol from tens of thousands of acres of sugarcane:

This community was advised by a government official to sign away a substantial piece of productive land next to a river. During the interview I was presented with a stack of unorganised legal documents, all written entirely in English, that gave the company a 50-year lease on the land and complete freedom to indiscriminately use and pollute the soil and water supply. In addition, the contract mandated that any subsequent legal arbitration would be handled in South African courts and that the community received only a small percentage of the profits. The community leader, an 82 year old woman, was illiterate, did not speak Portuguese (let alone English), was not given independent counsel and was genuinely surprised when I outlined some of the details of the contract to her.[54]

A second academic account of the same project, ProCana, cites the leader of another village inside the investors' concession area: "ProCana just came here and met with the leaders of the communities and in the first meeting leaders had to sign. Some of them just wanted to drink so they took their 300 meticais because they thought it was a government project and that they had no choice at all. But then when the community found out, they were very unhappy. They were upset with the leaders for signing before being informed and they were upset with the project because they would be left with very little space for their cattle."[55]

Even local leaders who take bribes to give projects their stamp of approval are acting on the basis of terribly little information. ProCana ultimately fell apart for other reasons: investors came to see its promises of sky-high ethanol yields—held in secrecy in proposals submitted to the Mozambican government—as unachievable.[56] The project was dissolved, but not before thousands of Mozambicans were moved off land by the Limpopo River, the water they used to grow rice and graze cattle turned over to a higher purpose.

In Namilepe, Regalo, too, is having doubts about Nova Algodoeira's future prospects. In his office in Alto Molócue, he got out a binder with a xeroxed map that said "ARCOPA" at the top and pointed to the hillside in dispute. With one finger, he traced the outline of the tract where ARCOPA had hoped to expand. Growing cotton couldn't be viable in the long term without access to more land and better irrigation, he said. "I can't predict the future, but we need to get bigger to have a viable production unit, to keep machinery there, to keep a technician there. Somewhere on the order of five hundred hectares. We're not going to go all the way there from here only to keep a *machamba* that can't produce anything." He couldn't see giving up the land. "It was in ARCOPA's plans to expand and expand," Regalo said. "We just want to carry out our plan. I'm old. Really, we want to do things that are worthwhile. So, if we see that corn is more productive than cotton, we'll do corn."

At vastly different scales, the plight of people displaced by Nova Algodoeira and ProCana reflects a failure to hold corporations accountable. Investors can gain access to land cheaply and generally keep it with taxes of less than a dollar per hectare per year. And in spite of what the land law allows, there's not much penalty for promising results and failing to deliver.[57]

Sixty days a year, Kutula and his neighbors pick cotton for Nova Algodoeira on their old land. Scarce as cash income is, they can't afford to refuse. They and Regalo disagree about how much he pays. Three or 3.5 meticais per kilo, he said; they insisted it was 2. As I left Regalo's office in Alto Molócue, I came alongside a man in the street and asked whether it was common to see so many people gathered outside. The women had been promised 10 meticais per hundred-meter row they weeded, he said. As it turned out, he was also waiting to be paid. After they weeded, they were told they'd be paid only if they transplanted and spaced the cotton seedlings evenly. So they did, he said. It's a hirer's market.

4

Confessions of a Human Smuggler

NAMPULA

One of my favorite haunts in Nampula is a windowless Somali restaurant near the colonial downtown, the only part of the city where you'll find structures taller than two stories. It's a drab concrete box painted turquoise and surrounded by decaying modernist apartment buildings built for officers in the Portuguese Army during the 1960s, when Nampula became the hub for Portugal's losing battle to stave off Mozambican independence.

Inside, sitting at tables with pink water pitchers and vinyl tablecloths decorated with fruit, men eat with their hands and sip juice boxes imported from Dubai. They laugh and carry on in a mixture of Somali, Swahili, English, and Portuguese, and congregate in groups of three and four at the windows of cars idling at the curb. Sometimes someone will run out of the restaurant and whistle up at the balcony of an apartment building across the street, gesticulating excitedly with a napkin clutched between his fingers. It's a run-down, treeless block, charming in its own way. V-shaped trails of soot left by the rain run down the facade of each apartment building to a sidewalk patrolled by Mozambican teenagers. Just standing in one spot, you can buy fake Ray-Bans, peanuts, school supplies, phone credit, cigarettes, and green coconuts. The neighborhood is known as Bairro dos Poetas, or the Neighborhood of Poets, and sometimes as Bombeiros—Firefighters—after a fire station there.

Over the years, Bombeiros has become a hub for immigrants from all over Africa. Nampula's well-heeled will tell you to not to set foot there after dark, or to avoid it altogether. But during the months I spent in Nampula, I lived just around the corner. Bombeiros was where I went to get internet access when it was out at home, or to get my fill of street life. The center of the neighborhood is all market, with the Somali restaurant sitting on the uphill edge. A dozen intersecting alleyways crisscross the hillside below it, crowded with cubby-like shops manned by immigrants from around the continent: Somalia, Ethiopia, the Democratic Republic of the Congo (DRC), Burundi, Tanzania, Kenya, Malawi, Guinea, Senegal, Mali, and only a few Mozambicans.

Some came to Mozambique as asylum seekers; others were drawn by Bombeiros' flourishing trade in gemstones and Chinese goods. Sitting cross-legged on rugs or perched on tiny wooden stools, most shopkeepers in Bombeiros deal in both categories simultaneously. Each stall overflows with household appliances, fabric, and cheap clothing, but a jeweler's glass is always within arm's reach, to inspect the rubies, emeralds, and garnets that rural people dig up in the countryside and carry into Nampula wrapped in bits of paper.

For three weeks running in June and July 2011, the Nampula police made weekly sweeps in Bombeiros, pulling up in a cloud of dust just outside the restaurant and detaining groups of foreigners as quickly as they could. Each time, during the lunch rush, a dozen officers appeared with their charcoal-gray uniforms and ancient assault rifles, riding in the open back of a large truck. People in Nampula call the patrol cops *cinzentinhos*, "little gray ones." There is a joke Mozambicans tell that says that all the patrol cops, or *cinzentinhos*, are small and skinny, because they are poorly paid, but that all the traffic cops, who stop cars along the highway, are fat, because they have better opportunities to solicit bribes. "Have you ever seen a skinny traffic cop?" someone will ask you, and you will say no, because, in fact, you never have. During their lunchtime sweeps, the *cinzentinhos* scattered along the block and down the alleyways behind the restaurant, flushing out Somalis and Ethiopians, whose light skin and aquiline features made them easily recognizable in the street.

Ostensibly, the police were looking for forged IDs among the neighborhood's many foreigners. The document in question is called a Declaração de Circulação, or Travel Declaration, which gives asylum seekers the right to move freely throughout Nampula Province, or, in some cases, all of Mozambique. They are printed in the back room of a one-story bungalow near city hall, at the Nampula office of the government's Instituto Nacional para o Apoio aos Refugiados—National Institute for Refugee Support, or INAR. The documents are simple black-and-white printouts with the bearer's name and photograph and a few lines of text. But INAR and the police both said that there were Somalis doing the job with home printers somewhere in Bombeiros, and they were determined to find the counterfeits.

Whether they found Travel Declarations or not, the police didn't stop to inspect them. Instead, they tucked the papers away in their shirt pockets and hustled the men off to load them in the truck. Each time, groups of fifty-odd Somali and Ethiopian men were arrested and spent twenty-four hours in a holding cell so small they had to take turns standing and sitting. Always, the following day, the men were released in Marratane, Mozambique's lone refugee camp, which lies twenty miles to the south.

At first, it was hard to get the police to admit that any arrests were taking place at all. The morning after the second sweep,

I made a visit to the *cinzentinhos'* whitewashed fortress of a head-quarters, rising high above the city a few blocks from Bombeiros. A cadet at the gate led me upstairs and back down again as superiors of higher and higher rank each declined to comment, one after the other. One of them finally insisted that I was in the wrong place: the police department only makes immigration-related arrests, he explained, at the behest of the Interior Ministry's provincial migration office. Ten minutes later, the provincial director of migration assured me that no arrests had been ordered.

When I returned to the provincial police headquarters that afternoon, I found a handful of Somali men whispering in a huddle beside an empty flatbed truck parked across the street. These were the envoys of the Somali business community in Bombeiros, who delivered thermoses of tea and buckets of spiced rice to the men detained inside, and who hoped to negotiate with the police for their compatriots' release.

Almeida Canderinho, the second-ranking cop in Nampula Province, received me in a wood-paneled office by the entrance to the compound. Asked about arrests in Bombeiros, Canderinho spread his arms wide, as though he were measuring a fish. Ripples of disbelief spread across his forehead. "Is it a crime to walk down the street?" he gasped. "Is it?" No one's documents had been taken, he assured me, and no one had stayed the night. Perhaps, he thought, some people had been told to "sit and wait" for INAR and the UNHCR to clear up the matter of identification, but the only incident he knew of had been miles from Bombeiros, on the highway, near Morrupula.

When noncitizens were held by the police, Canderinho said, they weren't detained, but *re*tained. "If you want to use the bathroom, you go. If you want to go buy something, you go—but the door is not locked. We can't take anyone's documents," he went on. "We're not allowed to." Even so, Canderinho allowed, the department had been having some trouble with foreigners lately. When people get to the refugee camp at Marratane, he explained, "they don't even stay there for three days. Someone shows up with a container truck and starts to take people away. Now, we don't know who these people are or where they come from. So, are you a refugee or are you a militant? Are you using Mozambique as a transit country or are you staying here?"

While we spoke, a few yards beyond Canderinho's office door, the compound gate was raised to make way for the same blue flatbed I'd seen outside, inching backward up the narrow driveway. When it exited a few minutes later, three dozen Somali and Ethiopian men rode in the back: the truck was headed to Marratane.

Nampula's police spokesman, an effusively polite man named Inácio Dina (who has since been promoted to serve as the national police spokesman), eventually spoke freely about the arrests in Bombeiros, taking up Canderinho's line of argument. The men the police had picked up were in fact "alleged" and "so-called" refugees: they had no intention of seeking asylum in Mozambique, as they claimed, but only wanted to use the country as a corridor to get to South Africa.

Since 2010, Marratane had been flooded with thousands of migrants from the Horn of Africa, including nearly four thousand arrivals in the first half of 2011. But the vast majority quickly disappeared from the camp altogether or were later discovered heading south under the cover of night. And in this, Canderinho and Dina both were right: the migrants were headed for South Africa, known to many in Bombeiros as the "USA of Africa."

What the police never seemed to consider was *why* this was happening: with few hopes of finding a better life through the world's overburdened official refugee system, Somalia's "so-called" refugees have devised their own informal workaround. Those who can afford it hire smugglers to do what the UN can't or won't do for all of them: send them to the USA of Africa, or to the USA itself. They get there by way of Tanzania, Mozambique, and half a dozen other "transit countries" along the way. It's illegal, it's risky, and it costs far more than applying for asylum through the official channels, but it works enough of the time that many migrants from Somalia have come to see it as the best among several bad alternatives.

The UN calls this mixed migration—a flow of people across borders in which there is a mixture of different types of immigrants: refugees, asylum seekers, and economic migrants, as well as victims of trafficking, who have been deceived or coerced into leaving home. On the one hand, mixed migration involves refugees fleeing political persecution or armed conflict. They hire smugglers to avoid the indignities of being a refugee in a place like Kenya, where they are unlikely to find a life outside of crowded camps. On the other, it includes people in search of a better livelihood, portraying themselves as refugees to enjoy the privileges that label can afford—ideally, citizenship or residency in an affluent country. Over the years, the cumulative weighing of odds by people fleeing Somalia has built up a well-organized smuggling industry, based in Nairobi and bankrolled by the diaspora, ever growing and famously entrepreneurial. In 2008, an estimated twenty thousand Somalis and Ethiopians hired smugglers to help them reach South Africa.[1] Mozambique, which covers nearly two thousand miles of the route from Mogadishu to Johannesburg, has become involved mainly as an accident of geography.

One vexing consequence of mixed migration, for destination countries and transit countries alike, is the need to figure out who is who: which migrants deserve special benefits or exemptions from the immigration process, and which ought to be turned away? While I was in Mozambique, for instance, nearly all the Ethiopians and Somalis attempting to enter South Africa were young, able-bodied men, traveling without their wives and children. When they told South African authorities they were seeking asylum—

that they had fled home because of war or political persecution—
immigration officers began to ask the obvious question: where are
your families?

To get as far as the South African border, the men had traveled
thousands of miles and crossed three countries or more—well beyond what they needed to do to outrun Al-Shabaab in Somalia
or political repression in Ethiopia. Were these refugees or simply
"so-called" refugees? Or were the categories of economic migrant
and asylum seeker mingled within each individual?

South Africa, through a combination of its wealth, its asylum
laws, and its proximity to some of the world's poorest countries and
refugee hot spots, has become one of the globe's strongest magnets
for mixed migration. In 2010, and again in 2011, it received more
applications for asylum than any other country in the world.[2] By
the end of 2012, the government faced a backlog of more than
three hundred thousand applications awaiting a decision.[3] Recently, South Africa has begun to reevaluate the policies that have
helped to make it so appealing to asylum seekers: historically, ap-
plicants for asylum have been registered at the border and issued
temporary ID, which allows them to seek work or start a business
wherever they choose, regardless of whether their applications are
ultimately approved. But by the spring of 2012, advocates noted
that South Africa was no longer accepting asylum applications
from Ethiopians and Somalis who showed up at the border. As an
observer with the group Lawyers for Human Rights put it, "They're
not willing to accept the entire continent's refugee burden."[4]

When it became clear that South Africa's policies were becoming more restrictive, officials at the International Organization for
Migration worried about "knock-on" effects in neighboring countries. They observed that border controls in Zimbabwe and Malawi,
to the north, also seemed to be tightening as a result of behind-
the-scenes diplomatic pressure from South Africa.[5] The police
sweeps in Nampula could be seen as part of the same reaction.

Yet whether they admitted it or not, it was hard to see what the police hoped to resolve by making arrests. A government lawyer at INAR candidly told me that claiming to seek asylum, even under false pretenses, is not a crime in Mozambique. Moreover, after detaining more than a hundred men, the authorities found no false documents, issued no fines, and filed no charges.

The police spokesman, Dina, revealed these details sheepishly the week after the third sweep, with a reluctance that suggested he was often in the position of explaining away his colleagues' excesses. Periodically, he gazed out the window of his fourth-floor office down onto the wreckage of a dozen impounded cars and decommissioned police trucks that filled the yard behind the building. The detainees said the police had also taken dozens of working cell phones, a tidy pile of cash gleaned during intake, and bribes paid to avoid arrests, but Dina didn't mention it.

As the sweeps in Nampula made clear, mixed migration has its own complications. Migrants who hire smugglers run the risk of ending up in circumstances that are no better than the ones they fled: they may face exploitation and abuse by their handlers or corrupt officials they encounter en route. As smuggling becomes bound up with applications for asylum, mixed migration threatens to unravel existing protections for asylum seekers and refugees—and indeed, to increase nationalism, corruption, and overall hostility to the presence of any refugees at all. This is the brew that has helped strengthen Europe's resurgent Far Right at precisely the moment when the need for shelter and support among Syrian refugees is greatest. In Mozambique, the government faces a quandary: if thousands of people claim to seek asylum only to disappear across the next border, how do you determine whose request for asylum is sincere?

More than 85 percent of the planet's refugees live in the developing world.[6] For the most part, they are concentrated in a handful of poor countries that lack the resources to provide for them and which have long shouldered more than their share of the global problem of displacement. These countries—Turkey, Pakistan, and Lebanon, but also Mozambique's neighbors Malawi, Tanzania, and Kenya, among them—are often said to suffer from "hosting fatigue," which means that they have gradually rolled back the rights afforded to refugees and asylum seekers on their soil, or become wary of granting them in the first place.

Hosting fatigue may be at its worst in Kenya, which has hosted large numbers of Somali (and, at times, Ethiopian and Sudanese) refugees ever since 1990. Though Kenya has never fully honored the protections guaranteed refugees under international law—few countries do—the plight of refugees living there has steadily worsened as the conflict in Somalia draws on. Today, more than half a million Somalis live in desperately crowded camps in eastern Kenya, deprived of the right to seek work or travel in society at large. Many have lived that way for years. In 2010, Human Rights Watch published a report called *Welcome to Kenya*, more than one hundred pages devoted to the illegal "interception, detention, abuse, deportation, and extortion of asylum seekers" by the Kenyan police.[7] The following year, at the height of a refugee crisis sparked by the region's worst drought in sixty years, Kenya refused to open a new $13 million camp funded entirely by the UN.[8] In 2016, the Kenyan government moved to close Dadaab, often described as the largest refugee camp in the world, citing concerns that it played host to Al-Shabaab fighters and depressed the local economy. Kenya's high court struck down the government order within months.[9]

It was around this time that I got to know Liban Ali, a chubby man nearing forty with a gray goatee and a worn, pockmarked face. The owner of the Somali restaurant in Bombeiros introduced us, saying he thought Liban had a good story to tell: Liban was

Nampula's foremost *mukalas*, or human smuggler. No one in the city bore greater responsibility for the mass movement of "alleged" and "so-called" refugees through the camp nearby, or for the ensuing corruption and resentment that led to the police sweeps in Bombeiros.

Now, though, Liban said he was retired and already had been for most of two years. He wanted nothing more than to work as an everyday trucker, hauling potatoes or bales of used clothing, but his reputation continued to haunt him: "Always, my name is going far," he complained. "Everywhere, everywhere, they know me I'm working this job."

Liban's reedy voice was shaped by a classic Somali accent, with rounded vowels and a mixture of pillow-soft and rock-hard consonants. It was over ninety degrees outside, but Liban wore sweatpants and an anorak over a black fleece. "Now, anywhere when they get problem, everywhere, they say 'Liban people, Liban people,'" he said. "I come like boss, but I don't know nothing, I'm not working. No one give me money!"

When Somalia's government fell, in 1991, Liban was only nineteen years old. For a year, he'd been a soldier in the army of Mohammed Siad Barre, a socialist general who took power in a 1969 coup and ruled for twenty-two years over an increasingly repressive military regime. Siad Barre's ouster came under pressure from a coalition of militias tied to Somalia's various clans, or ethnic groups. When Siad Barre fled Mogadishu, the militias turned on each other in the ensuing struggle for power, leading to the outbreak of the Somali civil war. The army disbanded, and Liban went immediately to fight with the Somali National Front, a militia founded by loyalists of the toppled president.[10]

For the next eight years, he manned a machine gun mounted on the back of a pickup truck and dodged shrapnel on the crumbling streets of Mogadishu. Recounting the experience, Liban rose from his stool and began to show off his scars. "I was fighting, nine years!" he said proudly, including the year he'd spent in the army prior to the civil war. There were scars from stitches on the back of his head; indents where shrapnel had gone through his upper lip; foreign matter lodged in his left shoulder; and large splotches on his torso marking the entry and exit of the bullet that ultimately landed him in a hospital in Nairobi, in 1998. Liban displayed all this with a lightheartedness that must have come from long exposure to violence. He spoke to me in jilted, broken English, but after more than a decade in Mozambique, he had picked up the nonverbal exclamations of a Portuguese speaker— "That time I was ready to die, because life is strong, *ne*? But now, *eeeeeee*, even I don't want to go back."

Liban was the last member of his family to leave Somalia, which, he said, made it far easier for him to get as far as Mozambique. For the first person in a family to leave, he explained, "they have to sell cows, house, whatever they have, they have to sell to take him out. . . . The boy when he reach other place, if he work, he send you money, to take his brother. The one you push, he has to push the other." As Somali refugees have been resettled at a trickle and established small businesses throughout the developed world in the last twenty-five years, funds have become available for the flight of family members who remain inside the country.

At the time, the smuggling networks were not so organized as they are now, and Liban continued south from Nairobi on his own, a practice now known as traveling "private." Using money a cousin had wired from Stockholm via Western Union, Liban made his way through Tanzania by bus. He stopped in Dar es Salaam to buy a fake passport, then continued traveling south into Mozambique. For fifty dollars, a gregarious Somali smuggler named Al-Wez helped him cross into South Africa in the middle of the night. Then he took a train to Cape Town, where he lived with an acquaintance from Mogadishu. Other Somali merchants from Liban's ethnic group banded together and gave him $300, which he used to start a small business.

He bought a folding table and sold cigarettes and shoes at the market in Mitchells Plain, one of South Africa's largest townships.[11] There was good money to be made, but almost daily, fellow Somali merchants were robbed at gunpoint. Some were killed. "I don't like the life of South Africa," Liban said sternly. "Example, South Africa you don't have enemy, you don't have problem. . . . You can't come out nighttime, always there is gang-ee, always they have gun." A look of alarm came over him. "South Africa, Somalia there is no different!" he exclaimed. In South Africa, Liban heard bullets every night, and he recalled thinking that Mitchells Plain was nearly as bad as Mogadishu. "In South Africa, I can kill you anytime. Kill someone, anyone, anytime. That's why," Liban concluded, "I say, eh, better then I go back Mozambique."

Liban's introduction to human smuggling involved a lot of waiting. When Liban returned to Maputo, Al-Wez sensed an opportunity to expand a flourishing business and took him in on the condition that Liban work for his keep. Each morning, he rose and made his way to Missão Roque, a hectic crossroads just north of the city. All day, he stood on the side of the road and scanned the arriving buses for people who looked like him—the toothy, light-skinned faces of Somalis standing out in a sea of Mozambicans. During the day, he lived on a diet of roast corn and peanuts he bought from hawkers who flocked to the open windows of departing buses. When he saw Somali faces through the bus window, Liban called out to them: "'Come, come.' When we talk Somali language, they come out," Liban said. He brought them to Al-Wez, and Al-Wez brought them to South Africa, passing through a sliver of Swaziland on the way.

These Somalis were coming as he had, "private"—on a series of jitneys through Tanzania, Zambia, Malawi, and Mozambique. At times, they traveled alone, and at times, they banded together in small groups, navigating on the strength of a few words in English and Swahili. Border crossings were the only segments of the trip that required much discretion. There, they negotiated with handlers they met on the spot, hiking through the countryside to avoid immigration officials.

After a few months, as he made contacts with peers in the business, Liban came to the conclusion that Al-Wez's generosity wasn't quite what it seemed. Smuggling is a lucrative line of business; doing Al-Wez's legwork for pocket money and room and board soon lost its appeal. Let Al-Wez get fat on his own, he thought. Liban rented a small house and stopped bringing Al-Wez business. "I come against with him," Liban said smugly. In retaliation, Liban claimed that Al-Wez began using the Maputo police force as henchmen for hire: "When I get three, four Somali in my house, he's coming with police. . . . He show my house the police, *ne*? They take the guys to give him." Each time, Liban pleaded with the police and claimed that he was only giving a bed to Somalis in need. The circus played out daily for months. Liban gradually befriended the officers who came to arrest his charges. "Now already I know small *português*," he recalled. "Every day. You know, no one can come every day to arrest you, *ne*? I know *all* police already. After . . . I start to fuck him," Liban went on. He began bribing the police himself, so that they raided Al-Wez's house and brought the customers to him instead.

As the conflict in Somalia wore on and members of the diaspora sent money back home, the stream of young men being "pushed" out by their relatives only grew, and Liban's business grew along with it. Cell phones facilitated the creation of a tighter, more efficient smuggling network. "*Eeeeeeee*, it's facilitate, mobile—everything," Liban said. "I told you, that time, I was Missão Roque, to wait the bus. No connection. Now, you don't wait. Now you receive the call. That time, I was staying what they call first bus station, I staying there, all day, my friend. Suffering!" Liban grimaced, then made a look of hopeful surprise.

"After, we get the phone. Telephone . . . Bus is coming—" He held out a thumb and pinkie to his right ear, miming a telephone: "'I'm in the bus, my friend, I'm here Inhambane, now we sleep, tomorrow we come.' Okay, give me driver, I want to talk the driver, or what they're calling another one's working bus, okay. '*Amigo, está a onde?* Where are you?'" Liban imitated a high-pitched Mozambican bus driver: "'*Amigo, está aqui, Maxixe, estamos a vir, a noite.*' Okay, I wait nighttime there."

Liban Ali, pictured outside a Somali restaurant in the Bombeiros neighborhood of Nampula, claimed to have "retired" after years spent smuggling migrants from end to end of Mozambique in a fleet of jeeps and minibuses.

By working with associates along the whole route instead of employing lookouts to check for new arrivals at each juncture, smugglers were able to organize the entire itinerary from Mogadishu onward, cutting down on the need to haggle with customers at every stop, and reducing everyone's chances of being caught. The top smugglers in Nairobi soon formed what Liban mundanely calls "agencies," as though they booked package trips to Club Med. He rattled off a list of names: "Biggest agency is Al-Jabr, second is Dahare, Bachir." A few smugglers even opened offices in Mogadishu, Liban said.

What kind of offices? I asked. Liban seemed confused by the question.

"Human trafficking office, like normal office," he said. Above the storefronts, there are painted signs that say things like, "Wherever You Want to Reach, We Can Take It You." There is a northern route—through Sudan, Libya, and Malta, to "whatever place you want" in Europe and North America, at roughly $25,000 a head—and a road south, to South Africa, which, at the time of our conversation, cost $3,200.

The smugglers, as Liban described them, are not strict competitors. They pool their customers to make a full load, and they each specialize in a portion of the itinerary, bundling passengers for discounted rates and paying one another on commission. This allows them to share equipment like cars, trucks, and boats and to move customers reliably even when there are fluctuations in business.

By 2002, Liban aligned himself with Al-Jabr, a smuggler based in Nairobi, but who had employees throughout the route. Liban no longer worked alone, and he was no longer confined to the short stretch of road between Maputo and the South African border. Traveling exclusively at night, he worked on commission, driving all the way through Mozambique in cars belonging to Al-Jabr and filled with charges from as many as three or four agencies. In his characteristic halting patter, Liban explained the routine:

"Sometime you sleep in Rio Zambeze, in the bush. Because the people, no one can see. Night is driving. When they come daytime, example five o'clock, six o'clock, you put the bush. You go bringing water, bread, they stay there." He put both hands in front of him, as if to tell me to stay put. "Nighttime load again . . ."

Liban was paid handsomely: $400 a head, minus a fee for renting one of Al-Jabr's cars. Payments were arranged through an informal network of Somali-owned "banks" known as *hawala* that make immediate transfers among cities throughout East Africa. To verify each transaction, *hawala* bankers rely on predetermined bits of personal information, like birthdays and the names of relatives. "They ask you questions, same like Western Union: when you reach Somalian bank, my name Liban Ali, I waiting money from there, exactly capital city or that city, who send is my friend *flan-flan-flan*, his name. Telephone number is *is-is*. Password number is *is-is*. They give you money!" Liban exclaimed excitedly. "How you know? It's same like Western Union. . . . You don't need even document to show."

On the road, Liban confirmed his movements by cell phone, receiving half his pay at pickup and half at delivery to the next of Al-Jabr's associates. "Because this is connection, they controlling from Nairobi, all the way. Nairobi, they got all office there." If anything went wrong—car problems, checkpoint police that demanded larger-than-usual bribes—he said, Al-Jabr withheld payment or subtracted it from the next job. "When you catch problem on the road, he catch you his money," Liban warned. "His money, he never lose."

Smuggling routes are notoriously elastic. When he first began working for Al-Jabr, Liban's portion of the trip took him from the Malawian border, in Milange, along a boomerang-shaped route that cut through most of Mozambique. A dozen Mozambican towns rolled off his tongue with familiarity: "I take his people Milange: Mila-

nge, Morrumbala; Morrumbala, Chimuara; Chimuara, Rio Zambeze; Rio Zambeze, Caia; Caia, Inchope. Inchope—" He broke off
laughing before he could get to the route's end, in Maputo.

Soon after he started working with Al-Jabr, Liban recalled, a
growing number of police checkpoints in the south made it fool-
hardy to travel along the highway outside the capital. Liban began taking men to the Zimbabwean border instead, allowing for
a different point of entry into South Africa. At the Zimbabwean
border they relied on Mozambican boys and teenagers: "You drop
them the border. Three kilometer the border. You drop. There's small
boys there. Those Somalian and Ethiopians, they don't know the
road. The boy Mozambican, *ne*? He know how to jump the other
side, still he bringing, immigration."

Later, Al-Jabr and the other smugglers began to use a coastal
route as weather permitted. Migrants traveled overland from the
border town of Doble, in southern Somalia, to the Kenyan port of
Mombasa; then, by dhow—a large wooden boat with triangular
sails—from Mombasa all the way to the northern beaches of
Mozambique. "Very dangerous," Liban said. "The boat is going
with air. It's not engine on this boat."

In traveling south with their human cargo, these dhows re-
versed a trade route that Arab merchants first plied more than a
thousand years ago, carrying ivory, gold, and slaves north from
Mozambique.[12] It was the southernmost extension of a trade network stretched all the way up to the Red Sea, along the Arabian
Peninsula, and down the Indian coast. Although the destinations
and terms of the trade have changed, the Mozambican coast remains a point of transit for much the same cargo—ivory, precious
stones and metals, and able-bodied men.

At times, Liban said, the men were let off in the middle of the
bush, and Al-Jabr's associates hired locals to spend days walking
them through sandy forest and thorny scrub to the nearest road.
Sometimes, the dhows were able to continue farther south to the

small port of Moçímboa da Praia, a picturesque town bordered by white-sand beaches and mangrove forests. There, eighty kilometers from the Tanzanian border, Liban waited in a guesthouse near the colonial slave market in Mocímboa Velha, and he loaded his passengers as soon as they were off the boats. Tapping an open palm against his fist, Liban made the hand signal that jitney drivers use when they can't take any more passengers. "*Cheio!*" he said—"Full."

Over the years, Liban came to take police corruption for granted. He paid the police well, gave them few surprises, and gradually built up a thriving business, using four cars of his own to lead nocturnal convoys through the country. He had two Toyota minibuses and two double-cabin Nissan pickup trucks—"D40!" Liban said proudly—which made for a total capacity of more than 110 people on any given trip. Often, Liban acted as the "spotter," driving ahead in a small car to negotiate a smooth transition for the unusual cargo behind him. Arriving at each checkpoint, Liban paid the officers according to the number of people he was transporting, and in return they let the other cars pass without pause.

Then, shortly after midnight a month before Christmas of 2009, according to Liban, police stopped four minibuses carrying one hundred Somali migrants as they approached the Zambezi River from the north. Liban, who had been "spotting," was a few minutes ahead. "My cars, *ne?*" Liban said. He soon noticed that something was wrong, and he pulled off the road before he crossed the bridge. In the morning, he learned that his passengers would be sent to Marratane, the refugee camp outside Nampula, and that his cars had been impounded at the police department in the town of Mocuba, nearby. After only a night in jail, the Mozambican drivers Liban had hired were allowed to walk free. But Osman Sheik Mohammed, a Kenyan associate of Liban's, called to tell him that his cars would soon be needed in Mocímboa da Praia once again: more migrants were already on their way. Liban could even get a bonus if he managed to find a solution. So rather than wait things out, Liban decided to travel to Mocuba and negotiate his vehicles' release.

As Liban saw it, this negotiation was not all that different from the less ambitious efforts he'd undertaken in the past at hundreds and hundreds of checkpoints throughout the country: it just required a larger payoff. Liban had been given a limit of $10,000 to secure the vehicles' release. But when he arrived in Mocuba, he attempted to bargain with the wrong cop. "It was one new guy," Liban recalled, his voice still full of surprise. He was arrested and promptly thrown in jail. "I'll show you what—I go prison, three months, to beat me, my whole body, I find the problem." Again, Liban rose to show off scars on his arms and back.

Within a month, Osman, too, was arrested on trafficking charges. He'd been stopped not far from Mocuba while shepherding a cohort of seventy-two Somali migrants through the district of Nacarôa.[13] Upon arrest, Osman tried with no more success than Liban to bribe a police commander with about $4,100 and the promise of a car.[14] It now seemed to Liban that the "new guy" he'd tried to bribe was more than an anomaly; police were facing pressure from the government to crack down on smugglers. Still, Osman continued to lobby for his freedom even while he was in jail. By February, he had brokered a deal that allowed both him and Liban to walk free without standing trial. Liban decided to leave the trade all the same: "I'm tired, that job, you know?"

In January 2010, while Liban and Osman were both in prison, dhows continued to glide onto the sand near Mocímboa da Praia, and farther north, on the banks of the Rovuma. Yet there was no one on hand to load the men into cars. Suddenly, the region was home to scores of bewildered Somalis and Ethiopians wandering in bands along the coast. In a single month, the police in Cabo

Delgado Province, where Liban was accustomed to loading passengers, detained more than five hundred undocumented migrants
from the Horn of Africa. All were young men aged thirteen to
thirty-five who presented themselves as asylum seekers. But
the police were not convinced: "Don't the women and the older
people flee from wars too?" a police spokesman wondered at a press
conference.[15]

Liban has a simple explanation for the skewed demographic
among Somalis who hire smugglers. He says they are "running
from Al-Shabaab," which forcibly recruits young men. "They want
twenty, under twenty. Twenty-five—Al-Shabaab when they come to
you they say, 'Let's go to jihad.' If you say, 'No,' they kill you. That's
the problem. That's why all they are running out the country." Yet
the demographic is largely the same with Ethiopians, who are
seldom seen as political refugees. The prevailing opinion on the
Mozambican police force was that the men were "in search of
life," as Mozambicans usually put it, or *a procura de vida*. Families
undertake the sacrifice of hiring a smuggler, they argued, so that
their sons, brothers, and husbands can go abroad, make a living,
and one day begin to send money back home.

Responding to the influx of migrants in early 2010, the police
attempted to repatriate Somalis and Ethiopians by sending them
back north across the Rovuma. But Tanzania responded by closing its border and reinforcing patrols on the frontier. So the migrants slept in the courtyard of the nearest police station on the
Mozambican side, in Palma, a backwater coastal town set amid
coconut groves and dry veldt.

Until recently, Palma was known mainly for its beaches. José
Raimundo de Palma Velho, the first Portuguese governor of the
area, for whom the town is named, conquered it from the sultan
of Zanzibar in the late nineteenth century.[16] Afterward, he wrote
that it sits on "perhaps the best bay on the East coast of Africa," with
deep, uncommonly clear water, and a long beach of "fine, white,

hard sand."[17] In 2006, a subsidiary of the Texas oil company Anadarko began drilling off the coast of Palma, and it has since become the base of operations for exploratory wells in an undersea basin thought to hold 65 trillion cubic feet of natural gas, enough to supply the planet for twenty years.[18] Now Palma is known as the place that will make Mozambique rich. To Somalis in Nampula, it is known as a sort of purgatory.

At the police station, dozens of men lounged, listless, in scraps of noonday shade, and they slept on rice sacks and bits of cardboard. A few followed mimed instructions from the officers and swept or scrubbed the station floor. But there were far too many of them to stay there, even when the UNHCR brought emergency shelters and rations to create a temporary transit center. "Our budget didn't include this situation," the police spokesman said.[19]

The *mukalas* farther north, in Mogadishu and Mombasa, didn't immediately react to the new status quo in Mozambique. Though there was no one to pick the men up in Palma or Mocímboa da Praia, dhows filled to the brim continued to ply the coast of Tanzania.

UNHCR and Mozambique's refugee agency, INAR, were obliged to charter buses to bring the stranded migrants to the refugee camp at Marratane. When the buses were delayed, some men walked the three hundred miles from the border to the camp, surviving on mangos and whatever else they were given by the perplexed locals they encountered along the way. When they arrived, many men were in desperate shape, malnourished and severely dehydrated from a week or more at sea, with swollen feet and slack skin.

The impounded cars were released on the same day as Liban and Osman, in the middle of February. "When I come out, cars come out, same day," Liban recalled, grinning. Returning to Nampula, he promptly spread the word of his retirement and sold his cars to his former competitor. He bought a large truck and found work for a commodities company hauling cotton to port. Liban said Osman took up the old business again.

But for whatever reason—perhaps because of the fierce government attention now focused on Mocímboa da Praia and Palma, or perhaps because hundreds of paying customers had already been relocated to Marratane—Osman no longer loaded his men from the same spot. Instead, smugglers began using the refugee camp at Marratane as a staging ground.

Set back about a half mile from the main road, Marratane covers a broad patch of shady savannah surrounded by dome-shaped granite peaks and small fields of cassava. The bulk of the camp is composed not of tents, but of small mud and cement houses much like the homes of the Mozambican farmers who live nearby. The camp is funded by UNHCR and administered jointly by the Mozambican government and the UN. Except for the policemen at the gate, and a handful of buildings painted with UN and government logos, it looks nothing like what I imagined a refugee camp to be. Instead, it seems strikingly permanent, with shops and an elementary school, like a sprawling Mozambican village.

Marratane was created in 2001 primarily to house families of refugees from the Great Lakes region—the DRC, Burundi, and Rwanda. They arrived throughout the year in small groups of anywhere from one to ten people, traveling slowly on foot, on public transport, or, often, escorted by police who intercepted them near the Tanzanian border. The Great Lakes refugees made it as far as Mozambique largely because they were afraid that camps closer to home, which already held their compatriots in large numbers, might succumb to the same ethnic violence they were fleeing in the first place. Many had already lived in camps in Uganda and fled, or they'd attempted to settle in Tanzania, where they encountered hostility from the local government.

By the time migrants from the Horn of Africa began pouring into Marratane in large numbers, in early 2010, many of the people living there had been in the camp for most of a decade. Over time, the refugees from the Great Lakes managed to work out a basic means of making a living. They subsisted on meager rations from the World Food Programme and farmed small plots on the camp's periphery, though growing conditions were poor. A Burundian man I met in Marratane told me with dismay that "the soil here produces nothing but peanuts and cassava." Those who could started small businesses, and if they obtained permission from INAR, they moved into Nampula, where Congolese refugees have carved out a niche with barbershops and small hair salons.

People in Marratane complained of mismanagement and routine corruption: bribes at the elementary school, shortages at the medical clinic, delays in processing IDs and other important paperwork. Their gripes were not too different from those of Mozambicans themselves in rural areas across the country. In fact, several of the camp's amenities compared favorably with the isolation of much of the countryside. It is accessible by road; some buildings are connected to the electrical grid; and though they are few, there are bore wells with cement coverings and hand pumps. One difficulty of supporting refugees in a place like Mozambique is that almost any level of public services they are provided runs the risk of alienating locals accustomed to receiving next to nothing from their government. In the years after the camp was built, some Mozambicans even moved onto adjacent lots to gain access to water and electricity. "Marratane is a real city!" one Mozambican farmer would tell me later, sitting outside his newly built house on the edge of the refugee camp.

* * *

Marratane's transformation into a smuggling hub threw the ordinarily sleepy camp into turmoil. The core of the problem was that the Somalis and Ethiopians arrived and disappeared in unpredictable waves. The camp's population ballooned to more than ten thousand in July 2010, then quickly plummeted to four thousand, only to see seven hundred new migrants from the Horn of Africa appear in a single two-week period in December.[20] Even with funding and technical assistance from UNHCR, government officials at INAR struggled to keep pace, hastily expanding their facilities and appealing for more supplies only to find that the intended beneficiaries had gone missing. Out of nearly ten thousand Somalis and Ethiopians registered at Marratane over the course of 2010, more than 80 percent vanished before the year was out, escorted out of the camp by Liban's old associates.[21]

According to camp administrators, the new residents from the Horn of Africa didn't fit in with the refugees who were already living there: they were unruly at food distributions and they didn't wait in line at the well. Crowded into a camp built for half as many people without the necessary infrastructure for so many new arrivals, they defecated in the surrounding fields and threw sticks and rocks during disputes. They spoke no Portuguese, no English, no French, and for the most part no Swahili, which made it nearly impossible to communicate with the other residents, and even with the camp's staff. INAR was able to hire translators to work with the Somalis, but to conduct intake interviews with the Ethiopians, they had to rely on two separate interpreters—from Amharic to Swahili, and from Swahili to Portuguese.

More arrived every day. The October rains in the Horn of Africa had failed for three years straight, since 2007, and dhows continued to deposit legions of exhausted migrants on the beaches of Cabo Delgado or the banks of the Rovuma. The boat traffic reached its peak in February 2011, when, UNHCR estimates, Palma and Mocímboa da Praia held more than three thousand asylum seekers without any infrastructure to support them. Many of the men had been robbed of the meager belongings they had kept through the sea voyage—cell phones, small amounts of foreign currency, and clothing—and they'd been beaten by the police before being led to the station. UNHCR lobbied the government to set up a transit center where INAR would conduct prescreening interviews to determine who might be eligible for asylum. But the transit center was never set up. The government argued that a transit center was unjustified because of the lack of new arrivals—hundreds and hundreds of "asylum seekers" had already disappeared, and there was no telling when the next group would come. Jesus Sanchez, a Spaniard who worked for UNHCR in Maputo, recalled this period as a sort of catch-22: "You found yourself in the position of lobbying for asylum on behalf of people who aren't interested in seeking asylum in Mozambique," he told me.

Meanwhile, Mozambican government officials were under pressure to tamp down on irregular migration by any means necessary. The police made highway busts as routinely as they could: inside of a month in November 2010, police detained a total of 346 Somalis and Ethiopians at checkpoints in Nampula and one neighboring province.[22] In December, there was a high-speed car chase in which cops followed two trucks carrying a total of 108 migrants until one of the drivers lost control and the truck rolled off the road. Miraculously, only one migrant died. The man at the wheel of the spotter's car was Liban's old associate Osman—less than a year after he'd been let out of jail.[23] In January, busts followed at a crossroads in the highland province of Manica and at the scene of a car accident in Tete.[24] Yet there were no trials and no convictions on charges of smuggling or human trafficking. Liban's old associate Osman was even arrested once more.

Throughout the first half of 2011, Mozambican newspapers were filled with reports of migrants from the Horn of Africa dying in inhuman circumstances as they made their way through the country: in January, off the coast of Mocímboa da Praia, some of the men in a group of 8 Ethiopians and 3 Somalis drowned after being thrown off a dhow by the boat's owner.[25] In February, 8 Somalis suffocated in a shipping container carrying 16 of their countrymen and 4,000 gallons of cooking oil.[26] Less than two weeks later, another boat carrying 129 Somalis and Ethiopians capsized off the coast, killing 51.[27]

Then, in April, and again in July, groups of four Somalis were shot dead by Mozambican border guards who were trying to force them to cross into Tanzania.[28] After the second incident, the owner of the restaurant in Bombeiros told me that Somalis in the neighborhood had known for days about a group of more than a hundred migrants stranded on a spit of sand in the Rovuma River, but that there was little to be done for them. They were caught between Mozambique and Tanzania; government patrols prevented the migrants from entering either country.[29] Witnesses said it was only once several of them drowned after being beaten by Mozambican border guards that the men were allowed back into Tanzania, where they were herded into a small prison near the border.[30]

Without fail, the migrants who survived these gruesome incidents or had their trips interrupted for any other reason ended up in Marratane. By May 2011, the camp was once again home to roughly five thousand migrants from the Horn of Africa. At times, the authorities found themselves locked in an absurd cycle with the smugglers, repeatedly trading custody of the same groups of people—from Marratane to police interception en route to the border and back to Marratane again. On the one hand, it seemed smugglers and migrants seldom gave up the quest to reach Johannesburg even after being caught by the police several times over. On the other, Mozambican police had no way of sending migrants home or preventing them from making serial attempts to get to South Africa.

"Your money is still working until you reach Joburg," Liban assured me. Whether it takes one attempt or five, and whether you are in prison or in a refugee camp, a smuggler will continue to "push you" to South Africa as long as you are alive, he said. Liban also said that the men who hire smugglers and die en route never lose their money either—that the offices in Nairobi and Mogadishu contact their families and return the original fee: "When they die these people, the family who they give you in Mogadishu agency, you have to call them," Liban said. He mimed a cell phone once again: "'Family, hello, yeah, how are you?' 'Fine, yeah, that guy, he got problem, he's sick, he's hospital, he's died.' . . . Understand, *ne*? Example like that, when they die, the guy in Mogadishu, he have to confirm the family. . . . Understand, *ne*?" Liban asked again. "Return back that money. Why you take the money? Which way you take the money?"

I found all this hard to believe. Migrants arrived in Mozambique already at wit's end, ground down by hunger and fatigue. Many had recounted violence and abuse at the hands of smugglers like Liban. It was hard to fathom much compassion in the business model. But Liban's version did offer some explanation for migrants' cycling in and out of police custody in central Mozambique. Without smugglers' help, the migrants who came to Marratane wouldn't have been able to leave again and again.

The other part of the problem was that although the law calls for repatriation, it has never been a practical option: it was unthinkable to send Somalis back to Mogadishu, into the midst of an ongoing civil war, and the Mozambican government was unwilling to bear the costs and responsibility for sending hundreds of undocumented Ethiopians back to Ethiopia. In the first six months of 2011, more than 3,000 people were admitted to Marratane,

while only 102 foreigners were sent back to their countries of ori-
gin.[31] More than half of those repatriated were Bangladeshis who
had reached Mozambique via Ethiopian Airlines, hoping to start
businesses. The government was able to convince the company to
fly them home.[32] Of the remainder, 5 were Ethiopians, and none
were Somali.

Even when migrants fled Marratane several times over, there
was no provision (beyond repatriation) to penalize them for claiming asylum under false pretenses or for repeatedly abandoning
the process of legal recognition. So, while the police often boasted
of the "arrest" of Somali and Ethiopian "illegals" and kept them
for a time in crowded holding cells, there was nothing to prose-
cute them for, and nowhere to put them other than the transit
center, a ramshackle grid of tarp tents and small wood fires on the
edge of Marratane.

I made my first visit to Marratane a week before meeting Liban,
thanks to the living Yellow Pages maintained by the owner of
the restaurant in Bombeiros, known to much of the neighborhood
as Kaiser, or London Boy.[33] Kaiser, who grew up in London in a
family of Somali refugees, sat at the register just inside the doorway, acting as a kind of fixer for the neighborhood. He helped
fellow foreigners extend their visas without incident. He knew
someone who could get you a desirable cell phone number—with
a long string of eights or alternating ones and fives—and someone
else who could help you pass a vehicle emissions test without having to bring your car in for inspection.

When I started asking about Marratane, Kaiser introduced me
to a friend who made his living delivering goods to the shopkeepers at the refugee camp and buying sacks of World Food Programme rations (all clearly marked "Not for Sale") from staff
and residents both. Another friend of Kaiser's, a Kenyan Somali
named Abdul Raman, came along to translate. On the road

before the main entrance, we passed a small makeshift cemetery with sand mounds and wooden markers. These were graves, the driver said, of Somali and Ethiopian migrants who had succumbed to malaria gone untreated. At the camp gate, he stopped and handed 100 meticais, just over three dollars, to the policeman so that he could continue, against the camp's regulations, with his car. Then he took us to the transit center, at the end of the road. A gaggle of Ethiopian men eagerly surrounded the car as it stopped, then backed up and stared at us quizzically when we got out. The driver left. I stood with Abdul Raman and took in the miserable scene around us, which I imagined to be much the same as it had been, intermittently, for the last year and a half. Groups of sallow Ethiopian men huddled over frying pans fashioned from steel oil barrels, cooking maize flatbread and watery pots of beans. Others, laid out with malaria, limply waved the black flies from their faces and rolled back and forth on straw mats inside lean-tos made from plastic sheeting.

One of the men standing nearby was a lanky farmer named Watiro Wachamo, aged thirty, who, as it happened, was one of the few Ethiopians in camp who spoke Swahili. Wachamo was just returning from a burial at the graveyard we'd passed on the way in, and he said that five or six people died each week. In early 2010, Wachamo left his wife and two kids at home in southern Ethiopia and walked across the border into Kenya, hoping somehow to make a better living than he had growing maize and sorghum at home. For five months, he did the piecemeal menial labor that is readily available for Ethiopians in Kenya: offloading charcoal trucks and hauling water in restaurants, carrying rebar and concrete as a porter at small construction sites. With a bit of cash to show for it, Wachamo made his way to the coast.

"I was looking for a good refugee camp to live in," Wachamo said, so that he could eventually find a way out of Africa altogether. In Mombasa, he met a man who told him that if he made it to Marratane, he could get to the United States or to Canada. He gave the man $500 and boarded a dhow to Mozambique. For a week, he crouched in the hull with one hundred others as the boat headed down the coast of Tanzania. During the second half of the trip, he said, several fellow passengers were thrown overboard when they became too weak to help bail water. Landing on the Tanzanian side of the river, Wachamo and his cohorts were robbed, then chased into the water by border guards. They managed to swim across to Mozambique at low tide, but several of Wachamo's companions didn't make it. Now, after four months in Marratane, Wachamo was penniless, and clueless about his prospects for resettlement.

When the police call the Ethiopians and Somalis in Marratane "alleged" and "so-called" refugees, Wachamo is the type they have in mind. In a sense, they are right. Wachamo did not flee persecution, armed conflict, or war. Even under the expanding definition of "refugee" brought into play by the treaties signed since the UN's 1951 convention, Wachamo doesn't qualify. At most, he might be considered a "climate refugee," born into a farming family in a place where farming has become next to impossible. Soon after Wachamo left Ethiopia, a terrible drought in the region renewed the Somali refugee crisis in Kenya and brought the idea of climate refugees to the world's attention for the first time. But if Wachamo shares something with Somali climate refugees, it is not a category recognized under international law, or by Mozambique's government.

Danilo Mangamela, a lawyer and protection officer for INAR, conducts many of the interviews that determine the legal status of irregular migrants arriving in Mozambique and says it is common for migrants to claim refugee status whether or not they are justified in doing so. The Ethiopians, he told me, always cite political reasons for their flight from Ethiopia, because "they know that if they mention drought that they will be sent to Immigration."

What he means is that they will be repatriated, even though, in fact, they won't be: they will end up at Marratane one way or another.

Somalis are more likely to qualify for asylum. An American woman I met in the UNHCR office in Nampula came to her post after four years conducting asylum interviews in Nairobi. "The Somalis, before you even speak to them," she said, "you already know what they're going to say: 'Tall men came into my house, they killed my father, then raped my mother and sister.'" Whether or not this story is always true, it does usually work to obtain asylum.

On another visit to Marratane in July, I met with the new camp administrator, Francisco Chihale, a barrel-chested man in his late forties with a soft voice and distaste for confrontation. Chihale is a former employee of the World Food Programme who had been in his post for only three months and said gravely that he took over at a "very complicated time." He was trying to avoid speaking directly to the consequences of the fact that smuggling routes had become entangled with the government's system for receiving asylum seekers. Marratane had become a repository for people of vastly different legal statuses—refugees, who have the same (nonpolitical) rights as Mozambican citizens; people whose asylum applications have been rejected but could not be repatriated; those with unresolved claims, some dating as far back as 2001; and economic migrants in transit who were caught by the police. "They are all here and they all receive the same treatment," said Chihale. "What are we supposed to do with the [nonrefugees]?"

A few weeks into his new job, Chihale spent an afternoon speaking with the leader of a group of thirty-three Ethiopians who had been discovered in the woods one hundred miles south of Marratane, apparently on their way to South Africa. "He told the whole story," Chihale recalled. "The smugglers were two

Mozambicans and one Ethiopian—he even had their phone numbers. They took the Ethiopians to a place he'd never been and let them out in the middle of the night, at three thirty a.m. They said, 'No one can speak, no one can cough, and no one can stand up. A car is going to come for you.' But the locals heard something going on, and they called the police. At the end of the day, I gave him something to eat and sent him back home, but he's already left camp."

Chihale had not tried the phone numbers. As we spoke, though, I couldn't help but think that he might learn something by talking to Liban. At Marratane, smuggling had thrown the camp's basic functioning into disarray. For a subset of migrants to Mozambique, the informal system moving them about had completely taken over the one run by the government and the UN. "Last night is going five car, last night is going 120 people," Liban said at the end of our first meeting. Evidently, he still kept his ear to the ground; it seemed likely that he missed being a *mukalas*.

Chihale said he had trouble even learning how many Ethiopians and Somalis were in the camp at any given time, which complicated the task of providing basic services like shelter and rations, let alone issuing Travel Declarations. "The camp is not closed, so people come and go as they please," he told me. Chihale pointed to a chart on the wall that showed that four hundred Ethiopians had left the camp in the last month. He didn't yet know how many had come there. After all, it was hard to tell who was arriving in Marratane for the first time and who had been there once before. It didn't help, he said, that so many of the migrants shared portions of their names: Mohammed, Ahmed, Ali.

In July 2011, the minister of the interior visited Marratane with a fleet of Indian-made SUVs and a couple dozen strong men who formed a security barrier everywhere he walked. He was accompanied by the entire staff of the Nampula offices of INAR and the

UNHCR, and though he'd never set foot in the camp, he strode deliberately through it, dictating his own itinerary without comment. He said hello to Congolese market women selling cherry tomatoes and plastic baggies of vegetable oil by the road, then jumped back into his Mahindra jeep and sped off, two hundred yards farther into camp. With a single sentence, he thanked the teachers from Marratane's elementary school, and made an about-face. They remained in receiving line formation until he was out of sight again. A crowd formed at a respectful distance from his entourage and followed him throughout, chasing after the jeeps. The mob was thickest at the transit center, where hundreds of Ethiopians looked on from beyond the security cordon. There was not a woman, child, or man over fifty in sight. The minister walked down long lines of ragged tents chatting with Chihale. "They come from Ethiopia to here by themselves?" an aide asked one of the INAR employees. "Is there a map or something?"

Beyond the transit center, the minister strode off on a foot-path that led into a cassava field, with soldiers and barefoot Ethiopians fanning out among the crops. After twenty yards, he narrowly avoided stepping in human feces, and the Ethiopians grinned eagerly while the entourage turned back toward camp, chuckling about "land mines." The minister stopped briefly in front of a group of Ethiopians. "*Como está?*" he asked. How are you? They murmured, as one. The man standing directly in front of the minister stuck his fingers in his ears. "Language!" someone shouted, in English. The minister continued walking. I asked a bystander what the people had been saying in Amharic. "Hungry!" he said.

The minister went to greet a Mozambican family living on the edge of camp, then turned back once more to address Marratane's remaining Ethiopians, a group of roughly four hundred, who squatted en masse under a large mango tree. "I want to talk to all of you," the minister said. "We are visiting you here . . ." An Ethiopian man translated stoically for the crowd. "We are visiting you here to change ideas, to know how life is here in this center." The crowd erupted in a hundred conversations.

Minister: "What did they say?"

Translator: "Continue, continue."

Minister: "No, I want to know what they say."

Translator: "Yes, yes, continue, no problem."

The minister gave up. "I want to talk with you and hear what you have to say, but I see that we'll need more time. So I'll come back another day, and we'll talk, and talk, and talk." The crowd applauded loudly, looking thoroughly amused. As I walked away, I heard one man speaking angrily to a friend. What did you say to him? I asked. "I said, 'Why are you doing this clapping? We have things to say. Why you are only clapping?'"

After we met that first day, Liban and I spoke on the phone every week or so, though our conversations never lasted more than a minute. He'd call me from Cabo Delgado, or Niassa, or some other far-flung corner of the country and explain where he was headed next. He hauled cotton, sugarcane, coconuts. "Yes, *amigo,* where are you? *Tudo bem?*" Everything good? "I am, Montepuez, that side, now. I'm coming, Nampula, one week. Yes, okay, *vou ligar pra ti.*" I'll call you. Inevitably, when I called back, we had missed each other, and Liban was on the road again. We finally met up in Maputo, two months later. He picked me up at a sidewalk liquor market in Baixa and had me throw my bicycle on a jumble of papers and cardboard boxes in the back of his Nissan Pathfinder. Together, we drove to the Maputo International Airport, a gleaming glass and concrete box where I'd arrived in the country in March.

Marratane, Liban said, was dead. Police scrutiny in Nampula had forced smugglers and migrants to reshuffle. There were no boats landing near Palma or Mocímboa da Praia, and the camp

Watiro Wachamo, thirty, left his wife and two kids behind on their farm in southern Ethiopia in hopes of making it to the United States or Europe.

had returned to the dreary routine of its long-term inhabitants from the Great Lakes. Jesus Sanchez, the UNHCR officer in Maputo, told me that there was a "practical seal" on the northern border of Mozambique for migrants from the Horn of Africa. Similar crackdowns had taken place in Tanzania, Zimbabwe, and Malawi, he said, evidence of a so-called knock-on effect from South Africa itself. When the UNHCR high commissioner met with President Armando Guebuza at an African Union summit to voice his concern over the treatment of refugees and asylum seekers in Mozambique, "the official version was that no one was being deported unless they were suspected of a crime," said Sanchez, "but in fact, deportations are happening. Unfortunately, it's a regional trend."

Liban was not so sure: he thought there were still migrants going through Malawi and Zimbabwe. But there was also a growing contingent of *mukalas* working through the regular Ethiopian Airlines flights into Maputo. This was why he was taking me to the airport. Already, Ethiopian Airlines was gaining a bad reputation around Mozambique as the carrier of choice for drug trafficking and illegal entry into the country. A single flight to Maputo in January 2011 carried 133 Bangladeshi and Pakistani migrants with forged entry visas, on their way to South Africa.[34] After suspect police and customs officers at the airport were replaced that July, nearly every week brought new headlines about cocaine seizures, including that of one South African who deplaned with more than thirty pounds of cocaine in his suitcase.[35] The very week I visited the airport with Liban, police made four

By the beginning of 2012, these men were some of the only Ethiopians left at the refugee camp in Marratane: everyone else, they said, had gone with smugglers to South Africa.

separate cocaine seizures from passengers transiting through Addis Ababa.

Liban pulled up against the curb just outside the parking kiosk, at the front of a long line of cars seeking to avoid parking fees by stopping short of the gate—the Chinese government funded the construction of the airport, but evidently, the Mozambican style of management still prevailed. By the entrance, young hawkers in MCel and Vodacom vests lingered with their pockets full of cell phone credit and backpacks full of pens, lighters, and glitzy plastic watches. Arms outstretched, they sold knock off Ray-Bans and other trinkets for the business set. On the other side of the sliding glass doors, the terminal was nearly empty. We were an hour early, so we waited at a café at one end of the hall with espresso and grilled cheese.

Soon, Liban began pointing out men he knew from his old trade—"That one, little one, Ethiopian one, he is *mukalas*. He is coming to tell *flan-flan*," meaning so-and-so, "I have coming, five people, six people." After a while, Liban grew impatient, and he beckoned me to follow him to see how things worked on the inside. He strode confidently up to the bay of doors leading to customs and immigration, used exclusively as an exit for arriving travelers, opened one, and brushed by a young security guard who protested but didn't bar his path. By the tables where baggage is searched and disembarkation cards are turned in, Liban shook hands and chuckled with a familiar customs officer, then turned to me to say that the plane wouldn't be long. "They coming this side, you say, I have this many people. . . ." He made it sound very easy. We went back out through the customs exit, and Liban crossed the hall to greet more old friends. Three detectives, he said, from the police criminal investigations unit. I was beginning to believe that Liban really did know all the cops in Maputo.

When the flight finally did come, the passengers scattered like marbles, but Liban pointed out two small groups—two Ethiopians and four Somalis—carrying only small backpacks. The foreign *mukalas* he'd pointed out earlier were long gone, but each of the groups was promptly met by a Mozambican handler who led them out of the terminal. "Already, he is waiting in the car," Liban said of the *mukalas*. "*Vamos lá?*" he asked, in Portuguese. Should we go? "If you want, I follow them."[36]

5

Where Have You Hidden the Cholera?

NAMPULA

Stones and brickbats were thrown at the premises, several windows were broken, even in the room where the woman, now in a dying state, was lying, and the medical gentleman who was attending her was obliged to seek safety in flight. Several individuals were pursued and attacked by the mob and some hurt. The park constables were apparently panic struck, and incapable of acting.

—*LIVERPOOL CHRONICLE*, JUNE 2, 1832

Rioting and social unrest in response to cholera was not entirely confined to Britain. Civil disturbances arose in Russia in 1830, and were followed elsewhere in mainland Europe in 1831. In Hungary, castles were attacked and nobles murdered by mobs who believed the upper classes were responsible for cholera deaths.

—GILL, BURRELL, AND BROWN, "FEAR AND FRUSTRATION"[1]

It was a story of bicycles.

—DOMINGOS NAPUETO

In October 2010, a government laboratory in Port-au-Prince confirmed Haiti's first cholera case in nearly a century. The Ministry of Health quickly flooded the airwaves with spots urging residents to wash their hands and treat their water. International observers who were surprised that cholera would resurface after such a long absence reacted skeptically at first, but the disease's path of devastation quickly proved them wrong.[2] The outbreak tore through the central plateau and up and down the coast of the Gulf of Gonâve, the bay that forms the hollow middle of Haiti's horseshoe-shaped map. Four thousand five hundred people died, and nearly three hundred thousand fell ill.

Cholera was a second, shattering blow to a country already crippled by an earthquake that had struck earlier that year, destroying much of the capital and leaving more than a hundred thousand people dead. Where had the disease come from? Had the jostling of tectonic plates during the earthquake unleashed cholera-carrying waters in the Gulf of Mexico? Had benign strains of the cholera bacterium already present in Haiti somehow morphed and become virulent? Suspicions quickly fell on a contingent of Nepalese soldiers with the United Nations Stabilization Mission in Haiti, MINUSTAH, whose camp was in Mirebalais, near the outbreak's start, and where sewage was said to have leaked into a tributary of the Artibonite River. Cholera outbreaks occur in South Asia every single year, and it was presumed that UN soldiers had unwittingly carried the pathogen with them to Haiti.

The UN waved off the accusations, but protesters reacted violently. "The reason we are protesting is because the UN is doing illegal things in the city," a man named Marcel Jean told a TV crew in Cap Haïtien, where the airport was shut down and barricades of burning tires were erected in the street.[3] "They bring the U.N. to give us security, but this is not security. This is devastation." A police station and cholera treatment center were burned to the ground.[4]

People threw stones at UN trucks and looted warehouses belonging to the World Food Programme.[5]

Presidential elections, first delayed by the shattering earth-quake that had laid waste to the Haitian capital earlier in the year, again seemed in doubt.[6]

"The way in which the events unfolded leads to the belief that the incidents had a political motivation, aimed at creating a cli-mate of insecurity on the eve of the elections," MINUSTAH said cryptically in a press release. "MINUSTAH calls on the popula-tion to remain vigilant and not let itself be manipulated by the enemies of stability and democracy in the country."

Presidential candidates insisted otherwise: "The Nepalese [peace-keepers] are their target," the politician Lesley Voltaire said of the protests. "People believe the cholera came from Nepal."

It would take five more years for the UN to admit fault.[7] What people had been saying all along turned out to be true—albeit unintentionally, UN peacekeepers had brought cholera to Haiti.

I think of this story as a parable of sorts. There were other vic-tims of the violence that accompanied cholera, too: by one account, more than forty voodoo priests were killed by mobs who believed them to be responsible for spreading the disease.[8]

But inevitably, our view of the protests anxious people led against the UN's cholera outbreak—and the destruction they visited on human targets—is colored by the fact that they turned out to be right. The purpose of this chapter is to ask what difference it would make for them to be wrong.

From the campaign for polio eradication in Pakistan to efforts to contain the Ebola epidemic in Sierra Leone, violent responses to public health interventions have become a tragically familiar part of health crises around the world. Nowhere has the phenom-enon been more consistent than in cholera outbreaks in northern Mozambique.

Every year since 1998, cholera season in Mozambique has brought a rash of violence that spreads like the disease itself. Convinced they are being poisoned by the people treating their water, farmers and fishermen across northern provinces attack the health workers trying to prevent cholera's spread and the machinery of their efforts. Government nurses have been beaten and bound with rope. Health centers have been burned to the ground as angry crowds blocked roads demanding to know, "Where have you hidden the cholera?" They are still waiting for an answer.

Explanations for the violence often center on a simple misunderstanding: that the Portuguese words for chlorine, or *cloro*, and cholera, *cólera*, are close enough to cause confusion.

"I know where the problem is," one NGO employee told me confidently in Nampula. Ailton Muchave had spent years working on WASH (water, sanitation, and hygiene) programs for the Christian charity World Vision alongside the provincial government's health and sanitation agencies. "In Portuguese, you have the word *cloro*, for the substance that treats water. But people who only speak dialect," as local languages are often called, "when they hear *cloro*, they don't make the distinction."

Imagine a health team from outside the community shows up during an outbreak to spread messages on cholera prevention, Muchave explained, and "an agent will say, 'to get rid of cholera, we need chlorine.'" He pantomimed the reaction with a frown. "The people are perplexed. They think, 'But chlorine causes cholera!'"

"When you say *cloro*, they think *cólera*, and that's where the problem begins," José Eduardo Miguel, a technician with the Red Cross in Nampula, told me. To reduce the confusion, he explained, the Red Cross office in Nampula had adjusted its strategy during outbreaks. They no longer distribute generic chlorine—the cheapest option for water treatment—but branded Certeza chlorine solution. In some places, they had switched off chlorine altogether, distributing bleach instead.

Do you really think that the chlorine/cholera explanation is sufficient? I asked Miguel. *"Acho que não,"* Miguel replied. I don't think so. "There is probably some other cause, something hidden."

"It could be ignorance," Ailton Muchave mused in response to the same question, "but it could also be political."

That politics plays a role seems incontrovertible: cholera violence has been concentrated in areas with strong Renamo support. The worst episodes have occurred on either side of elections, times of high tension when the state apparatus controlled by Frelimo seems most transparently to function as a political party rather than a government. The targets of violence are not random scapegoats, but the specific people and places—of and associated with the government—tasked with responding to public health crises.[9]

Even today, after close to twenty years of episodic cholera-related violence, it's not hard to find people who do think chlorine is to blame for the disease, or who speak of cholera as an invention of the political class. But hanging the explanation on *cloro* and *cólera* or on misinformation spread by Renamo obscures a more important question. How is it that so many Mozambicans have come to believe NGOs and government workers are out to kill them?

Some of the worst violence in recent memory took place along Nampula's coast in 2009. The year before, parts of the region had been flattened by Cyclone Jokwe, which uprooted cashew trees and washed fishing boats out to sea on its way to leaving tens of thousands of people homeless in one of the poorest areas of Mozambique.[10]

Domingos Napueto, a compact, muscular man with a baby face and a high voice, led efforts by the Red Cross to survey the damage in the district of Mogincual. When a German delegation visited a month later, a project was approved to distribute cashew seedlings and mosquito nets and to train locals in building houses that stood a better chance of surviving a storm. Volunteers chosen for the effort were given bicycles to help them cover the long distances between communities where they were helping with construction.

Napueto had been a Red Cross volunteer since the end of the civil war. He had a day job doing supplies and inventory at the district health center in Liupo, and many of his fellow volunteers were also drawn from the ranks of the civil service—health workers, teachers, and so on.[11]

Volunteers pitched in 10 meticais a month to support the organization, but they also acted as a conduit for aid from the International Federation of the Red Cross. As people returned to areas they had fled because of the fighting, Napueto and a handful of colleagues organized distributions of oil, cornmeal, and bales of used clothing and gave away hoes and machetes to farmers trying to start over.

In 1992 and 1993, hundreds of people in coastal Nampula suffered an outbreak of konzo, or tropical ataxic neuropathy, a form of paralysis caused by cyanide poisoning; Napueto said Red Cross volunteers responded with education and outreach about the disease, as they would do later for sanitation and hygiene.[12] Cassava, the staple crop in Nampula, is drought-tolerant and does well in poor soil, but it can also contain toxic levels of cyanide that have to be leached out by rinsing, drying, or fermenting the crop. Konzo occurs in periods of drought or war, when people are forced to subsist on a diet of bitter cassava alone, or eat it raw.

The rainy season of 2008–9 was shaping up to be another difficult time. Exacerbated by drought, the damage from Cyclone Jokwe had produced a terrible harvest for many farmers in the area, and local officials were bracing for a return of the disease in the midst of widespread hunger.[13]

Meanwhile, cholera outbreaks sparked unrest in other parts of northern Mozambique. In Pemba, Cabo Delgado, an angry crowd had burned down three cholera treatment tents set up on the beach in the midst of an outbreak there, forcing two local officials to take refuge in the police station. In another Cabo Delgado town, eight people were beaten up for distributing chlorine and spreading cholera prevention messages, accused of spreading the disease.[14]

In Mogincual, Napueto recalled, people had heard vague rumors about the violence, or listened to cholera prevention messages on the radio, but the Red Cross had never encountered any overt hostility. As Napueto's colleagues told me, before the bicycles, "we'd never had any problems with jealousy—but from that time until now, they've never gotten it out of their heads."

The first signs of trouble came on a Friday in January when Napueto accompanied a group from the provincial office of the Red Cross to a coastal community outside Quinga to watch the construction of a demonstration home. They were clearing a lot for the house when morning prayers let out at the mosque, Napueto said, and a group of irate young men approached them. "They said, 'We don't want your house here,'" Napueto recalled. "'You didn't come to help us. You came to bring us diseases.'"

As the confrontation threatened to degenerate, the delegation left and told the volunteers to postpone work for the time being. The house did not need to be built at all, or it could be built another day.

Juma Raimundo, a Red Cross volunteer who was living in Curuhama, remembers the day in February when the first cholera cases showed up in Mogincual.

The Red Cross had learned of an outbreak spreading in a neighboring district the day before. Volunteers were in the midst of planning a chlorine distribution when people from affected areas began trickling in on foot, terrified at seeing their neighbors racked by fatal, uncontrollable diarrhea. Several people died on arrival.

Raimundo's village, Curuhama, began to empty out as people fled.[15] Those who could afford the fare walked out to the main road and hailed motorcycles and trucks to Liupo. One man from Curuhama told me that even some relatives of those who died fled "like ants before a flood." Some stayed to assist neighbors and loved ones in burying the dead—with no protective equipment. Others looked for a culprit.

Raimundo mans the health post in Quinga, a picturesque town on a hillside three miles from the Indian Ocean. Once upon a time, under the Portuguese, Quinga was the administrative seat of the district, and the town square is still dominated by the pastel pink and blue skeletons of a dozen or more large art deco buildings, their roofs long gone, with a scattering of tailors and cigarette sellers making use of the shelter afforded by their overhung porches. You can still make out "Tribunal," or courthouse, written on the facade of one, and imagine "Correios" painted above the entrance of the old post office.

Raimundo waved me inside and had me sit behind the doctor's desk while a young woman stood on the steps with a tiny coughing baby swaddled in a *capulana*. When the first cholera cases appeared in Curuhama, Raimundo said, people became uneasy and approached the *líder comunitário* (community leader) to express their suspicion that the Red Cross might be involved. "'We've lived here for so many years, and we drank the water without becoming sick,'" they argued.

There had been PSAs on the radio there explaining the basics of the disease and spreading prevention messages too, but, if anything, that made people more suspicious. As one young woman participating in a focus group on cholera violence told a sociologist years earlier: "I think the problem is that the radio anticipated that there would be a cholera outbreak this year, which made people say, how can they know a disease is coming on such and such a day?"[16]

In Curuhama, "When the outbreak began, people felt the Red Cross volunteers already *knew* it would," Raimundo explained. The community leader tried to dissuade them from accusations against the Red Cross, but he was beaten up for his trouble. On February 25, the mob grew to something like two hundred young men from Curuhama and surrounding villages, Raimundo estimated, as they burned down houses belonging to volunteers.

The secretary of the Quinga chapter of the Red Cross, Cassiano Muquinone, had gone to Liupo by bicycle the day before to get chlorine water treatment solution—called Certeza, or "certainty"— to distribute. When he returned, he was tied up, beaten, and locked with two other volunteers inside a house as it was set on fire. The ultimatum given, as recounted by a provincial representative for the Red Cross at the time, was this: "Either you take out the cholera, or you'll die."[17] Muquinone and one other person were killed in the attacks, and several were badly injured.[18]

Raimundo himself was bound, beaten, and forced to drink Certeza by the capful as neighbors turned aggressors interrogated him. "You better talk now and tell us where the cholera is coming from," he recalled being told. Raimundo managed to free himself during the night and left for Liupo on foot early the next morning.

As the ordeal unfolded, Domingos Napueto's information came to him from wounded Red Cross volunteers who arrived one by one, first at the hospital in town, and then, with no other port of call, in his tiny thatch-roofed home across the street, where fourteen terrified volunteers ultimately took refuge.

The first word arrived with a volunteer who had had the good fortune to be away from home when the disturbance started, Napueto said. He returned at dinnertime after restocking on medical supplies in Liupo, and he was warned people were coming for him. When they did, he escaped out his back door and walked in the bush through the night, returning to Liupo the following afternoon.

From here, accounts of the next several weeks began to diverge. Had the police heard about the destruction in Curuhama in real time over the radio or from volunteers who fled? Did reinforcements come from Nampula straightaway, or only twelve or even twenty-four hours later? Who exactly was involved, and why?

"When something like that starts to spread," Napueto told me, "everyone speaks in his own way."

Paulo Ipo, a lanky Liupo policeman who was among the first to respond to the cholera violence, recalled his own experience with a kind of breezy matter-of-factness you might expect from an officer at the end of a weeknight patrol.[19] He, too, pinned the disturbances on the chlorine/cholera misunderstanding.

At the time, Ipo said, the police force in Liupo did not have a truck of its own, so they piled into a pickup belonging to the provincial department of agriculture and headed for the coast. They reached a mostly deserted community near Curuhama and stopped at the ransacked house of a Red Cross volunteer, whose wife was still there cowering in fear, and whose equipment—first aid supplies, tarps, and so on—had been strewn around the yard.

According to one report, police made a handful of arrests and picked up three wounded Red Cross volunteers to take back to Liupo.[20] On their way, though, they had to stop at a small bridge that had been blocked with logs. When the officers got out, they were met by a group of cholera vigilantes who seized their guns and their truck, attacked two policemen, and forced the whole group to flee on foot.[21] A unit of the Força de Intervenção Rápida—Mozambique's equivalent of a SWAT team—came from Nampula and went back again.

By the afternoon of February 26, the district police commander in Liupo was reassuring reporters that calm had returned to the area.[22] But after that, Ipo said, "the situation generalized."

Protests and vandalism continued over the ensuing weeks, with logs and stones dragged across the roads and "checkpoints" set up by groups of angry residents to keep health workers from getting to areas affected by the cholera outbreak. Or, in the words of Manuel Tadia, a man who proudly told me he'd been one of the checkpoints' main instigators, "to defend our area."

Sporadic violence continued too. In a neighboring district, Angoche, where cholera raged on, people burned the houses of thirteen Red Cross volunteers and turned with machetes and spears on policemen who were protecting health workers accused of spreading the disease. One officer was killed and disemboweled; two others were badly injured.[23]

On March 14, a mob marched out of a community near Curuhama, holding Sandra Assuate—a Red Cross volunteer they accused of spreading cholera—hostage.[24] Her description of the ordeal is tragically similar to what Juma Raimundo had seen in Curuhama weeks earlier: "I found myself faced with about 50 people all armed with machetes," she told members of a legislative commission investigating the incident later, asking, "Where have you hidden the cholera?"

Assuate's captors undressed her, tied her up, and marched her to a house ten miles away, torturing her by setting a fire around her before leaving to deliberate about whether to kill her. Police discovered her just in time, buried alive up to her neck.[25]

The social contagion brought on by cholera-related violence seemed to have overtaken the disease itself. Staff at a medical clinic in Quinga abandoned their patients out of fear of being attacked.[26] The district education director, Agostinho Mendes, said fifteen schools had shut down after the lion's share of their students stopped showing up. Just as they had during the war, families fled the violence and hunger of the countryside to take refuge in Liupo and other larger towns.[27]

Some thirty men were arrested in connection with the attack on Assuate and the murder, by another group involved in barricading the roads, of a storekeeper whose body was thrown down a well.[28]

What happened next only reinforced the paranoid rage that sparked so much violence in the first place. On the night of March 16, somewhere between thirty-four and forty-nine men—reports vary—were arrested as cholera agitators and brought to the police station in Liupo, many of them bound with rope or handcuffed in pairs. There, they were crowded into a Liupo holding cell built for nine, scarcely over one hundred square feet.[29] A good chunk of that space was occupied by a communal latrine.[30]

The two policemen on duty, doubtless terrified themselves, ignored the inmates' calls for help, even as a struggle broke out as the men jockeyed for position beneath two small openings near the roof that provided ventilation in the heat.

When at last they opened the door in the middle of the night, eleven men had suffocated to death inside. A twelfth stumbled out and took his last breaths in the courtyard of the police station. Thirteen men died in all.

As Juma Raimundo remembered it, word of the jailhouse deaths spread like a pall over the district, calming the nerves of the young angry men who had led the witch hunts over the previous several weeks. "From there," he said, "the subject was closed."

Both the officers on duty were ultimately sentenced to a year in prison on manslaughter charges; they served jail time alongside some of the prisoners who had survived.[31] The legislature launched a commission of inquiry into the whole sordid episode in Mogincual, but the seams of the effort at fact-finding and reconciliation soon began to show. Frelimo politicians dusted off their standard argument over cholera-related violence and accused Renamo of spreading misinformation about the disease. However the tragedy came to pass, one Frelimo deputy charged, "Renamo is the moral author of the deaths in Mogincual." Afonso Dhlakama, always one to embrace a poetic flourish, said Frelimo was trying "to hide the sun with a feather," persecuting the opposition in order to deflect its own responsibility to protect people from cholera.[32]

When I asked later whether Frelimo and Renamo were using distress over cholera to do what the district administrator in Mogincual called "making politics," he told me, "I can't say yes or no, but I can say all politicians are opportunists."

Others, though, pointed out basic shortcomings of governance that let the situation in Mogincual get so bad in the first place. As the columnist Mouzinho de Albuquerque wrote in the state newspaper two days after the jailhouse deaths, "The top brass of the PRM [Mozambique's national police force], both nationally, and at the provincial level, knew the outlines of the unrest around cholera in Mogincual, but none of them went there in time to see for themselves. It was only after these twelve [sic] people died that the provincial commander, for instance, went to Mogincual."[33]

Public officials, he suggested, seemed to have condemned Mogincual through sheer indifference.

Other questions surfaced from the report of a local human rights organization that conducted interviews with the police and focus groups in the field that very week. How could it be that police arrested more than thirty men but didn't see the need for a contingency plan given that they had room for a fraction as many? Why were only two officers left on duty that night? Poor conditions and inadequate infrastructure, it noted, could be blamed for previous deaths in nearly every jail or prison in Mozambique.[34] Why hadn't something been done sooner?

Two weeks after the violence subsided, in timing that seemed too fortuitous to be accidental, a doctor showed up for work at the health clinic in Liupo—the first physician ever to be permanently stationed in the district.

* * *

The hospital in Liupo is a constellation of bright-white single-story buildings set in a large red-dirt courtyard and bounded by a row of massive mango trees. While I waited there one morning to meet Josué Chicara, who became Mogincual's first resident physician in 2009, I struck up a conversation with a young male nurse entering the twenty-sixth hour of a forty-eight-hour shift.

Others had told me that the standard twenty-four-hour shifts—common for ER residents in the United States, though not for nurses—contributed to exhaustion and stress among health workers, exacerbating the difficulties posed by low wages, disdain for patients, and well-documented corruption throughout the health system.[35] I hadn't imagined what twenty-four-hour shifts would mean in rural clinics where no one was available to fill in for employees who couldn't come in.

In this case, the nurse said he was covering for a colleague whom he imagined to be home with a fake illness, likely, he said, to be seen in one of Liupo's kiosk-like bars in a few hours' time. He looked weary to a point past physical exhaustion, standing in baggy hospital whites with his hands in his pockets, his blank expression disturbed only by the disorderly beginnings of a wiry mustache. "If I could amputate an arm and go back to Nampula city, I would," he told me when I asked how he liked Liupo. Then, reconsidering, he added, "Or cut off a finger and go back.

"The countryside" he said, "is complicated."

Chicara walked out a few minutes later, extending a strong handshake and a broad smile, and invited me to sit on a plastic patio chair outside the pharmacy. When he'd first come to visit Mogincual, he explained, he'd only agreed to stay when he saw that there was cell phone service. Broadly speaking, Chicara was optimistic about the direction of public health in the district, though, he added, "Mogincual is known for having a difficult population."

There had been a handful of cholera cases in 2010, he said, but only isolated instances of unrest since the "events" of 2009. In one incident, a group of men in the town of Namige had burned down the home of a Save the Children volunteer working with the Ministry of Health, and attacked a nurse while they vandalized the health post there. In another, this time in the town of Liupo itself, a schoolteacher woke up to find a ring of white flour on the ground outside her home, a kind of warning that she was bringing cholera to the area.

In 2011, a year when there was no cholera in the whole district, one neighborhood simmered with rumors that a Frelimo party official was spreading cholera in the dead of night, and he was ultimately threatened with a crude note tacked to his front door: "Marcos Prata—distributor of cholera. Attention: If anyone gets sick and dies, you'll be killed with a machete."

Nevertheless, nurses who had had to steer clear of parts of the region following the unrest in 2009 had recently resumed visits to Quinga and elsewhere. In 2010, Chicara himself had gone to Curuhama as part of a childhood vaccination campaign and found the community eager to participate.

Sidestepping politics, Chicara framed all this in the context of a broader national struggle to reconcile Western-style medicine with the care offered by Mozambique's *curandeiros*, or traditional healers. Since 2009, he said, the Ministry of Health had started to embrace collaboration with traditional health practitioners: a nurse in each district had been assigned to act as a liaison for traditional medicine, meeting with *curandeiros* monthly to try to coax them to refer patients to the government health system.

Mozambique has made undeniable strides in public health in recent years. There have been sharp decreases in child and maternal mortality and a steady uptick in child vaccinations.[36] Although HIV/AIDS remains the leading cause of death, access to antiretroviral treatment has expanded dramatically.[37] At the same time,

UNICEF estimates that more than 40 percent of children in Mozambique are chronically malnourished.[38] According to the World Health Organization, nearly one in three women aged fifteen to forty-nine dies from maternal causes.[39]

Fully 45 percent of Mozambique's population is younger than fifteen.[40] It will be hard for growth of the medical system to keep up. In 2009, Mozambique had one doctor for every 33,000 people, and one nurse for 5,000.[41] It has one practitioner of traditional medicine for every 200.[42] Accordingly, the Ministry of Health estimates that more than two-thirds of Mozambicans are their patients.[43] Yet the relationship between traditional healing and so-called biomedicine has been fraught for a long time.[44]

"The state ignores traditional doctors while civil servants frequently resort to them," writes the Portuguese anthropologist Maria Paula Meneses. The institutions, she argues, operate in strictly rational terms; their employees are more practical. Meneses relays a story from a patient from the professional class who's visited *curandeiros* for serious ailments: "Anything goes. You never know if they will work, but one certainly will; we can't risk not trying."[45]

In 2010, the Ministry of Health created the Institute for Traditional Medicine to build ties with traditional healers and conduct research on herbal and plant-based remedies. It created a national registration system to get some account of the number of *curandeiros* operating around the country and to give them a modicum of recognition from the government. The ministry has conducted a series of tailored trainings for traditional healers on recognizing symptoms of HIV/AIDS, malaria, and tuberculosis.[46] It's largely a one-way street: "The knowledge of the traditional doctor is only seen to be valid as a complement to biomedicine," Meneses observes. "The traditional doctor is seen as one who needs to be trained, but who does not participate in the training of biomedical doctors."[47]

Mistrust remains a challenge on the other side too. Two weeks before we met, explained Josué Chicara, the doctor in Liupo, a seventy-year-old cook had died in his care, having arrived at the hospital in the terminal stages of tuberculosis. Over the two preceding months, the man had been admitted to the hospital and fled treatment a total of seven times, dragged to the health center by family members or neighbors, weakened, groggy, in the midst of a crisis of symptoms, only to run home on his own when he began to get his strength back.

When I visited Mogincual for the first time, in 2012, I was anxious to see what scars had been left by the outbreak and ensuing violence. Similar if less widespread unrest has followed cholera around the region every year since 1998. Usually, as in Angoche and Mogincual, unrest moved in concert with the scale of the outbreak, though sometimes it arose in places with no cholera cases at all.

"Ironically, there were no cases of cholera reported in Alto-Maganha," reads a 2010 story describing cholera riots that destroyed a newly constructed health center in a town along the coast of Zambezia Province.[48] "But there were outbreaks elsewhere in the province, and in neighbouring Nampula. So the Pebane district health authorities embarked on an education campaign, telling people how to avoid cholera."

Within days, "a mob marched on the health centre, smashed all the windows, tore off the roof, and destroyed the medical equipment."

When the governor visited the town two months later, residents apologized for destroying the clinic and asked him to rebuild it. "You used to complain that there were no health services here," the governor, Francisco Itai Meque, replied. "When it was thought that the problem had been solved, you fell for the wave of disinformation and rose up against your own interests."

Did anyone in Mogincual feel contrite, or somehow wiser for the tragic events of 2009? What, at bottom, had driven the resentment and suspicion that boiled over into such rage?

I got a ride to Curuhama on the back of a Chinese motorcycle belonging to Hermínio Alexandre, a community court judge in Liupo who had agreed to drive and translate. It was a luminous, cloudy day. A sprinkling of rain left the road a bright brick red, majestic mahogany trees rising on either side with a tangle of vines and underbrush below.

Past the crossroads leading to Quinga, Hermínio and I took one hopelessly zigzagging shortcut between cassava fields and gnarled cashew trees and nearly fell repeatedly. But we soon emerged in a wide lane of small *matopi*, or thatch-roofed shops,

Hermínio Alexandre, a community court judge in Liupo, was a witness to the aftermath of the cholera outbreak in 2009 and acted as a guide and translator on visits to villages affected by the violence.

where we found the home of the *líder comunitario,* Gregorio Passarinho, at the bottom of a slender wooden flagpole.

Passarinho is in his fifties, lean and muscular and, at our meeting, circumspect, with a creeping hint of a smile that suggested a lingering expectation of my saying something impolitic or treading on precarious ground—which, of course, I was. Passarinho has a gray beard, hollow cheeks, and a long, refined nose that gives him the look of Jules Verne or some other nineteenth-century baron of ink sketches in profile.

That Passarinho was still living in Curuhama was remarkable to me. Less than three years earlier, he'd been rounded up and beaten alongside Cassiano Muquinone, the Red Cross volunteer who was ultimately killed, and left bound by the wrists for forty-four hours as his neighbors set fire to the houses all around him. Afterward, he'd spent three months recovering in the hospital.

Passarinho suggested speaking to a few people in the market. Was it necessary to gather them? he wondered. No, I explained, I found it easier to talk to small groups. Even so, he led me, my government credential letter folded between weathered fingers, to the steps of the fishmonger's and proceeded to read the contents out loud in Makua for a crowd of fifty young men who had gathered to learn the purpose of a foreigner's visit.

Anxious to keep a mellow mood, I said a few things myself: that I had no secrets, that I didn't come to muck anything up, that I found it hard to do an interview with so many people at once, and I proposed to Passarinho that we begin by chatting on his verandah one-on-one.

"If the government didn't have any power here," he said, "the whole area would have been destroyed."

Still, he'd returned to Curuhama to reclaim his neglected fields and resume his humble duties as *líder comunitario,* being a liaison to the district government and a first port of call for visitors.

There hadn't been any trouble since. As Juma Raimundo put it, "The people who spent time in prison are the ones who keep everyone else calm." When I asked Passarinho whether his neighbors' views of cholera had shifted in the intervening years, he broke out laughing. Where do people think diarrhea comes from? I asked. "Even today," he said, "people think diarrhea comes from the government, that only Frelimo knows. That's exactly what they say: 'Frelimo knows where it comes from!'"

Outreach and education work around hygiene has continued in Curuhama, he said, albeit with some careful parameters. "The government comes and talks about latrines, about cleaning wells, about hygiene, but they never say the word 'cholera,'" Passarinho said.[49]

After Passarinho and I spoke, I said I wanted to walk around the village to try to speak with people one-on-one, but I soon found myself on the porch of the fishmonger's surrounded by a crowd. Once again, I explained that I was a reporter, not a politician, and that I'd like to just walk around and chat with people one-on-one or in small groups. But in Passarinho's translation from the Makua, at least, everyone was too uneasy to do things that way: it would cause suspicion and gossip for me to have private interviews, they said. At an impasse, I proceeded to ask my questions of the group.

How have things here been since 2009? Has your relationship with health workers changed? After a stirring silence, a man in a blue knit cap with a long goatee spoke up: "From 2009 up through today, we have been living happily, because things have changed." What has changed? "From that time until now, that illness hasn't returned."

Where does that illness come from? Murmurs, nervous chuckles. "They want to know which illness you're talking about," Passarinho explained. The illness they call cholera, I said. "They are saying some people know where the illness comes from, but they're afraid to say."

How had the outbreak in 2009 affected life here? A volley of translations moved through the crowd, as the group churned in consideration of the question. I rephrased: in 2009, some very serious things happened here. Some people died, others were badly hurt, and others went to jail. That kind of thing doesn't usually happen in a village. Has it changed what it is like to live here? More murmurs. Finally, if this illness were to return, do you think that your reaction here in Curuhama would be the same? This elicited a much firmer response. A man in Muslim dress in the back row spoke for his companions: "That depends on the spirit that enters the population at the time, whether it will provoke us to react a lot or a little." What do you mean the spirit? "Whether we'll be inclined to accelerate or remain calm."

Will you go to the health center if you get diarrhea? The reaction was unanimous: "No! If you go to the health center, you'll get worse and die." Watching my expression strain the edges of earnest belief, someone made a comment Passarinho tactfully neglected to translate. Bit by bit, I and the crowd descended into a contagious fit of belly laughs. When it finally subsided, I forged ahead: would you go to the health center for other diseases? "Yes, we do, and you usually get better."

How is it that the hospital would make you sicker for some things and less sick for others? "Perhaps the medicine for that illness does not exist. Perhaps they only have medicine for fever and headache."

A young man piped up to say they would take up *armas brancas*—or "shiny weapons" like knives and spears—to fight those responsible if and when cholera returned to Curuhama. "If it's the water, we'll fight the water, if it's wood, we'll fight the wood, and if it's a person we'll fight them." But how will you know? "We're grown up," he said. "We know how to tell who is evil."

* * *

The only one-on-one interview I managed to secure with a perpetrator of Curuhama's cholera violence was with Momade Mutumuara, a fifty-one-year-old farmer who invited me to sit on a straw mat outside his home surrounded by tall grasses and rows of fleshy cassava plants. Mutumuara had spent three months in jail in Angoche after the riots. He did not deny taking part in vandalism but said he hadn't been convicted of participating in any actual violence and wouldn't say exactly what he had done.

Even so, Mutumuara's gripe with the Red Cross seemed deeply personal, a vendetta over a long record of neighborly grievances.

Mutumuara described Cassiano Muquinone, the Red Cross volunteer who was killed, as "showing off" when he came to the village in a Red Cross jeep, asking for credit at Mutumuara's *barraca*, or bar, and making jocular threats about bringing ill health on people in town. "At your *barraca*, he'd come in and say, 'If you don't give me what I need—patience, careful, watch out. You'll get diarrhea.'"

He was also skeptical of the expanding reach of the state and NGOs as they responded to Cyclone Jokwe. Why was it they distributed mosquito nets from house to house rather than allowing people to collect them at the hospital? he wondered. Why did they bring food aid directly to Curuhama rather than have the villagers pick it up somewhere? Equally suspicious was a cache of shovels and gloves the Red Cross had left in a nearby village. Mutumuara had never seen anything like it before.

The connection between cholera and the wave of distributions following Jokwe was, to him, obvious and indisputable: "They distributed mosquito nets to everyone, and four months later, this illness appeared," he declared defiantly. How could one draw a different conclusion? "Not even fifteen days ago, they distributed more mosquito nets and I refused," he ventured. "*Tenho medo*. I'm afraid, I'm afraid," he said, repeating the phrase three times over. "If I feel I need one, I'll go out and buy one."

Momade Mutumuara spent two months in jail after taking part in the cholera-related violence that spread throughout Liupo in 2009. To him, the link between cholera and the Red Cross's relief work after Cyclone Jokwe was obvious and indisputable: "They distributed mosquito nets to everyone, and four months later, this illness appeared," he said.

Mutumuara was similarly suspicious of Passarinho, seen during the outbreak as a co-conspirator of the Red Cross volunteers—in part, of course, because the Red Cross used *líderes comunitarios* as liaisons to plan trainings and demonstrations. As a community leader, Passarinho had traveled to Inhambane, in southern Mozambique, for a special workshop with the government. When people in Curuhama asked about it, Mutumuara said, "He just said to us, 'Don't complain: when you see me eat rice, I'm eating my pen. When you see me eat cookies, I'm eating my pen'"—a swipe, as Mutumuara understood it, at illiterate neighbors like him.

Most telling of all, though, was Mutumuara's response to the twelve bicycles given to Red Cross volunteers in Curuhama to assist with their work after Cyclone Jokwe, a subject he raised unprompted. "Could it be that the government only knows twelve people in all of Curuhama?" he asked. "Is that supposed to be help? If it's help, it's supposed to help everyone."

This last gets at a fundamental question over the basic relationship of people in places like Curuhama with their government, which is to say, at best, almost none at all, and, at worst, a hostile one, with interactions perverted by patronage and bribery or run through with a kind of arrogance. In this context, a violent response to a public health campaign takes on a different sheen, as Joseph Hanlon writes in an essay called "The Panic and Rage of the Poor":

> Objections to chlorine may be scientifically unfounded, but reflect a well-founded social and political understanding. If a nurse or health post worker normally demands a bribe to provide proper treatment, why should they be trusted when they say they are giving chlorine free? If an arrogant NGO helps only a select few, why should it suddenly be trusted to help the poorest on a key health issue? If government actions have only led to increasing poverty and loss of jobs, why trust the government now? And if local chiefs and party secretaries have used their links with the outside to collect taxes and increase their own power, why should they be trusted to help now? The poor have every reason to ask if the sincere priests and health workers and NGO staff sent into rural areas are not just an attempt to build up trust so that the poor can be better exploited. And they have every reason to distrust the local leaders who ally themselves with the new outside exploiters.
>
> In a time of hunger when people see no hope of improvement in their lives, perhaps the passive and violent resistance to putting chlorine in local water supplies should be seen as local people making a desperate attempt to regain some power; as a disempowered group finally taking a stand to defend its very lives.[50]

In 2002, a team of researchers led by the sociologist Carlos Serra undertook an ethnography of an even more destructive wave of cholera violence that swept across Mozambique in 1998–99. Serra called the resulting book *Cólera e catarse*, or "Cholera and catharsis."[51] In one exchange, in Memba, where residents had risen up to resist a water treatment campaign by Save the Children, a *régulo* explains their point of view as follows: "People ask the government to spray their cashew trees"—presumably to cut down on the losses from pests. "The government doesn't do it, because they say it costs a lot of money. So then people start to question things: *'They can't spray our cashew trees, but they can find money for chlorine.'*"[52]

Serra finds the roots of the mythology that drives cholera riots in a sweeping tableau of deprivation: bad water, agricultural pests, declining fisheries, literal hunger along with hunger for basic infrastructure like brick-and-mortar schools (as opposed to straw and mud), the arrogance and derision of public officials. The list goes on and on.

Out of all this, Serra argues, arises a potent symbolism hostile to the state and everyone who touches it. "It is not the State as such that is targeted," he writes, "but the absent, non-dialoguing state, with no sustained contact with communities, incapable of giving up its demands for political loyalty in exchange for providing of basic services."

Cholera is caused by the *Vibrio cholerae* bacterium, believed to have originated in the Ganges River delta, in India, and now endemic in more or less virulent strains throughout much of the world. Like new strains of influenza, or citrus psyllids, cholera has become an extraordinarily successful migrant in the age of world travel, finding a foothold in Africa in the early 1970s.[53] With proper hygiene and/or immediate access to basic medical care (mainly rehydration), cholera is a preventable and highly treatable illness. But it can also prove fatal in the span of a few hours and spread incredibly quickly.

Cholera first appeared in Mozambique in a Maputo hospital ward in 1973.[54] It was a tiny outbreak—five cases and one death—but by year's end, cholera had surfaced in half the country's provinces, affecting eight hundred people. Abetted by war, drought, and massive population growth, it would spread throughout the country over the next two decades.

Between 1980 and 1991, the aggregate population of Mozambique's largest cities doubled as fighting in the countryside drove people to the security of urban centers. The plumbing was not ready for them; the incidence of cholera over the same period tracked neatly with population growth.[55] This was the same trajectory cholera followed in nineteenth-century Europe, as it spread along waterways and railways that connected the booming population centers of the industrial revolution. "As [cholera] arrived in the mushrooming towns and cities of a society in the throes of rapid urbanization," writes the historian Richard Evans, "it took advantage of overcrowded housing conditions, poor hygiene and insanitary water-supplies with a vigour that suggested that these conditions might almost have been designed for it."[56]

By 1991, one survey of Mozambique's piped water systems—already few and far between—found that 80 percent had no way of treating the water that traveled through them.[57] In the countryside, drought disrupted an already precarious water supply: rivers and wells dried up. New wells had to be dug, sometimes in areas already dotted with latrines.

During the first months of 1992, while negotiators were hammering out the terms of a peace deal to be signed in Rome that year, a cholera outbreak in Tete Province was on its way to infecting more than thirty thousand people and killing seven thousand.[58] Cholera continues to be a major problem in Mozambique: in the decade ending in 2015, there were more than fifty thousand cases and five hundred fatalities from the disease.[59] Still, both the incidence of and the mortality from cholera have declined incrementally since the late 1990s, suggesting both hygiene and sanitation and access to treatment during emergencies have improved.[60]

"Overall, the tendency is toward fewer diarrheal illnesses," Francisco Sumbane told me. Just how much is hard to say. Sumbane is a WASH engineer with the Swiss organization Helvetas who has worked on sanitation in northern Mozambique since 1979. In Cabo Delgado, he told me, "you could look at the statistics and think that a whole community is without latrines, even though everyone has one." Official figures on sewage and latrines kept by Mozambique's public works ministry don't include unprotected (i.e., uncovered) wells and traditional latrines, making it hard for organizations to get an accurate picture of practices on the ground.[61] Distribute large cement disks used to cap so-called improved latrines, Sumbane said, and you might return months later to find them used as washboards for doing laundry.

Alternately, drill a well in a community where there's only a precarious living to be had from the soil and no technical or financial support for agriculture, Sumbane said, and it could soon outlive its usefulness. "There are some places [in the countryside] where you'll find pumps that are very isolated, with no houses nearby," he said. "The people have moved: you could be building WASH infrastructure every year for new communities."

Even in areas where people stay put, he said, "The population is growing faster than the level of services being provided."

Sãozinha Paola Agostino, who was chief medical officer for the provincial health department in Nampula when we met in 2012, told me then she believes the incidence of cholera-related violence is diminishing too, though it's not something the government has studied directly.

In Nampula, the provincial government and its nonprofit partners have accelerated hygiene education campaigns using pamphlets, workshops, and radio spots. "The population must understand the pathology," she said.

But the contours of the problem go beyond the scope of the Ministry of Health. "We will not be the entity to solve these problems," Agostino said. "You can't say that people are doing this out of a lack of understanding, because violence happens in areas where there have already been efforts at sensitization." Here, Agostino seems to be caught up in a fallacy that assumes that education efforts are effective. The core issue isn't whether information on cholera is available, but whether it's credible.

On a second trip to Mogincual during the rainy season in 2016, I visited Iaué, a community a short ride from the district seat in Liupo, and the one that suffered the heaviest losses in the debacle that followed the cholera unrest in 2009.[62] Seven men from Iaué were among those who died in the police station that March, having been arrested, in the police's version of the story, for doing "night patrols" and stealing a motorcycle belonging to a Red Cross volunteer while they blocked the road.

Many people in Iaué, it turned out, had been to a WASH workshop put on at the hospital in Liupo. The basic message on cholera they'd taken away from the event, in the words of a woman named Terezinha Momade, was that "this disease comes from filth, from not having a latrine, not washing your plates and pots. But," she countered, "when our ancestors lived here a long time ago, they didn't wash their pots and pans or their plates, but that illness never came. Now that hygiene has started to show here—everyone has latrines, everybody cleans their house— that's when cholera comes. Well, where does it come from? If they say this illness comes from a lack of hygiene: we always keep our homes clean with hygiene, and it still comes." When people made this comparison for the health workers giving the presen-

Terezinha Momade, center, and her neighbors in Iaué remain skeptical of the hygiene and sanitation workshops they've attended at the hospital in Liupo. "When our ancestors lived here a long time ago, they didn't wash their pots and pans or their plates, but that illness"—cholera—"never came." Seven men from Iaué were among those who suffocated to death in the holding cell in Liupo in 2009.

tation, Momade said, they were told, "You can't count on old logic."

There was truth on both sides. Diarrhea writ large has been a scourge around the world for centuries, helped along by the "old logic" of going without latrines or antibacterial soap, or drinking untreated water. But to the people in Iaué, cholera was something different—diarrhea that could spread from village to village or rip through a neighborhood overnight, bringing quick and certain death. Both the disease and the quick population growth that made it so deadly had come to Mozambique within living memory. Even without access to a timeline of cholera's spread in Mozambique, people in Iaué had made an important observation: cholera was actually a relatively new phenomenon in the region, virtually unknown in much of the country until the 1990s.

I'd been talking with Momade and a group of women under her porch while a hard rain fell outside. The group shook with laughter when I asked if they trusted the answer they'd been given at the hospital. "If you tell the truth," Momade said, "you can go to jail." Of course, they might have been misremembering the exact words, or misunderstanding their meaning in the first place, but the takeaway was the same. To them, the information they'd been given about cholera—or, at the very least, the messenger—simply wasn't convincing.

Over time, cholera riots can be expected to wane along with the prevalence of the disease in Mozambique. But it is too soon to discern the future of either phenomenon: in the past, large outbreaks have been separated by intervals of as many as five or more years. Mozambique's declining economic fortunes, high population growth, and vulnerability to the floods and droughts of a changing climate all serve to exacerbate the challenges the country faces in addressing the underlying public health needs.

The relative calm officials have noted among communities where violence has occurred in the past may have as much to do with the absence of cholera as it does with a shift in attitudes about the disease and the people working to prevent it.

While cholera violence is, of course, linked to the disease's spread, it is also controlled by another mechanism altogether. Contagion, fundamentally, is about whom you believe, and for close to two decades, disenfranchised people in the remote areas and urban slums where cholera violence has taken root have often chosen to believe their peers and their lived experience rather than their government.

One tragedy of the chaos in Mogincual and Angoche is that the official response to unrest seems in some respects to have reinforced the underlying problem of government credibility.

A report by the Mozambican League of Human Rights (Liga dos Direitos Humanos) based on fieldwork done in March 2009 concluded that press accounts of the unrest left out crucial parts of the story. Cholera prevention efforts during the outbreak in Angoche, for instance, had been undertaken without knowledge of the local community leaders: "Some health workers were discovered in the middle of treating wells with chlorine. Having little information, residents of Sangaje [in Angoche] thought they'd discovered a plot to contaminate the water with a drug that causes cholera. The misunderstanding resulted in a popular protest against the health workers that led to a deadly response by the national police."[63]

"In putting down the protest, police fired on unarmed citizens, resulting in an unknown number of deaths, and detained 38 people in the district jail." According to the authorities, the report continues, only eight of those detained were involved in the related violence—police, the report concludes, believed from the start that members of the opposition, Renamo—were to blame, and acted accordingly, rounding up people involved in the opposition.

In Iaué, a man named Danilo Martín said his brother, his uncle, and his nephew were all killed in the holding cell in Liupo. Afterward, people from the village spent four days outside the police station there demanding that the government return their relatives' bodies, only to be told they had been sent to Nampula for an autopsy.

Ultimately, Martín said, people from Iaué had to scrape together money to get to Nampula and transport the bodies home for burial themselves. But the autopsy results were never revealed.

"I don't know how long an autopsy takes to deliver results," Martín told me, nearly seven years later. "We never got a judgment or anything at all about why our relatives were killed. That's why we blame the government," he said. "We'll never stop saying the government is guilty of some things, because it is."

The UN voted to draw down the peacekeeping mission in Haiti in April 2017, a few months after acknowledging MINUSTAH's role in the cholera epidemic there.[64] The announcement coincided with another damaging revelation from the Associated Press, that UN soldiers had spent years luring children in Port-au-Prince into a sex ring, and that UN investigations into similar misconduct were often closed inconclusively.[65] The formal rationale for the UN's withdrawal was that after a presidential election in November 2016, Haiti was finally on a path to political stability—that MINUSTAH's job, in other words, was complete. But many in Haiti took the news to mean the opposite, welcoming the UN's departure as vindication after years of unheeded criticism.[66]

There's been no evidence of similarly malevolent plots by NGOs or by the government in Liupo since 2009, but that hasn't stopped each side from drawing exactly opposite conclusions from the cholera violence. For officers of the Ministry of Health in Nampula, the absence of further unrest in recent years is an indication that medical knowledge of the disease and its causes has increased. For the people in Iaué, the lack of closure on their relatives' deaths at the Liupo police station is ample proof that you can't safely speak your mind to the government; and for the people in Curuhama, the fact that cholera hasn't come back since the Red Cross stopped talking about it shows they were right to defend their community against outside meddling.

Florencio Vasco, a nurse in Nampula who supervised a health post in rural Mogincual until the cholera violence of 2009, argued that education on hygiene should be integrated into primary school, a lesson learned year-round and beginning in childhood. "Sensitization cannot simply be during outbreaks, because then the population will begin to say: 'Here comes the time for them to kill us,'" he said. "Children should grow up knowing how cholera is spread. As long as the population doesn't understand the means of transmission of the disease, things will not improve."

Perhaps a government that can deliver on that promise, though, will have the means to form a different relationship with the people of Mogincual altogether. To flip Vasco's proposition on its head, you might say the population won't understand the means of transmission until they feel they can trust the teacher.

6

Go Tell the Crocodiles

TETE

To some of the Egyptians, then, the crocodiles are sacred and to others not, but they treat them as if they are enemies.

—HERODOTUS[1]

Fairy tales still play a considerable part in molding the average person's ideas about natural history.

—RAYMOND DART[2]

The King of Crocodiles

When we met, the King of Crocodiles introduced herself as Mae Rosa, "Mother Rose." She smiled broadly with a show of gums and folded her hands in her lap. She is frail and leathery from a lifetime of menial work under hot sun, and shy with outsiders in the same way as many women in northern Mozambique: not a matter of personality so much as a learned form of politeness. The king wore an orange bandanna over her hair and a purple polyester blouse printed with images of roses, tulips, and hibiscus flowers. I had trouble imagining that there was anything dangerous about Rosa, but the neighbors' children gave her a wide berth.

Since losing her husband in 2005, Rosa has lived alone with a grown daughter in a mud and thatch hut at the western end of Bawa, where she cultivates a plot of millet, maize, and cassava near the Zambezi River. The soil near Bawa is sandy and acidic; on the whole, it makes for terrible farming, but annual floods deposit a new layer of silt along the riverbanks and on the labyrinth of reed islands opposite the village, making these the only areas where the locals successfully grow food year after year. Otherwise, they tend to change fields every one or two years, returning to fields left fallow for several seasons or burning a new clearing in the surrounding woodlands to plant before the rains. Rosa has one plot on the river and another on high ground, where yields are less reliable, and she works them both with a hoe and a machete from Zambia. *Capinar*, "weeding," is how she describes making a living. Rosa eats what she grows. To buy soap, oil, and salt, she occasionally sells a sack of maize or small bundles of greens.

Mae Rosa earned her sinister nickname in 2010, in the days following the disappearance of her brother's daughter, Amelia, who had been washing dishes on the riverbank one morning that August. Bawa is home to only a few hundred families, but the village lost nearly fifty people to crocodile attacks in a single decade, from 1999 to 2009, making it the deadliest place in Mozambique, and possibly the world over, for human-crocodile conflict. Amelia had been taken by a crocodile, and the whole village thought that Rosa was responsible. Rosa was the owner of a charm that became a magic crocodile and obeyed the whims of its master. It was Rosa, the neighbors said, who'd killed her own niece and several others before her.

Bawa is the westernmost village in Mozambique, on a broad peninsula below the confluence of two major rivers: the Zambezi, which meanders lazily down from the highlands of Zimbabwe, and its tributary, the Luangwa, which merges with the Zambezi as it flows out of Zambia. Known to locals as *zungunukei*, meaning "eddies," or "whirlpools," in the Chifunda language, the spot has been an important trading site since at least the seventeenth century, when the Portuguese began buying ivory, gold, and slaves on excursions upriver from the Indian Ocean. The town on the Zambian side is still called Feira—the Portuguese word for market—after the ugly trade that led to its founding.

To the south of Bawa is a flat plain that fills with elephants and Cape buffalo in the late afternoon. Fish eagles perch on scarecrow-like trunks on the bank, and reeded sandbars provide aquatic grazing for pods of hippos. Bawa is at the edge of a large wilderness that stretches deep into Zambia and Zimbabwe, home to leopards, lions, hippos, and crocodiles as well as hundreds of smaller animals. People in the region have always had to cope with the dangers of living side by side with large wildlife, but the problem has grown far more intense over the past twenty-five years.

Since the end of the Mozambican civil war, in 1992, Bawa and scores of other villages along the Zambezi have seen a steady stream of returnees. The war sent more than a million refugees over the border into Zambia and Zimbabwe, and those who fled fighting during the 1980s are now returning from exile with grown children and grandchildren in tow.

As the human population around Bawa swells, the custom of farming and living beside the river has brought locals into more frequent conflict with the animals around them. Farmland has eaten away at hippo and lion habitat and cut off the corridors that elephants and buffalo use to reach the river to drink. Fishing, bathing, and washing all take place in waters patrolled by large crocodiles. Lions eat livestock; hippos raid crops; elephants trample fields and houses; buffalos charge when they feel threatened. All four have killed people in Bawa. Yet no animal has aroused more anger and suspicion than the crocodile. The elephants that kill people, Bawans will tell you, are "god's elephants"; destructive hippos are "god's hippos." Only crocodiles belong to other humans.

Biologists, trophy hunters, and government wildlife officials in Mozambique all view crocodile attacks as a perilous consequence of human encroachment on the wilderness. Crocodiles face increasing interference from fishermen who cast their nets in nesting and breeding areas and habitat loss from deforestation along the riverbank as farmers struggle to grow their crops in poor soil. In this view, crocodiles attack humans simply because we are easy to prey upon: we are far less vigilant than other animals and far more given to steady routines, like bathing and fetching water in the same spot day after day. Bawans tend to take a different view: "If a crocodile knows your name," one ferryman told me there, "then your day has come."

The attacks in 2010 followed a familiar pattern: fishermen went missing from their dugouts, and women at their washing never returned from the riverbank. Amelia was only the last victim in a spate of disappearances during the dry season. Distraught, villagers turned to Bawa's headman, Merinho Gregor, for a solution. It was in front of Gregor's house, sitting on rickety wooden chairs with Rosa and a toothless man introduced as the community policeman, that I came to learn the details of Rosa's case.

The day before she disappeared, Amelia was making fried dough balls on a small charcoal stove in front of her house. Rosa walked by as her niece took the first donuts, or *bolinhos*, out of the oil and asked to have one. "No, Aunty," the young woman said. "I am making them to sell." The girl was twenty years old, pretty and popular with her peers. She was dating a man who worked on a small barge, the *Santa Maria*, which makes erratic trips from Zumbo, across the river, to the nearest outpost of Mozambican civilization, two hundred miles downstream. On return trips, the bargeman brought his girlfriend cooking oil, soap, and sugar; Rosa, according to her neighbors, became jealous.

After Amelia went missing, her family consulted Gregor and sent away for the services of *curandeiros*, or traditional healers, who could make a determination of guilt. According to Gregor, a *curandeiro*'s credibility in such matters depends on the distance he travels to get to Bawa, so messengers were dispatched on foot across the border to Zimbabwe and to Zambia. *Curandeiros* culled from villages closer to home might have a family member involved in the case, or foreknowledge of the facts or surrounding rumors. The more far-flung the judge, the more impartial the verdict. Still, rumors began to circulate even before the *curandeiros* reached Bawa. It was not the first time Rosa had been accused.

In 2005, another brother of Rosa's lost a daughter to the river. As in England and colonial America, widows are often the first to be accused of witchcraft, and suspicions fell on Rosa even without a specific motive. She was soon at the mercy of a mob: beaten, stuffed into an empty rice sack, and nearly dumped in the river before the national police came over from the county seat in Zumbo and threatened to arrest her persecutors. But the case went no further. Until Amelia disappeared in 2010, Rosa continued to live in Bawa undisturbed.

Speaking through an interpreter in Chifunda, Rosa kept her nervous gaze on Gregor as she told the story. "When [the *curandeiros*] got to my home, they said, 'This is the one with the crocodile charm. The charm was here in the house, but it ran away to the forest.'" Rosa was given a concoction brewed from foraged roots and leaves and herded to the forest at the center of a growing crowd. Arriving at a potent spot, a *curandeiro* instructed family members of the deceased to dig a hole, and they uncovered two cloth amulets filled with flour: sure signs of Rosa's guilt.

Neighbors call Liveness Mandar, who introduced herself as Mae Rosa—
"Mother Rose"—the King of Crocodiles. In 2010, she was accused of
casting a spell so that a crocodile would kill her niece.

The people's judgment delivered, it was the community
policeman—now sitting next to her—who laid on blows, with the
approval of the headman, Gregor, and Rosa's own family. Hoping
to avoid a repeat of her near death five years earlier, Rosa said, she
quickly admitted guilt. Gregor stopped the beating, and the community police brought her across the river, where they handed her
over to "community court."[3] There, before an audience of relatives
and neighbors who had wanted to banish her, she was sentenced
to a week of spiritual healing with a traditional doctor and ordered never to use her crocodile again.

Miguel Wilson, a gentle gray-haired farmer in his seventies, presided. "It's very challenging to resolve problems of magic in the justice system," he said. The community courts are the unofficial descendants of the popular courts that Mozambique's ruling party, Frelimo, set up in liberated zones during their war for independence from Portugal. Then, as now, the courts were intended to operate as a counterweight to the abuses of traditional authority in places beyond the reach of the justice system.

The community courts have established a fixed price table at a national level for the most common village infractions—adultery, domestic violence, livestock theft. There are no set penalties for acts of witchcraft. In 2010, Wilson said, the court in Zumbo heard nearly a dozen cases involving magic crocodiles, not to mention sundry other accusations of witchcraft. One case, later transferred to criminal court, he said, was presented by a woman who had walked more than eighty miles carrying the dismembered leg of her grandson wrapped in a new shawl after her husband discovered it in their grain silo. There was no outpost of the Mozambican justice system closer to the woman's home.

"Sometimes, even without concrete proof, the court will hand out a small sentence or penalty in order to satisfy the community— it might be cleaning, or gardening at public buildings," Wilson explained. The courts follow Mozambican law, but they are staffed by volunteers and receive no funding or specific guidelines on procedure or hours of operation. Hearings typically take place in local schools, which are often without electricity or adult-sized furniture.

In Mae Rosa's case, reaching a productive resolution was made more difficult by her own admission of guilt. "That woman, Rosa— *she* said, 'I have a crocodile,'" Wilson recalled, disbelieving. "She told the court that she sold the victim's meat in Zambia!" Wilson fingered a packet of cigarettes lying on the table between us.

Periodically, he beckoned the waiter at the bar where we met and sent him into the kitchen to light one.

"You can't witness witchcraft," Wilson said. "But almost everyone was against Rosa, because her niece's family was enormous. It's always the greater number that prevails in villages." Even after Rosa's hearing, most of Bawa was intent on banishing her, but the law forbids it, and she did not want to leave the only place where she had ever lived. So the court handed Rosa over to the police, who had her clean the station for three days and told the chief, Gregor, not to let people exact any further revenge. Rosa was forbidden from ever using her crocodile again. Incredibly, Rosa told me she has made up with her brothers and has good relationships with Gregor and the community policeman. The crocodile attacks have continued all the same.

Crocodile attacks come without warning. Crocs swim silently at the surface of the water, their eyes protruding like tiny periscopes, or submerged, where a translucent third eyelid allows them to see beneath the surface. Even more important on the hunt are the thousands of tiny black specks dotting every scale on a crocodile's body, where spools of nerve fibers allow them to detect tiny vibrations and disturbances in water pressure. These freckly nodes, called dermal pressure receptors, enable crocodiles to hunt effectively even in complete darkness: like an aquatic version of sonar, the receptors allow crocodiles to navigate around obstacles in murky water and pick out prey in their vicinity.

At full size, Nile crocodiles are the largest predators in Africa. Their life span is similar to a human's, except that crocodiles continue to grow throughout adulthood, so that males over fifty routinely reach well over a thousand pounds and twelve feet long. The largest Nile crocodile on record, shot in Tanzania in 1905, was more than twenty-one feet long and weighed 2,400 pounds, though there have been plenty of reports of larger ani-

A child collects water inside a makeshift chain-link enclosure Bawa residents put up to protect themselves from crocodile attacks. During my visit in 2011, after a decade in which crocodiles had killed nearly fifty people in Bawa, the only working water pump was broken.

mals still.[4] A crocodile like that was probably more than eighty years old. Crocodiles' diets vary as they grow: bugs and other invertebrates early on; fish, birds, and amphibians in middle age; and anything from mongoose to kudu, wounded hippos, and even other crocodiles when their size allows. As a rule, only crocodiles over ten feet, measured from snout to tail, are likely to attack humans.

When they are close enough to strike, crocodiles snap their jaws around their quarry with lightning speed and incomparable force: the Nile crocodile's jaws are among the strongest on the planet, capable of producing more than three thousand pounds of pressure per square inch.[5] But they must take care not to lose their teeth, which come unmoored far more easily than a mammal's. A crocodile can clamp its mouth like a vice, but it can't pull or tear flesh

The vast majority of crocodile attacks in Bawa take place on the river's edge, where women and children come to fetch water, do laundry, and wash dishes.

like a hyena or a lion, so it swallows its prey in large pieces with great gulps. With larger, terrestrial prey, a crocodile will attack not with its jaws, but with a violent strike of the tail, knocking the animal into the water before grabbing it in its mouth and twirling, corkscrew fashion, until its prey is drowned.

The Rancher

The crocodile biologist Richard Fergusson calls the area near Rosa's home "crocodile heaven." Confluences, where two bodies of water come together, are often sites of particular importance for biodiversity and wildlife habitat. The flow of one river into another creates turbulence and slows the water down. Plant life, insects, and microorganisms that would normally be carried along in the current are instead caught up in eddies, where they float to the surface, sink to the bottom, or simply hang suspended in the flow. Fish and larger animals—humans and crocodiles among them—congregate nearby to gain access to what Fergusson calls the "nutrient load" a river deposits as it slows.

At the confluence of the Luangwa and the Zambezi, this effect was enhanced with the construction of the Cahora Bassa Dam in the early 1970s. The reservoir above the dam, Lake Cahora Bassa, stretches for more than two hundred miles. At the upper end, the Zambezi slows to the speed of maple syrup, leaving a cloud of rich, food-filled sediment from both rivers in the area near the confluence.

The dam was envisioned as a way to irrigate tens of thousands of acres in the mountains in Tete Province, the linchpin in a program to settle Mozambique with Portuguese farmers and boost the sluggish economy back home by way of the colonies. The project displaced thousands of Mozambicans, and Frelimo, then leading a guerrilla war against the Portuguese, attacked the construction site repeatedly, deriding the dam as a symbol of imperial arrogance. Today, it has walls five hundred feet high and generates 17 billion kilowatt-hours of electricity annually: just over a third of what it takes to power our least energy-hungry state of Vermont, yet far more than what Mozambique used in 1975, or even today—Mozambique still sells most of Cahora Bassa's output to South Africa.[6] But the dam turned out to be the empire's last folly in Mozambique: the colonial government fell just six months after it was completed, and the Frelimo government inherited Lake Cahora Bassa.

Thanks to the nutrient load near the confluence, the lake's headwaters are one of the richest fisheries in Mozambique. But Fergusson says the dam brought particular advantages to crocodiles in the area. When the lake was created, it filled in countless narrow valleys between the ridges that rose from the river, giving

Cahora Bassa the intricate, fractal perimeter of a snowflake. Crocodiles thrive in the shallow bays and inlets at the lake's edge, where they find ample vegetation for cover and suitable sandbars for basking and laying eggs. As the lake filled, what had been a stretch of river with a couple hundred miles of crocodile habitat became a vast underwater wilderness with hundreds of new appendages. Though the dam initially destroyed important nesting habitats by flooding, crocodiles have done exceptionally well ever since.

Fergusson is a wiry white Zimbabwean in his fifties, with a piercing stare and acerbic wit. He's a veteran of what insiders call the "reptile leather industry." For many years, he led the Crocodile Farmers Association of Zimbabwe, and more recently, he's devoted much of his career to nurturing a nascent croc-farming industry on the shores of Lake Cahora Bassa. Plentiful access to fresh water, cheap electricity provided by the dam, and proximity to large breeding populations of Nile crocodiles—one of the "five classic" species used for crocodile leather—all recommend the spot.[7]

Today, Fergusson hopes to establish a niche market for "eco-friendly," "sustainably sourced" crocodile leather, if such a thing is possible. The conceit relies in large part on the transition from croc farming to "ranching," using crocodile eggs laid in the wild instead of those produced in a hatchery. Even wild hatchlings have a dismal survival rate—about 10 percent—but many croc farmers have already embraced ranching on that basis alone. Hatchlings born of parents in captivity do even worse. Any damage done to natural reproduction, Fergusson says, can be managed as it is in Zimbabwe: by reintroducing a controlled number of hatchlings to the wild.

The term "ranching," though, may give the wrong impression. Eggs laid in the wild still hatch in a bed of warm sand inside a styrofoam box kept in a temperature-controlled room. Instead of learning to hunt, the crocs spend their days slithering around in a heap with hundreds of other juveniles, crawling through a slurry of lake water and feces in a heated, glass-smooth concrete pen, the better to protect their hides from the abrasions and clawmarks that are commonplace in the wild. "Wild skins are buggered," Fergusson told me when I visited the farm he oversees on a peninsula beside Cahora Bassa. Rather than hunt for bugs, fish, or even smaller crocodiles, as they would in the wild, ranched crocs get a mix of frozen fish and skinned crocodiles on a regular schedule. Cannibalism accounts for 30 percent of their meat intake.

Crucially, for Fergusson, ranching gives crocodile leather producers a stake in protecting habitat for wild crocs: without viable nesting grounds, there will be no eggs to collect. What's good for crocodiles, he says, is good for crocodile leather. And protecting crocodiles, Fergusson will tell you, can only be achieved by protecting humans from them.

Other work makes him well positioned to act as an ambassador for these ideas. Through a trade association called the Crocodile Specialist Group, Fergusson has conducted surveys of wild crocodile populations across sub-Saharan Africa, and as a side project, he maintains a database of reported crocodile attacks around the world, now running to well over a thousand separate incidents. In Bawa, I spoke to people who worried that crocodiles could chase you over land, but one of the more striking patterns in Fergusson's data is that crocs invariably attack humans in the water or on the bank, where surprise and terrain both play to their advantage. Fergusson thinks this sense of mystery is part of what separates attitudes around crocodile attacks from the rest. "With elephants and lions you generally see them before there's a problem. That's all I can put it down to." According to his records, people who struggle or beat the crocodile across its sensitive snout are likely to escape attacks alive, but few people do.

The crocodile, Fergusson says, is "a tremendously powerful animal." When, in the midst of fieldwork, he has had occasion to wrestle crocodiles with his bare hands, he has never single-handedly subdued a crocodile that weighs more than thirty pounds—a fraction of the size of the crocodiles responsible for attacks on humans.

The Inspector

On the wall of his office in Tete's Provincial Directorate of Forests and Wildlife, Florencio Gerente Sixpence keeps an eight-and-a-half-by-eleven-inch color photograph of human remains arranged neatly on a reed mat: a man's right leg, severed below the knee; his right arm, a bloody mess of tendons where it once attached at the shoulder; his disconnected left hand; and sundry unidentifiable internal organs, all pulled from the stomach of a fifteen-foot crocodile. Beside the photograph hangs a series of charts detailing the frequency of human wildlife conflict (HWC) throughout the province, so far as it's known. Since most incidents occur in remote areas, Sixpence takes it as a given that HWC is underreported.

"In Mutarara, it's crocodiles and hippos," he says, rattling off the specifics of the problem by district. "In Changara, elephants, crocodiles, lions, and hyenas. In Zumbo, elephants, hippos, and crocodiles. In Marávia, lions, leopards, and sometimes hippos. You know, co-habitation between men and wildlife has never been peaceful, but then, the human population has never been what it is now."

As the ranking wildlife inspector for the province, Sixpence coordinates the work of Tete's Problem Animal Control (PAC) teams, rotating groups of three rangers drawn from a staff of twelve, charged with shooting animals that pose a danger to humans. Usually, the PAC teams respond to reports relayed by the local governments in what Sixpence calls "conflict zones," where large wildlife populations live alongside human settlements. Sixpence may learn of conflict before it occurs—when an elephant or a hippo is seen on the periphery of an established village—or only days, even weeks, after a given incident. Rogue elephants, for instance, tend to stalk the same terrain, returning repeatedly to the villages where they have found a source of food. With elephants, Sixpence told me, "We fire in the air first, and if the animal isn't scared by the shot, then we know they'll be a problem." The problem with this approach, according to Sixpence, is that "there are places where the animals have always been and where they are not going to leave."

The core of the government's response to crocodile attacks has been to conduct annual culls, or crocodile hunts, along the Zambezi River, where the vast majority of attacks occur. In 2009, with funding from the UN's Food and Agriculture Organization, the Ministry of Agriculture set out a national strategy that called for killing a thousand crocs on the Zambezi over a period of five years. As the government's man in the province of Tete—which curves like a five-hundred-mile bird's beak to follow the arc of the Zambezi—Sixpence was responsible for more than two-thirds of the quota.

On the day before I arrived in Zumbo, across the river from Bawa, Sixpence had driven up from the provincial capital in a Land Rover pickup truck carrying 330 gallons of diesel fuel, six boxes of ammunition, and an ancient but seemingly well-served single-action .375 Magnum hunting rifle. For a week, he paid for the services of a fisherman with a fiberglass banana boat and a four-horsepower outboard motor and sent two local inspectors out on the river to shoot as many large crocodiles as they could. Sixpence and his colleague Isaac Omar stayed in a small guesthouse run by the local chair of the Frelimo party. Every morning,

Florencio Gerente Sixpence, a technician with the Provincial Directorate of Forests and Wildlife in Tete, oversees crocodile culls and Problem Animal Control teams that respond to human-wildlife conflict.

the team woke them with a knock at five to pick up the rifle and the day's ammunition.

A soft-spoken man in his fifties with a prominent scar below his right eye, Sixpence is a career civil servant who seems often to be caught between his wildlife expertise and the demands of following the chain of command. Late that morning, we walked to a large, twisted mango tree on a bare slope below the local government offices, whose entrances are decorated with crumbling elephant skulls. The spot functions more or less as Zumbo's town square, overlooking a forlorn outdoor market and, below it, the marina, a sandy beach where boats offload merchandise from Zambia.

Sixpence took a seat between the local director of tourism and the director of agriculture and fisheries, and we all cracked cold bottles of Coca-Cola. Without getting up, Sixpence took a phone call from a crocodile rancher on the lake, which immediately took on the tones of cat and mouse. "Don't waste your time talking with me. I've been sent here," Sixpence told him. "I'm *mandado*." *Mandar*, in Mozambique, is not only "to send" but to decide, to make fate, to call the shots. "Talk to the national office," he said. "There is no sense talking to me."

On a river that stretches through fifteen hundred miles of prime crocodile habitat, there's no guarantee that culls will make a dent in the population of dangerous crocodiles. To begin with, the hunts usually take place weeks or months after any given attack, so there's no way of knowing whether they target the specific animals responsible for the loss of life. More broadly, individual crocodiles rove over a large aquatic territory according to the availability of food—the headwaters of Lake Cahora Bassa will remain an attractive niche as long as the river holds fish and animals come to its shores to drink. Short of decimating the entire crocodile population in the Zambezi, any large crocodiles that are shot in Zumbo will be replaced within a few years by opportunistic crocs swimming down from other parts of the river. But the culls' most damaging impact is to obscure the true causes of the conflict. "We go and build our houses in the crocodile's habitat, and we kill all the fish they need to eat," Sixpence said. What, in other words, should we expect?

Today, much of the fish catch netted near the confluence is butterflied and smoked on sticks over an open fire, then trucked to Zambian cities and towns packed in large, cylindrical bales of hay. In an area where nearly everyone practices subsistence farming to survive, fishing is the primary source of cash, and it is almost entirely unregulated. As the catch diminishes in areas that are easy to access, local fishermen have ventured into the remote bays that are the crocodiles' preferred nesting habitat. Some men have taken to fishing at night, when they are less likely to be fined by government inspectors for using oversized nets—which cut off entire channels of the river—or nets with small mesh that capture fish before they are fully grown. This is also the only time of day when crocodiles hunt actively. Crocs regularly drown when they become entangled in the fishermen's gill nets; fishermen die when they are pulled from their boats while playing tug-of-war with the crocodiles, hoping to save their catch—and their nets—from being lost to the river. In a corner of Namibia where the Zambezi and several tributaries converge hundreds of miles upstream from Mozambique, it's estimated that crocodiles damage more than seventy thousand fishing nets a year.[8]

In 2005, Fergusson authored a report for the World Wildlife Fund comparing the results of two surveys of human-crocodile conflict he'd conducted a decade apart on the same stretch of the Shire River, a tributary of the Zambezi in Malawi. Little about the region had changed in the intervening years except that an aid organization had installed wells in most of the villages where women previously collected water from the river.

In comparing the two surveys, Fergusson found a similar density of crocodile attacks (attacks per year per mile of shoreline) in each period, but he noted a major difference in the demographics of each group of victims. In the first, the victims were largely women and children, washing pots and fetching water at the riverbank. In the second, more than half the victims were fishermen who hauled their catch in dugout canoes and slept on reed platforms above their nets in the river.

It wasn't that the crocodile population had grown or changed in character, but that their prey had changed behavior. With the addition of wells, Fergusson concluded, the women no longer needed to go to the river. "So, the women were easy and the fishermen were next easiest," he says. "Humans are [simple]. We go every day to the same spot to fetch water, and we're not nearly as alert as an antelope would be. When you think about human-crocodile conflict, you have to remember that you're dealing with two species." In 1992, researchers reported that the breakdown of a local water pump in a town in Tanzania had led to a death by crocodile attack once a week when people were forced to rely on river water.[9] In all Australia, by comparison, home to saltwater crocodiles even bigger than Nile crocs, there have been about two attacks per year since the 1970s.[10]

The best alternative to crocodile culls, Sixpence says, would be to create special residential and conservation zones, to resettle people away from areas with large wildlife populations in order to conserve habitat.[11] "But hunting is the only solution that the government considers cost-effective," he concluded. "It is better to compromise conservation than to compromise politics. Because the place where we get the most votes is there in the villages. If I, as a technician, say I won't do the cull, then I am complicating the work of the government. [If we don't cull], whoever comes to stand in the elections will go out to the villages and they'll say, 'Go tell the crocodiles to vote for you, go tell the elephants to vote for you.'" Sixpence was laughing at the thought, but he insisted that it was a serious possibility. "They will; they'll say it just like that," he added.

Tete is the second-most rural province in an overwhelmingly rural and underdeveloped country, and Zumbo, in turn, is Tete's farthest backwater. Once a hub of the international slave trade, Zumbo is now an outpost on the edge of Zambia, at the far end of a 220-mile dirt road from the rest of Mozambique. It's an area with few public services to speak of: there's a post office and some lackluster schools, but roads, electricity, and water are all unreliable, and none extends past the edge of the county seat. Nearby, or across the river in Bawa, wild animals seem to have more sway over day-to-day existence than the national government does.

As a result, culls have come to stand in for the more difficult long-term development work so sorely needed in the region. A crocodile cull won't improve farmers' yields, provide safe access to water, or encourage conservation. But in the absence of more meaningful measures to make people less vulnerable to attacks, it's a fine way for the government to show its populist colors; you might even think of it as a political campaign.

In that sense, Sixpence's cull was an undeniable success. By early afternoon, when the first two crocodile carcasses had been hauled to shore, a small crowd had gathered to watch them bake slowly in the sun. Neither one was close to the government's declared ten-foot threshold for dangerous crocs. Only one, perhaps, might have had the gumption to attack a child. As it was, giggling children ogled the sallow corpses and wondered aloud what would be done with the skins. "They're worth good money!" one boy offered. A half dozen guards from the Mozambican border patrol had just come off duty. They posed next to the carcasses one by one, snapping photos with their cell phones the way you might in front of a Ferrari or a bronze statue. One of the guards put his boot on a crocodile's head and crossed his arms triumphantly, wearing flashy sunglasses beneath an army-issued beret. "What an ugly animal," said another.

After the first two crocodiles were ceremoniously displayed near the center of town for a day, the hunters returned them to the water—to be eaten, presumably, by other crocodiles. On the local level, Sixpence and his colleague Omar considered the political aspect of the mission largely accomplished: by now, everyone knew that the government had come to town to kill crocodiles and that they had succeeded. There was no need for them to continue dragging carcasses out of the water or doing all the things that Fergusson and his colleagues insist on for the benefit of science—measuring them, determining their sex, examining the contents of their stomachs, or taking note of the precise spot where they were shot. It sufficed to take a few pictures and keep track of how much fuel and ammo the team used, which Sixpence did in

On the first day of the cull, Sixpence's team of crocodile hunters displayed their kills on the banks of the Zambezi River, in Zumbo.

a small notebook. This stance makes Fergusson livid. "Last year, Fauna Bravia"—Sixpence's department—"and the army slaughtered, to the best of my knowledge, 143 animals, and they did not even bother to recover the carcasses," he told me. "I know half a dozen researchers in South Africa who would have given their left ball to get some blood, some tissue."

A few days into the cull, Omar began to worry about satisfying the other side of the political equation—the people above him, in Maputo, who had never seen a crocodile carcass, who had no idea how difficult it was to hunt them, and yet who were terribly demanding when it came to the numbers. Omar sat on the edge of his bed as the afternoon rain sputtered on the tin roof: "Personally, I don't think that shooting crocodiles will solve the problem. What we need is a change of mentality. You still have people bathing with their backs to the water, fixing their nets while standing in the river. We've already shot 29. But you know, it's a lot of work without much benefit. I think the national target this year is round about 160 crocodiles. In Sofala they killed 67; in the city, near the bridge, they've killed 35, and we're going to try and complete the tally so that we'll get to 160, but I don't know if we'll make it, because the crocodiles are getting scarce, or maybe they're getting wary of going out in the river. It's politics." The president, Omar ventured, "is caught between the sword and the wall. I think he knows that killing is not the right path. Maybe he says, 'We want to continue to govern this country,' and he forgets, or pretends to forget, the technical side."

Crocodiles and humans have seldom gotten on well. Historians have theorized that the fearsome Leviathan, imagined as a whale ever since *Moby Dick* and described at length in the Book of Job, is in fact a crocodile: "Who can strip off its outer coat? Who can penetrate its double coat of armor? Who dares open the doors of its mouth, ringed about with fearsome teeth? Its back has rows of shields tightly sealed together; each is so close to the next that no air can pass between. . . . Strength resides in its neck; dismay goes before it. . . . When it rises up, the mighty are terrified; they retreat before its thrashing."[12]

Historically, the range of Nile crocodiles extended nearly throughout Africa, from Egypt and Mali to South Africa, Angola, and Uganda. Colonial governments hunted them indiscriminately: H.L. Duff, a British official stationed in Malawi (then Nyasaland) at the turn of the twentieth century, thought that crocodiles were "to be shot whenever and wherever they were seen."[13] A contemporary of his, the South African hunter R.C. Maugham, observed that there was "probably no more dangerous, more stealthy or more universally hated and feared branch of creation than the [crocodile]."[14] Maugham referred to crocodiles as "pest" and "vermin" and called them the "veritable curse . . . of the Af-

rican waterways." This view was reflected in colonial policies offering bounties for crocodile heads and eggs. Motivated by the
misguided impression that killing crocs would promote the fishing industry, the government of the Belgian Congo was the first
to declare an all-out war on crocodiles and advocate their total
extermination. Other governments followed suit. In the mid-
twentieth century, crocodile belly skins—used for handbags,
belts, shoes, and luggage—became an important export for many
African countries, including Mozambique. Total exports reached
well into the millions of skins.[15]

By 1975, *Crocodylus niloticus* was included on the CITES (Convention on International Trade in Endangered Species of Wild
Fauna and Flora) list regulating trade in endangered species, requiring countries to adhere to strict hunting and export quotas for
wild crocs. There has been extensive debate in the years since about
just how far African crocodile populations actually fell, and whether
adding the Nile croc to the CITES list was justified across the
continent. But the intervening years have brought evidence to
correct the impression that crocodiles deplete fish populations. In
fact, researchers have demonstrated just the opposite, that remov-
ing crocodiles can be harmful to fisheries, and crocodilians are
now widely regarded as "umbrella species" essential to the health
of freshwater ecosystems.[16] One recent survey of crocodile diets in
Lake Kariba, along another dammed section of the Zambezi River,
in Zimbabwe, found that crocodiles consumed just half a percent
of the lake's fish population (by weight) each year; fishermen took
in ten times as much.[17]

Nile crocodile populations have made a dramatic recovery in
parts of Africa since the age of unbridled extermination ended
forty years ago.[18] Today, doing surveys overhead in an airplane,
Fergusson says, "There are bits of Tanzania where you basically
can't count fast enough."[19] Crocodiles' resilience is driven partly
by their versatility as hunters. Fergusson describes Nile crocodiles

as "superbly opportunistic" predators, capable of eating every-thing from paperclip-sized fish and small turtles, shell and all, to full-grown cows and buffalo, aided by super-acidic stomachs that allow them to digest bones whole. In the wild, crocodiles can be avid scavengers as well: one researcher observed fifty-three crocs feeding on a single hippopotamus carcass.[20]

Circumstances are set for worsening conflict with humans across vast swaths of the Nile crocodile's range. The whole African con-tinent is in the midst of an unprecedented demographic boom, mirrored in the growing towns and villages that line the Zambezi River from Zumbo all the way to the Indian Ocean.[21] In the drier reaches of the continent's southern half, where crocodiles naturally thrive, they are in competition with people over access to our most fundamental resource: freshwater. As in Zumbo, the same rivers that are the backbone of human development are croco-diles' primary habitat. Rivers are often used as international boundaries, subject to differing environmental regulations and enforcement on either side, or as the buffer between protected and nonprotected areas, the interface of human activity with the wilderness.

Leave aside for a moment the big-picture consequences of human activity on rivers and lakes that threaten humans and crocodiles alike—pollution, toxic algal blooms, deforestation, blockages, and buildup of silt from dams and irrigation systems. In the words of one biologist, "Human crocodile conflict is the cherry on the top."[22]

The Administrator

In 1988, a safari operator over the border in Zimbabwe obtained a concession along the southern shore of Lake Cahora Bassa, near Bawa—the first hunting concession to be granted in postindependence Mozambique. Buffered by protected areas and wildlife corridors in neighboring Zimbabwe, blessed with plentiful year-round water sources, and relatively less touched by active fighting, the area was one of only a few in Mozambique where big-game populations were not decimated by the war. (On the northern shore of the lake, Richard Fergusson described making his first trip into Mozambique in the mid-1990s and seeing not so much as a bird.)

The people of Bawa returned to their land from Zimbabwe and Zambia in the early 1990s. "Soldiers, former soldiers, government officials, and police were surviving on their terrible salaries by hunting and using our resources and other ways," they told an audience of academics and land rights activists several years later.[23] Desperate for food and cash, locals, too, hunted unrestrained. Zambians "were looking hungrily at our resources and thinking how much they could sell our fish and meat for in Lusaka or the Copper Belt." In this context, you might have thought that the safari operator—in the midst of a campaign to crack down on poaching—would be a natural ally. Consider how the hunting concession looked from their perspective:

We found that our land had been given, by high officials who had never visited Bawa, to a foreign company to hunt wild animals. This company had hunted even during the war, but now that there was peace, they became more active and were worried because they thought that we would interfere with their hunting if we returned. Therefore, they tried to tell us where we could live and farm, where we could go, which paths we could use, and so on. But, most of all, they tried to stop us from hunting. So, we began another war with them and it was hot. Many of us were badly hurt, because this company had a kind of private army and our government could not see what was happening to us for a long time.

The "private army," as people would tell me when I visited Zumbo, had also run a kind of unofficial prison for people caught hunting in the concession, locking them up for days or weeks at a time and confiscating homemade muzzle-loaders they also used for protection.

A few years later, a young engineer with Mozambique's Ministry of Agriculture, Luis Namanha, secured funding from the Ford Foundation for a pilot program in Bawa and a handful of nearby communities to help reduce conflict with the hunting operation, Mozambique Safaris, and promote sustainable land use and stewardship. The project was called Tchuma Tchato, meaning "Our Wealth" in the local Nyungwe language.[24] In the industry jargon, it was Mozambique's first community-based natural resources management (CBNRM) scheme. As the war drew to a close, population growth created both economic pressure as refugees returned home and a ravenous market for fish and game meat over the Zambian border. The result was a strong push for the local subsistence economy to transition to a commercial one.

The promise of hunting and fishing revenue from foreign tourists offered a kind of escape valve: the potential to support a better livelihood than could be had by simply selling bushmeat and smoked fish directly, or by raising livestock on marginal lands. At first, this arrangement showed surprising promise. At the time, the provincial wildlife office was operating with "no computer, no telephone, no fax, no mail, no transport, no uniforms, no learning or reading materials, no working facilities," according to Namanha's master's thesis, which focuses on the early years of the project. Tchuma Tchato presented a source of support and outside funding.

The communities near the hunting concession were promised nearly a third of the revenue that came in from trophy fees. Namanha recruited local hunters and successful commercial poachers to form a team of game scouts who began work with no pay and no guns, living in tents in the bush.[25] Game scouts designated specific fishing areas to keep people out of sensitive breeding areas, and patrolled Lake Cahora Bassa's headwaters looking for unlicensed fishermen, illegal nets, and Zambians prohibited from fishing in Mozambique altogether. With Namanha's leadership, several government officials and local policemen were arrested for involvement in poaching.[26]

Lion, buffalo, and elephant populations quickly rebounded. "We worked so hard that, even after 1 year, the animals increased in number and also became less afraid of people," reads a community report on the early years of the project. "We were happy about this but, at the same time, began to face problems with elephants, which had learned quickly that we would no longer harm them. Therefore, the elephants came into our fields and destroyed them, and even came right into the villages."[27]

Namanha claimed the Ford Foundation spent $100,000 on a documentary about Tchuma Tchato before local communities had received their first dollar. Soon after the project launched, in 1996, the foundation was projecting that the annual community benefit would reach $300,000 within two years.[28] According to Anthony Maughan Brown, who conducted his master's thesis on the project a year before Namanha, "The community had the expectation that the project would deliver schools, clinics, shops and transport."

What Tchuma Tchato did deliver was a diesel-powered corn-mill to grind the harvest in two out of the six villages within Mozambique Safaris' concession. At that rate, Maughan Brown points out, aside from periodic bush meat, each community could expect to benefit from Tchuma Tchato once every six years; "a total population of approximately 9,000 people is having to find a way to share a total income of approximately $15,000 per year. That is, less than $2 per head per year."[29]

In theory, another 35 percent of government revenue from hunting was supposed to go to authorities—split between the national tourism office and the district—to use in the service of sustainable development. In 1996, the annual allotment disappeared from a government account, never to be found again; the following year, an official used the funds to buy himself spare motorcycle parts and for repairs on roads outside the project area.

By 1998, morale over Tchuma Tchato was faltering. A Land Rover purchased for the project sat with its wheels removed outside the office. Game scouts caught between their job and brewing frustration around them abandoned camp for days at a time. Some villages had waited four years for benefits that never came.

"When I speak about Tchuma Tchato, I get angry," Namanha said when we met. "It's like raising a child; you get attached." He felt he had been pushed out of Tete before Tchuma Tchato had achieved success. The project had been his life's work. In the years he spent in Zumbo, he'd ridden around the bush on a bicycle giving "conservation seminars" and engaging in running community conversations that lasted for days on end. Once, Namanha narrowly escaped from an encounter with an elephant that crushed his bicycle. He paid visits to the offices of local politicians to try to keep them informed of developments with the project, to give them talking points to defend it, or to at least shame them into supporting it. When Tchuma Tchato reached its peak, in 2003, it had expanded to eight hunting operators spread across four districts. There were twenty-seven cornmills and three tractors across the project area, with plans to purchase a truck in the works.

The next year, Namanha was promoted to provincial director of tourism in Tete, a clear step up, but one that required him to live and work ten hours from Zumbo. Much of the dynamism he'd helped to build up in Tchuma Tchato simply dissipated. After the Ford Foundation cut off funding, the number of game scouts ballooned and shrank with hunting revenues from year to year, many working months on end without pay. "Tchuma Tchato is dead," Namanha said.

He looked stricken when I told him about the crocodile cull I'd gone to Zumbo to see. "The hunting is not sustainable. For me as an ecologist, it's not controlled, and it won't do anything. More crocodiles can come down the Luangwa, down the Zambezi. So we are getting a bad reputation for nothing."[30]

Without a share of the money commercial hunting generates, rural people have little incentive to abide by the notion of conservation it imposes—one that requires them to give foreigners dominion over the wildlife that threatens their livelihoods so regularly, or to resist expanding their farms and settlements farther into the bush. As Maughan Brown observed of Tchuma Tchato's beginnings, people in Bawa seemed willing, even enthusiastic, about protecting wildlife, so long as they could look forward to some meaningful benefit. But their cooperation was contingent; it collapsed as soon as it became clear they were being asked to give up something for nothing.

In a recent email exchange, I told a safari operator near Zumbo that I was interested in understanding potential solutions to human-crocodile conflict. "The solution in my opinion is pretty simple," he replied. "Stay out of the water and the crocs will not eat you. Most of the attacks take place at the places where the villagers bathe and wash their clothes. They do this every day in the same place. It is like creating a feeding station. Is it not a simple task to take a bucket (or any container), quickly fill it with water and do all the washing a few yards away from the water's edge? But they insist on standing in the water. . . . So if they are not prepared to stay away from the water's edge they will get attacked."

The Hunter

"Conservation measures will never amount to anything in an area where people are starving," Carel Maartens remarked on his deck one evening as the sun sank over Lake Cahora Bassa. Maartens had spent seven years there, five miles downstream from Zumbo, at the camp he'd built on the banks of the lake. Time at Chawalo Safaris had taken a toll on Maartens's optimism about the prospects for conservation. Villages that began with fifty return-ees had grown to eight hundred or a thousand people. The wooded shoreline he remembered from his first visit to the lake had been steadily cleared for farmland, and still, he lamented, it wasn't enough. Bush fires raged each fall as people moved their *machambas* in search of more fertile soil.

"The land is so marginal that you can't possibly hope to support a family because it's all sand and rock," he said. "That's why they're expanding so much all the time. I keep investing here with the thought that maybe one day [the politicians] will wake up and say, 'Let's try and keep a little piece of this,'" he said coolly. "As long as you stay negative, then you can't be disappointed."

Each year, Maartens welcomes some hundred sportfishermen and six to ten trophy hunters (all foreigners) who are prepared to spend tens of thousands of dollars for the privilege of shooting an assortment of local wildlife. The animals fall into two categories: plains animals like kudu, Chobe bushbuck, and roan antelope, and big game including four of Africa's "Big 5"—elephants, lions, buf-falo, and leopard (there are no rhinos left in Mozambique). Hippos and crocodiles complete the "Dangerous 7."

Maartens and his clients have shot more than a hundred croc-odiles over thirteen feet since 2005, netting the Mozambican government close to $400,000. Modeled after Tchuma Tchato, 32 percent of that revenue is supposed to revert to the community.

But the more important benefit may well have nothing to do with money: Fergusson and others have shown repeatedly that only the largest male crocodiles—somewhere north of ten feet—are likely to attack full-grown human beings. Often well over fifty years old, these kings of the river expend less energy going after fast-moving birds and fish, and instead wait by the riverbank to ambush big animals on the shore. They are not easy to hunt. Maartens's clients have spent as much as two weeks going after a trophy crocodile, quietly stalking them through the mud and on the reed-covered islands where they bask in the sun. In and of itself, the death of more than a hundred dominant males on a small stretch of river has probably had a substantial impact on the incidence of crocodile attacks in the area. When Maartens began building Chawalo in 2005, he claims thirty fishermen were eaten in a single one-month period. Until Maartens got there, Miguel Wilson, the community court judge, confirmed, the river frontage along one side of Maartens's concession was considered so dangerous that fishermen dared not venture there at night.

Government hunters taking part in culls cannot afford to be so exacting. Sixpence, Omar, and company have a schedule that requires them to shoot a certain number of crocodiles on each trip, and only so much fuel and bullets to get the job done, patrolling the river with a spotlight powered by a car battery. "The big territorial males are extremely cautious," Maartens explained. "They're not going to let a boat approach. In the sixty crocodiles they shoot, I'll bet there's not one habitual man-eater."

As safari operators go, Maartens has tried hard to navigate the delicate politics of human-wildlife conflict. Local officials told me he lends his boat, and sometimes his crack shot, to their efforts to investigate conflict or get rid of "problem animals." He built schools and health facilities in neighboring communities and launched a mobile health clinic that visited twelve villages each month, providing prenatal care, immunizations, and HIV medication, with the help of a South Dakota casino man who donated a Toyota Land Cruiser after a hunting trip in Zumbo.

The nurse who runs that program, LiseMarie Cronje, has developed a sideline specializing in treating injuries from crocodile bites, which cause infections that often require months on

Government crocodile hunters go out at night, using a spotlight hooked up to a car battery to scan the water for crocodiles' telltale amber eyes peeking up above the surface.

antibiotics. "Most of what we do is hose you down and try and clean the wound with hydrogen peroxide," she said. "Then you go to [the operating] theater." Cronje recalled a recent episode in which a fisherman who survived a crocodile attack with a gaping chest wound sought help at Mozambique Safaris, close to where he'd been hurt. "He was not given so much as a glass of water," she said. "They told him, 'Go to Chawalo Safaris. They can help you there.'"

But this is only one part of the relationship. In the three years before my visit, Chawalo game scouts had seized more than five hundred rusty rifles and homemade muskets as they made their rounds of the concession. In Maartens's telling, the guns belonged to people abetting commercial poachers who crossed over from Zambia or, in some cases, subsistence hunters shooting animals they were not allowed to.

To Miguel Wilson, the community court judge in Zumbo, this narrative obscures why locals have always kept guns around: to keep animals away from their *machambas*. Wilson said broad restrictions on community hunting had made big game less wary of human settlements. "Now elephants come all the way into town," he explained—trampling houses and, once, venturing into the courtyard of Zumbo's high school. "If you shoot in the air, the elephant gets around to leaving when it wants to."

Wilson recounted an incident of a few weeks earlier when an angry crowd marched on Mozambique Safaris with machetes and picks after the owner, Simon Rogers, refused to shoot an elephant that had trampled a child to death.[31] Local people had no guns that Rogers and his game scouts hadn't already seized. A crowd stormed one of Rogers's camps, beat up a guard, and broke into a storeroom where Rogers kept the homemade muskets he'd confiscated, then set the place on fire. They wanted their guns back. Rogers fled.

"You know what I used to do when someone got killed?" Luis Namanha asked when I brought up the incident. "I went and rushed there and got a bag of rice and sugar, and said to the safari operator—'Please, one impala for this woman.' Local people are easy to convince," he said. "You just have to show up."

The Medium

One afternoon in Zumbo, I hired a banana boat to visit the papyrus island that shelters a narrow channel of the Zambezi just downstream from Bawa, a broad sandbar covered with reeds and tall grasses. At the island's tip, a pod of hippos rooted for grass on the river bottom, creating circular ripples on the surface as they exhaled. Onshore, I found a smiling, wizened old woman named Mariana Kumuezi, a spiritual healer who said she was possessed

Mariana Kumuezi, a spiritual healer who said she was possessed with *kolo*, or the spirit of the monkey, stands in her fields, on a reeded island in the middle of the Zambezi River. "Of course we're planting in the hippos' house," she said, of her fields. "Because if we plant in Bawa, there will be no food because of all the elephants and buffalo."

with *kolo*, or the spirit of the monkey. Kumuezi wore a head wrap and a tangle of necklaces and bracelets on each wrist. These were mementos of her trips to the United States: Kumuezi had been part of a delegation from Tchuma Tchato that traveled with the Ford Foundation in the 1990s and had returned twice since then to do work as a spirit medium. When I returned to America, she wondered, could I say hello to Doña Liz? Kumuezi couldn't remember exactly where in America she'd been, but a few details, like a large cemetery, she recalled vividly. "*Sheeeeee!*" she exclaimed, putting one hand to her forehead. "I was so surprised to see all those graves: I didn't know that white people died," she said, laughing. At a zoo, Kumuezi remembered seeing elephants dance. She stiffened at the elbows and swayed back and forth in imitation.

"*Cha. Cha. Cha.*" She repeated this tidbit four times, it was so unbelievable, and bent over double laughing at it.

Kumuezi spends six months a year here, surrounded by anemic fields of maize and squash and watermelon that look as though someone had planted a vegetable garden on the beach. It's hard to believe it's a better option than farming on the mainland, but the water table is high, and seasonal floods that wash over the islands during the rainy season leave enough sediment behind to fertilize the sand. In Bawa itself, Kumuezi's house is all concrete, built for her by a former president of Mozambique, Joaquim Chissano, after she'd forecast a favorable election result. On the island, she sleeps above her corn silo on a small platform made of reeds and wood, in order to keep the hippopotamuses out of her fields. Kumuezi showed me maize plants that had been chewed to small perforated stumps by the hippos and told a story that explained how hippos began raiding crops in the first place: "There was a man who got a charm that allowed him to transform into a hippo. So he went to his wife and said, I am going to turn myself into a hippo, and I will go around and get fat eating everyone's maize. When you see me, you must come and hit my belly with a cooking stick, and all the maize will come out, and I will become a man again. So the husband went ahead with the plan, but his wife never found him again."

Aren't you planting in the hippos' house? I asked. "Of course we're planting in the hippos' house," she said. "Because if we plant in Bawa, there will be no food because of all the elephants and buffalo."

"The problem," Kumuezi said, when I asked about crocodiles, "is that Simon has been giving the crocodiles zebra meat," referring to Simon Rogers, the safari operator whose camp had been raided a few weeks earlier. "They get used to eating things they shouldn't, and when there's no meat, naturally, they begin to go after humans." Miguel Wilson, the community court judge, had told me much the same thing about Carel Maartens, arguing that safari operators had made crocodiles more aggressive: "Sometimes, this Chawalo Safaris contributes to the problem," he said, "because when they kill hippos, they cut it into pieces and give the meat to the crocodiles." Whether or not this practice has an effect on crocodile behavior, it's true that partial carcasses from trophy hunts often wind up floating in the Zambezi. And for a community accustomed to seeing crocodiles as part of the human world as much as humans are part of the natural one, this explanation seemed every bit as plausible as the idea that things they had always done—fishing, bathing, washing—had suddenly become more deadly.

"The government team should start killing crocodiles on my island," Kumuezi went on. "There are crocodiles everywhere. Would you like to see one?" I followed her to the end of her field, stepped over an anti-hippo fence made of sticks stuck in the sand, and crept quietly to the edge of a small canal, its sandy banks crisscrossed with birdlike crocodile tracks and scratches. I asked Mariana who owned the crocodile that left the tracks. "This one seems to belong to god," she said. "If it belonged to humans, we would all be dead. But it is very big. If you see it, you will run away." I asked if the government's crocodile cull was effectively targeting those human crocodiles who went after people. "Human crocodiles do not stay in the river. Especially not now, when they know that crocodiles are being killed," she said. But some of god's crocodiles might be going after people as well now that they are used to getting meat from the safaris, she said, and especially now that the crocodile farms are collecting eggs. "When the crocodiles return to their nests and find them empty, they get angry and come after people," she said.

The temptation to argue against culls comes largely from the feeling of being right: based on the evidence, culls carry the risk of real ecological damage, and they seem unlikely to mitigate conflict or push people toward demonstrably safer behavior in crocodile habitats. But being right is not enough. Culls make for effective politics because they respond to reality as people at the confluence experience it: a struggle for use of land and water that pits them against dangerous animals. The people selling conservation as an economic strategy are selling hope for a scenario local people have never seen, one that hinges on government accountability and on cooperation with white foreigners who take their guns away and tell them they can't hunt.

At the end of 2013, the Mozambican government announced that some 350,000 hectares along the southern shore of Lake Cahora Bassa—a little smaller than the state of Rhode Island—would soon become Magoé National Park.[32] Luis Namanha was tapped to return to Tete Province to run the park. The move included pledges to strengthen Tchuma Tchato, which now includes adjacent land covering ten times that area, and imagines the park as a breeding area that can help stabilize wildlife populations outside its boundaries. But there's a long way to go. "New National Park in Mozambique Has No Money," blared the headline of an article in Voice of America's Portuguese news service recently, outlining the challenge Namanha faces in getting the effort off the ground.[33] He is wiser this time around and, as ever, committed to the cause. Namanha's been circulating a proposal for an overhaul of Tchuma Tchato to top brass in the Mozambican government.[34] It calls for doubling the share of trophy fees that goes to local communities— to 60 percent—and eliminating the share that gets sent to Maputo, a change he sees as crucial to getting more community buy-in for the program. As proof of the sustainability of Tchuma Tchato's model, Namanha's report shows that the revenue theoretically available to the program increased more than tenfold between 1996 and 2014: wildlife populations have rebounded, and trophy hunting has expanded enough that "if revenue is distributed and well-managed, it could sustain the operation of Tchuma Tchato." Any external funding, he writes, could go toward capital investments and infrastructure.

It's an optimistic vision at a time when commercial elephant poaching has accelerated its conquest of ivory in Mozambique, killing off nearly half the country's elephant population in just five years.[35] Another of Mozambique's national parks, Gorongosa, has been closed sporadically because of violence, as Renamo has returned to the bush near its old wartime headquarters. Donors ambushed by news of $2 billion in secret loans taken out by members of Mozambique's central government may be reluctant to fund the launch of a national park with grants made through Maputo. But Namanha kept on crisscrossing the bush to talk conservation even after an elephant crushed his bicycle. Perhaps he's the man for the job.

7

A Mercenary's
Retirement Plan

TETE

"If it weren't for Jesse Hickman, we all would have starved." This is what Danilo, who owns a bakery and a butcher shop in Tete, kept telling me about his upbringing during the civil war. "That man is a hero."

Hickman, as Danilo described him, was the American savior of western Mozambique. For four years in the 1980s, Hickman ran logistics along the Beira corridor, which connects Mozambique's most important port with the landlocked countries to its west—Zimbabwe, Zambia, and Malawi. It was a focal point of the Mozambican civil war, and Hickman was serving, improbably, as a lieutenant colonel in the Zimbabwean Army under Robert Mugabe. As the white commanding officer of a battalion of four thousand black troops, Hickman protected convoys of maize trucks from ambushes, land mines, and hand grenades, and ensured that some semblance of a food supply continued to move inland. So one day after eating lunch at Danilo's bakery, I went off in search of Hickman. There was an element of Lord Jim in his story—an expat who got there first and never left, who blended into the woodwork in a way that now seems inaccessible, or even out of time.

Fifteen minutes later, I found him at home in a rugby shirt and flip-flops, with two Yorkies and two spaniel mutts yapping at his knees. To me, Hickman looked a good deal younger than sixty-four. He's over six feet, with a big man's lumbering gait and long arms. Only a slight paunch hinted that he was finally beginning to slow down. He had flecks of gray in his brown crewcut, and taut, pinched features that remained all but motionless when he smiled. I found that his expressions still reflected a sort of macho military manner, or at least the Hollywood version of it. He seemed accustomed to answering questions with an impassive Clint Eastwood squint. Hickman lives in a comfortable stucco bungalow adjoining the kitchen of the Esplanada Why Not, a restaurant he used to own. The cook there prepares most of his meals, delivering them through the back door and across his driveway. Visually, Hickman's home resembles self-sufficient retirement somewhere in the Everglades, with central air-conditioning and an ice maker in the fridge. There is white tile in the kitchen, cherry-stained wood paneling on the living room walls, and a lush, minimal garden inhabited by a half dozen tortoises. His wife is a striking light-skinned Mozambican woman twenty years his junior, with a broad, heart-shaped face marked by delicate features. She answered the door in jean shorts and a red boat-neck blouse. She seemed to speak no more English than Hickman speaks Portuguese, though the two of them have been together for nearly twenty-five years.

"Jesse, there's an American at the door," she called out in Portuguese after I introduced myself, walking back into the kitchen. "Há um americano aqui à porta"—it came out nonchalantly, as though it happened every day. There aren't many Americans in Tete, but the house, I'm sure, receives more than its share of foreign visitors. Hickman emerged with a bemused scowl, surrounded by his canine entourage. His wife followed with two cans of Coca-Cola on a tray. "You're American?" he asked. "Have a seat."

* * *

When Hickman came to Tete in 1984, the surrounding country-side was nearly empty. A large share of Tete's rural population had fled the violence of the civil war, some to towns and cities, most over the border into Zimbabwe, Malawi, or Zambia, all of which border the province. The region was ravaged by the advances of Renamo, the guerrilla army funded by white-ruled governments in Rhodesia and South Africa, and its clashes with the army of Mozambique's Marxist government, Frelimo. The Catholic priests, from Italy and Portugal, had fled the change augured by Mozambique's independence, or they'd been pushed out in the wave of nationalization that claimed most of their missions for the state. The bridge across the Zambezi River, which connects Tete with the rest of Mozambique, had been damaged so that trucks—required to travel in convoys for security purposes—had to cross it one by one. Then, as now, Tete was dry, and stiflingly hot. "Tete is a terrible place," Hickman says now. But he stayed all the same.

Hickman was born in Pittsburgh, Pennsylvania, in 1938. He joined the army out of high school and took his first trip outside the United States aboard a navy carrier that took him across the Atlantic. He spent the next four years "cruising around the Mediterranean," he said, "doing a lot of bullshit." After that, he spent three more years, in Nuremberg—"doing bullshit." The bullshit continued with each new posting. Eventually, he said, he landed in Vietnam, doing two tours of duty as a captain. "Bullshit," he said wryly.

Hickman returned to the United States, where he made major and was posted to a base in Louisiana. But after thirteen years of service, he left to join the reserves and went home to work as an adviser to the recruitment office in Pittsburgh. This was at the height of the Vietnam War, and Hickman was disgusted at the maneuvering he saw in the draft office. "I saw all kinds of corruption there. They were getting guys who played football out of the draft, and things like that." What bullshit. "You know, I think I was having trouble adjusting to civilian life," he said, "just seeing the way these giant bureaucracies worked." Hoping to help other vets navigate the transition he found so difficult, Hickman became a claims adjudicator for Veterans Affairs. He stuck with it for the remainder of the war, though he often found adjudication just as frustrating as working in recruitment. "There was one case that made me sick," Hickman said. "Dennis Joyner. I'll never forget that name."

Joyner was a triple amputee from Vandergrift, Pennsylvania, who was injured in a land-mine explosion in the Mekong delta. In a war that killed 57,000 American troops and sent home more than 11,000 amputees, he was one of only 52 soldiers who survived the loss of three limbs. He spent scarcely more than a month in the hospital, including his twenty-first birthday. Back in Vandergrift, a small steel town east of Pittsburgh, Joyner enrolled in the local community college nonetheless and went on to earn a BA in accounting.

After graduation, Joyner sent a résumé to the VA office in Pittsburgh, where Jesse Hickman worked at the time. Attached on a second sheet were four photographs that Joyner hoped would show what he *could* do, in anticipation of the inevitable questions about his ability to work in an office setting: one showed him sitting, another showed him driving, a third showed him getting into his car, and a fourth showed him rolling his wheelchair down the sidewalk.

The VA made Joyner an offer, but it seemed they wanted him for little more than window dressing—to sit in the lobby, as Joyner put it later, "where the veterans would see somebody sitting there who was working, and missing three limbs—like 'Wow, I guess I'm not that bad off; look at this poor guy.'" Frustrated, Joyner withdrew his application and looked for work elsewhere, but it was more than Jesse Hickman could take.

Hickman stared gently off to my left as the memories came to him spontaneously. Revolted at Joyner's cynical treatment at the hands of his office, he decided to go to Washington, D.C. He would speak directly to the top brass at the Department of Veterans Affairs. He was determined to get a response. Hickman bought a ticket and boarded a plane to the capital, where he went straight to Vermont Avenue. "They blocked me," Hickman recalled wearily. "I couldn't get an appointment."

He went to a bar instead. "There was this guy there who was an intelligence officer for Ian Smith's army. He said, 'We can offer you the rank of major. Why don't you come to Rhodesia?'" Hickman glanced down at his folded hands in the retelling of the moment, as though he were still gripping a pint glass between them. "I said, 'Where's Rhodesia?' and he said, 'Africa,' so I said, 'Okay.'"

Nearly three hundred Americans served in the Rhodesian Army during the 1970s. Almost every one of them was a veteran of the U.S. Army. Yet they disobeyed a State Department travel advisory to go to Rhodesia and ran the risk of forfeiting their U.S. passports, all to receive ordinary pay in Ian Smith's army, starting at less than $800 a month. They left behind the integrated armed forces of the United States to fight black guerrilla soldiers who would eventually topple the minority-rule government and take power in an independent Zimbabwe.

Many of the American mercenaries learned about the "Rhodesian Bush War"—Zimbabweans now remember it as the Zimbabwean Independence War—from accounts published in the early issues of *Soldier of Fortune*, a right-wing quarterly that has grown to be the mythmaker and preferred classifieds outlet for mercenaries

around the world. Some were open and committed white suprem-
acists. Others had developed a paranoid, rabid hatred of communism during service in Vietnam. Still others simply couldn't adjust
to life outside the barracks.

Jesse Hickman seemed to be motivated mainly by a dismal
sense of the rest of his life back in Pittsburgh, a feeling that trying
to be "normal" would actually drive him crazy. He had grown
used to the stark mental landscape of enlisted life, and he couldn't
stand the moral compromises and hypocrisies of civilian society.

Hickman had a wife and two young children in Pennsylvania,
but he never managed to feel fully at home. And though he
was desperately frustrated with his work for Veterans Affairs,
he shrugged off my questions about why he decided to join Ian
Smith. Hickman flew home to Pittsburgh and broke the news to
his family, while the intelligence officer made their travel arrangements. In the space of four days, Hickman quit his job; packed,
sold, or discarded his remaining belongings; and boarded a flight
to Salisbury (now Harare), with his wife and kids in tow. There,
narrowing his eyes, Hickman skipped over the first four years of his
service to a moment in the spring of 1980.

"After independence, Mugabe said, 'If you want to stay, stay; if
you want to go, go.'" Hickman shrugged, smiling. "I stayed. I think
there were about thirteen of us." Within a few weeks, a black general approached him with some advice. "He said to me and one
other white guy, 'If you stay out of politics and just focus on doing
your job, you'll be fine.'" Now, looking back on his mercenary years
from the comfort of a patio chair, he appeared noncommittal and
reserved. Neither regret nor pride disturbed the calm of his face.
"I kept my head down," he said.

Under Mugabe, Hickman reached the rank of lieutenant colonel,
and in 1984 he was sent to Tete as the commander of four thousand
Zimbabwean troops stationed in Mozambique. His main task was
to protect the transport corridors between Zimbabwe and

Malawi. On the job, Hickman got to know the Indian Mozambican merchants, including Danilo's father, whose forebears came to Mozambique as cashew traders in the first part of the twentieth century. The businessmen relied on Hickman's protection to bring their goods to Tete, and he met Danilo as a young boy. At the peak of the war, it took a week for trucks to reach Tete from the port of Beira, a few hundred miles away. But Hickman and his troops kept the roads moving, surviving "a few dustups with Renamo," he said, in the process.

Renamo was founded the year after Frelimo won Mozambique's independence from Portugal, the same year that Jesse Hickman arrived in Salisbury. Initially, Renamo was sponsored by the Central Intelligence Organisation of the Rhodesian Army, the same agency that recruited Hickman. While Ian Smith still ruled Rhodesia, Mugabe and ZANU-PF fought the colonial army with Frelimo's support. Samora Machel, Mozambique's first president, was a vocal proponent of the Pan-African solidarity that had helped Frelimo take power the year before. Prior to independence, during a decade of guerrilla warfare with the Portuguese, Frelimo was based in exile in Tanzania, then under the leadership of its first black president, Julius Nyerere. With Nyerere's blessing, they ran a school for young apparatchiks in Dar es Salaam and conducted military training along Tanzania's southern border.

After achieving independence, Machel paid it forward: Mugabe's forces kept bush bases within Mozambique and even launched ambushes on Rhodesian forces from across the border. Renamo began as Rhodesia's response, a rebel group whose mercenary origins could be camouflaged and melded with homegrown grievances against Frelimo rule. By fomenting insurgency in Mozambique, Rhodesia hoped to disrupt the fledgling government enough that it would be forced to withdraw support from rebels across the border.

Over the next sixteen years, Renamo waged a brutal guerrilla campaign throughout Mozambique, focusing their disruptive violence on the institutions of Frelimo's new socialist state—schools, rural health posts, and *lojas do povo,* "stores of the people," or government stores. Without going so far as to articulate a coherent political platform, Renamo asserted itself as a defender of democracy and the people's ally against Frelimo's socialist agricultural policies. Scholars still dispute the extent of Renamo's popular support, but the group had important backers in the white-ruled governments of Rhodesia and, later, in apartheid South Africa, as well as in the CIA, which viewed the Mozambican conflict as a proxy war against the USSR. All three groups had reasons to fear the rise of a stable, leftist black government in Mozambique.

In 2007, Hickman suffered a serious stroke on his right side that left him "talking funny" and forced him to step back from the constant sale of meat and beer and potatoes by which he earned a living. He decided to put the Why Not? up for lease and asked Danilo to help him find a tenant. Danilo came back several weeks later with Louis van der Bank, whose name suggests just the sort of grandiose anecdotes that cling to the man like lint. Louie is a stout, flamboyant character with a rippling neck and a wiry, reddish goatee. He wears V-neck T-shirts and a Kangol hat and appears to make no effort to ward off the brutal sunburn that Tete can inflict on the pale-skinned.

People tell a story about Louie and the bridge that Hickman was charged to protect during the civil war. For much of the 1980s, the South African Army provided food, arms, and communications equipment to Renamo fighters in the bush. Van der Bank, a white Afrikaaner, served as a pilot flying tactical missions into Mozambique in support of Renamo. At a pivotal moment, the story goes, van der Bank, on a low-flying salvo over Tete, received orders to bomb the bridge that was the city's lifeline. The bridge's elegant pilons and cables stretched in a gentle arc over the eddying blue of the Zambezi. Beyond it, a nineteenth-century Catholic church overlooked an expanse of sandbars and tall reeds, humble mud houses stretching out across the veldt. Van der Bank couldn't do it. He couldn't let the bombs go on such a lovely scene. Tete was spared.

Nearly thirty years later, the city would reciprocate. In 2004, Tete made headlines in investors' newsletters and trade monthlies around the world as the site of one of the planet's largest undeveloped coal basins. Soon after, Vale do Rio Doce, the world's second largest mining company, and Rio Tinto, the third, each leased sizable concessions and are now in the midst of building multibillion-dollar mines nearby. Upscale hotels and restaurants have sprouted across town, and houses built to "Western" standards rent for upward of $5,000 a month. The street corners are clogged with young men shouting "Boss, boss!" at passing pickups, hoping to sell phone credit to the expatriates who have descended on the city with the boom. It is a far cry from the Tete that Hickman first discovered in 1984, when there were only a few dozen cars in the whole city, and Hickman was the only white man he knew of in the area who wasn't an aid worker or a priest.

Nowadays, the Why Not? attracts its most boisterous crowds on Sunday mornings, for the South African rugby equivalent of *Monday Night Football* in the United States. When I visited, the town was awash with the fortune seekers of the global mining industry—Australian and South African men in their thirties and forties with lots of money and little in the way of entertainment. So the Why Not?, with its Afrikaaner-friendly menu and rugby broadcasts, represents a sort of homecoming for them. "You wouldn't believe the business I'm doing over there," Louie told me.

Danilo got to know Louie while he was studying in Johannesburg. These were Louie's high-rolling days as a hotelier. Today, he still retains the expensive tastes of that profession. At bars, he drinks his whiskey from a personal bottle, ice bucket on hand, and he wears a large diamond earring on an otherwise bare head. As only a foreigner would, van der Bank wears shorts and flip-flops under expensive blazers. Beaming with paternal pride, he likes to tell the story of his daughter, Kandra, who has just bought a house with the proceeds of a shoot as Miss October for *Playboy South Africa*. "I didn't give her anything—she doesn't need to ask Daddy for anything!" he says.

Van der Bank is easy to talk to. He rolls his *r*'s and belly laughs heartily at his own jokes. He is also one of the only expatriates you will meet in Tete who seems to have an unabashedly positive opinion of the city. "I love it here!" he insists. But van der Bank might never have come to settle in Tete if it weren't for an incident, years ago, that put him flat out of the hospitality business at home: early in the aughts, he was pulled over in southern Mozambique driving two thousand tablets of Mandrax, a form of methamphetamine popular in South Africa, to Maputo. He served three years in a Mozambican prison, and when he got out, Danilo threw him a lifeline: Jesse Hickman was looking for a tenant.

"Louie's a good boy," Hickman said cheerfully when I asked him about van der Bank. He didn't dwell on it. Hickman has seen a lot over the years; perhaps he liked the idea of giving someone a second chance. Few trajectories of shifting political allegiance require a greater reinvention of purpose than Hickman's, though he remained in essentially the same position all the while. In five years, with only a series of stoic "yes, sirs" sent up the shifting chain of command, Hickman went from fighting to preserve minority white rule in Rhodesia to fighting in support of the black Marxist government of a neighboring country while it fended off an insurgency funded by apartheid South Africa. When ZANU-PF came to power in Zimbabwe (formerly Rhodesia), Renamo's backing shifted to Pretoria, where the government was incensed by Frelimo's support of black freedom fighters like Nelson Mandela and Steve Biko in the African National Congress. The apartheid government took up where Rhodesia had left off, funding Renamo's campaign of destruction to cripple Mozambique's lingering commitment to Pan-Africanism. But Hickman was basically unmoved by the shift he'd undertaken from the "white fellows" to the "black fellows," as he put it.

In 1988, Jesse Hickman turned fifty. In eight years of service in the Zimbabwean Army, he'd had only indirect dealings with Mugabe. He had shaken his hand at public events and sat in on a handful of meetings at the Presidential Palace. But he began to sense a sea change. "Mugabe was in the process of getting the white guys out," he recalled. It would be more than a decade before Mugabe began seizing white-owned farms and businesses around Zimbabwe, pushing many of the country's white settlers to leave as he reapportioned their assets among his allies. The full effects of this purge wouldn't be felt until 2007 and 2008, when hyperinflation emptied Zimbabwe's grocery stores and turned its "100 trillion dollar" notes into souvenirs. But it was undeniable that Mugabe had begun his transformation from freedom fighter to idiosyncratic autocrat, and Hickman thought it best to get out of the army of his own accord.

Hickman left his post in Mozambique, took his pension in one lump—$170,000—and bought a house in Harare. It didn't last. He and his wife divorced, and she returned to the States with their daughter while he stayed in Africa with their son. He moved to Beira, the Mozambican port that also serves landlocked Malawi and Zimbabwe, as well as being Renamo's historic stronghold. There, Hickman went to work for a transport company dispatching freight along the same corridor he'd protected in Tete, and he met his current wife. Together, they opened a discotheque and returned to her native Tete five years later, after the civil war ended.

Ever since, he has been "making good money" off a patchwork of businesses ranging from logistics to farming to bars and night-clubs. Twice or three times a month, he visits his farm in Cateme, thirty miles outside of Tete, where he raises pigs and chickens with the help of a Mozambican caretaker. At the farm, Hickman sleeps on a cot in a canvas tent like an enlisted man. He doesn't make much money from it, he says, but he likes it too much to give it up. Hickman's most famous venture is a club and motel called Paraíso Misterioso—Mysterious Paradise—that sits just beneath the bridge on the banks of the Zambezi. Hickman built the Paradise himself, and he remembers it as a fun place to spend a Sunday afternoon, drinking beer beneath a canopy of palms: the Paradise has one of Tete's only swimming pools, and a shaded courtyard filled with carved wooden statues—busts of koi fish and muscular men paddling a dugout canoe. These days, Hickman rents it out to the Hassam family, who also own gas stations, general stores, and rental homes around the city. It looks as though the Paradise hasn't received so much as a lick of paint since Hickman first opened it, yet it's undergoing a revival all the same. Mining money has been a boon to Tete's hospitality indus-try. Rooms at the Paradise go for more than $100 a night, and there are packed pool parties with live music every weekend afternoon.

But Hickman doesn't get out much. He stays home, in an air-conditioned room he calls his "little office," with a flat-screen sat-ellite TV and broadband Internet. The coal boom has done wonders to connect Tete to the rest of the world. And though Hickman has not returned to the United States since 1976—"I don't miss it," he insists—he has re-created something of the suburban base-ment hangout in his corner of Mozambique. He watches *Jerry Springer* reruns most days, and every Sunday and Monday in the fall, Hickman stays up until four a.m. to watch NFL games on DSTV. Unsurprisingly, he is a die-hard Steelers fan.

He hasn't seen his daughter in twenty years, but he remains in daily contact with her and the rest of his family in the United States, largely thanks to Facebook. His daughter is even considering a visit to Mozambique. "It's as if I never left," Hickman said. A few years back, Hickman's son, who managed the nightclub business with his father, moved to the United Kingdom in order to "have more white friends," Hickman said. He winced ever so slightly, knowing how this might sound to American ears, but Hickman insisted it was simply a matter of his son's finding a place where he would feel at home. The boy had grown up with the children of white officers in the Rhodesian Army, as far from a harmonious multiracial upbringing as you could find anywhere. He now works security at a nightclub in Leeds. "He's happy," Hickman said. That was enough.

Every couple of months, Hickman drives his Dodge minivan up into Malawi, where he visits a missionary hospital in Blantyre and receives medication for his stroke. He also visits Shoprite, for those necessities that are hard to find in the Zambezi valley: peanut butter, potato chips, cheddar cheese. "They've got a real mall up there," Hickman said. "You should check it out." His wife insists he's going blind, but she can't do much to stop him from driving. Do you ever think about going back to the United States? I asked him before taking leave. Hickman shook his head emphatically. "My whole problem in the U.S. is that I couldn't get used to civilian life. I can't imagine going back. Especially now," he added. "I'd be a social welfare case. No way."

By the time Jesse Hickman settled in Tete, he was already well-known there, beloved after a decade protecting the city through a brutal stretch of history. In Tete, Hickman became a successful restaurateur and a gentleman farmer. He found love again after his marriage fell apart. But his prominence was also tied up with a special kind of anonymity. Above all, Mozambique had given him what he wanted most—a quiet, contented retirement, a place to be suspended beyond the reach of American society.

For foreigners, anyway, that mix—of anonymity and opportunity, of carrying the cachet of a Western passport unmoored from life in the West—is still a core part of Tete's appeal. As much as the city has transformed in the years Hickman has lived there, it is no less a frontier town. The coal boom has slackened in the years since I was there, in 2011, but there's no doubt mercenaries of various stripes are still showing up in search of cash and cold beer.

The mercury scarcely dipped below ninety degrees in the two months I spent in Tete, even at night. Concrete walls radiated heat long after sundown. Locals often took straw mats out into their yards to sleep with a breeze. The weather dominated conversation to the degree that you might have thought the city was in the middle of a flood or a hurricane. "*Calor!*"—Heat!—was a kind of casual greeting. At noon, I would often take refuge for the price of an espresso on the air-conditioned top floor of the Hotel Zambeze, where you could meet South African security guards who had done stints in Iraq for Blackwater, and drilling contractors riding waves of industrial activity around the world.

"Tete is the ass of the world," a white South African woman told me in the air-conditioned bar atop the Hotel Zambeze one afternoon. "They must have forgotten this place." She took a drag of a Pall Mall looking out over a span of river where boys spent the day jumping off an old pier into the Zambezi. Women washed their clothes on the bank in the sun.

"Can you imagine what this place was like before all these companies rolled in?" she asked. "It's a proper taste of Africa, my friend." The woman had come to Tete a few months earlier for an exploratory mining venture that went bust. Now she was planning on opening a restaurant, which she seemed to see as a potent civilizing influence on the city. "Last year, we had Why Not?, we had Le Petit, and what else?" she asked. "It's expensive too—when phase two of the [Vale] project begins," she said, "this place—people aren't ready. It's going to become more expensive than Angola. These people, they have learned the word 'dollar' and gone crazy with it." She was eager to ride the wave.

One day I sat across from an old Portuguese man who grew up in colonial Maputo when it was still called Lourenço Marques. He'd built a career in Lisbon exporting hotel and restaurant equipment to Mozambique and Angola. Most of what he had to say about Tete could be summarized as "Weren't the colonies nice until we handed them over to the Africans?" It's a trope you hear all the time from white foreigners in Mozambique. When he was in Tete forty years ago, in his telling, the city was clean, there was no hunger, people had the opportunity to get educated, the buildings had paint on them. It was as though he couldn't fathom a connection between that city and this one, or the web of privilege that made either place pleasant for a Portuguese businessman.

Mozambicans have many of the same complaints: slow service at banks or restaurants, bribe-seeking policemen, broken plumbing, bad roads, intermittent blackouts. But a little money makes all the difference. For a price, someone else can drive your car, wash your clothes, keep a generator running, carry your water. "Everyone has maids here," I once heard a Portuguese man say at a sidewalk cafe in Maputo. "Even the maids have maids." In a way, there's no clearer explanation of class or privilege than the sum of one's exposure to these daily indignities.

How much better to enter a needy society at its upper crust, with access to the climate-controlled Wi-Fi and coffee on the top floor of the Hotel Zambeze? I was often amazed at the social capital the phrase "American journalist" seemed to unlock at stores or government offices—the access to authority, the gifts of time and goodwill. For Jesse Hickman, for the foreign drillers and miners, or for me, being an "outsider" in Tete is something of a misnomer. All too often, it's ordinary Mozambicans left on the outside of their society's caprices, striving for a seat at the table.

8

Neighborhood Headquarters

BEIRA

A Frelimo é que fez. A Frelimo é que faz.

It's Frelimo that did it; it's Frelimo that does it.

—PARTY SLOGAN

The Mapiko Lounge Bar occupies one of the older buildings in the oldest part of Beira, Mozambique's third-largest city. It's a stately two-story stucco affair built in the early twentieth century, repainted in lively pink, with elegant ironwork grilles on each second-floor balcony and an imposing wrought-iron gate outside. In the colonial era, it was a small hotel, nationalized after independence when the Portuguese owners left the country. Recent renovations have made the interior unrecognizable. Jazz combos, DJs, and stand-up comedians perform in an intimate hall with sparkly pink wallpaper and electric-blue cocktails served on faux-leather sofas. On the bar's Facebook timeline, you can see "before" pictures showing the building's roofless facade before the conversion got under way.

The club stands at one end of a street market in Chaimite, a bustling commercial neighborhood between Beira's downtown

and the port, built up a century ago as a railway link to move
goods in and out of the vast landlocked territories of the British
Empire. Today, sidewalk vendors clog the streets themselves,
dangling dozens of USB chargers and impossibly cheap head-
phones from crude wooden stalls set up on the pavement. Women
move through honking motorcycle traffic carrying plastic tubs
of pineapples and peanuts over their heads, or sit in the shade of
Indian almond trees on a slender triangular plaza across from
the Mapiko.

There, amid the bustle of cold-drink sellers and steaming pots
of rice and stew, a trio of faithful municipal clerks sit behind two
rusty desks counting change and checking IDs, doing their best
to ignore the detritus of bottle caps and discarded scratch cards
in the dirt around them. This is a local government office known
as the *sede de bairro*—the "neighborhood headquarters" for Chaimite.
The clerks' main line of business is writing out the declarations of
residency needed for all manner of interactions with officialdom:
to open bank accounts, to send or receive international wire trans-
fers, to remove the body of someone who has died at home, to obtain
a birth certificate when a child is born, to register a marriage, or
to request help resolving disputes between neighbors.

The lead clerk didn't want his real name to be used; I'll call him
Mr. Vicente. Vicente is a dignified man approaching seventy, with
a stern bearing and the cool good looks of an aging movie star.
He entered the civil service in the 1960s and still completes his
residency declarations—in triplicate, with two sheets of carbon
paper—with the flawless looping cursive of another time. "When
it rains, we take refuge in a hallway," he explained bitterly, gesturing toward a covered alley flanking a grocery store around the
corner. When the headquarters closes for the day, Vicente brings
the chairs and a few other necessities to be stored in space belonging to a soda distributor operating across the street. "And at night,
when we're done working, *malandros* like to come out here, eat

on our desks, urinate on the ground," Vicente said. He looked outraged.

It's customary for a *sede de bairro* to have a sort of community bulletin board as well, where clerks can post subpoenas to appear in court, marriage notices, and the like, to inform interested parties or give people an opportunity to object. Vicente gestured toward the MCel kiosk directly behind his desk, made from a slice of a repurposed shipping container. A faded flag of the city of Beira hung at eye level. "Where can we post any notices?" he asked.

Until a few years ago, the *sede de bairro* in Chaimite had a community bulletin board and much more: four walls, a bathroom, even benches where citizens could wait to be seen. For decades, the neighborhood headquarters occupied part of the Posto Administrativo de Chiveve, the next rung up the ladder of government offices, housed in the colonial building now enjoying a third act as the Mapiko Lounge Bar. But that was when Frelimo was in power.

In 2003, a charismatic thirty-nine-year-old organizer from the opposition, Daviz Simango, ran for mayor on the Renamo ticket— Simango was actually part of a smaller party aligned with Renamo at the time—and won. Suddenly, the ownership of government buildings around Beira became a matter of hot debate.

Renamo's electoral victory in Beira was the product of weeks of retail political organizing of a kind that the party had scarcely done before. Leading up to the election, one newspaper noted that hundreds of young people went door-to-door soliciting votes for Daviz Simango "tirelessly, night and day," while the bars and clubs were populated with men in Frelimo T-shirts.[1] But the election was marred by irregularities and allegations of corruption. Initial results from ten polling stations went missing. Vote counting was interrupted repeatedly as officials from each party refused to open warehouses where ballots were stored. A Frelimo technician was caught scribbling extra digits—for example, 142 instead of 42 votes—on the tally sheets being sent to Maputo. It took more than a week to reach a result.[2]

Municipal elections are a recent development in Mozambique: local officials were all appointed until 1998. That year, Renamo led a group of opposition parties in a boycott of the country's first local elections, voicing complaints about fraudulent voter registrations and partisan bias in the state's election agencies that have become a regular chorus in every election since. Frelimo candidates ran unopposed in 80 percent of city council races and more than half the country's mayoral elections, winning that post in all thirty-three cities where elections were held.[3]

As Simango's government prepared to take power at the end of 2003, incoming civil servants discovered that the outgoing Frelimo administration had simply locked the doors on many of Beira's municipal buildings. In Chiveve, James Domingos, the bartender at a restaurant next door, said Frelimo's *chefe do posto* and his family went on living on the *posto administrativo*'s second floor even as the incoming Renamo *chefe do posto* resorted to signing official documents and conducting the duties of his office on the staircase outside. While the building had functioned as part of the city government for years, this was the first time in Mozambican history that an opposition party actually controlled the machinery of government in any part of the national territory. Beira's civil service had crossed into the territory of a multiparty democracy, but the buildings it relied on were still stranded in a one-party state.

The details of this period—the start of a long-running political dispute—have long since slid into the depths of partisan memory, blurring and shifting like underwater objects seen from the surface in bright sunlight. Here, as best as I can tell, is more or less how things went. Downtown, Daviz Simango moved into the spacious wood-paneled mayor's office in city hall without incident. But in Chiveve, meanwhile, just a few blocks away, the work of the *posto administrativo* carried on in the stairwell. The *chefe do posto* and his staff, a former Renamo soldier who lived in the neighborhood told me with indignation, "took off their administration hats, and put on whose hats instead? Frelimo's! They didn't want to cede their places!"

Soon, Frelimo began to use the building to plan a celebration of Josina Machel, Mozambique's first first lady. The Organização da Mulher Moçambicana (OMM) and Organização da Juventude Moçambicana (OJM), Frelimo's women and youth organizing bodies, respectively, both held meetings there. Renamo supporters attempted to take the place by force. "We were tired of being attended to in the street," the soldier said. Partisans of either side gathered in the street—Renamo protesters huddled in front of a pharmacy, Frelimo supporters outside a funeral home by the market where Vicente and his staff now shelter in the rain. For two weeks, they beat drums and exchanged taunts with the other party. Finally, the standoff was resolved. Or, rather, it shifted to the courts: Frelimo would sue to regain control of the building, along with Beira's sixteen other *sedes de bairros*, and allow the municipal government to use them in the meantime.

So it went for seven years. Simango, a civil engineer who worked as a construction manager, had run on a platform of transparency and efficient management, pledging to combat corruption and fix the sanitation problems that dogged Beira during major cholera outbreaks two years in a row. The odds were long: when he took office, Simango inherited a city of five hundred thousand residents with only three garbage trucks and a government that did all its accounting with paper and pencil. Key staff in the outgoing Frelimo administration had resigned and taken the contents of their filing cabinets with them, leaving Simango's team in the dark about the nuts and bolts of city administration. Beira's sixteen hundred civil servants complained that they hadn't been paid regularly for a full year and promptly went on strike.[4] The central government, which funded more than half the operating budgets of all Mozambique's municipalities, didn't send money to Beira for a full six months after Simango took office.

There were similar patterns of obstruction in all five municipalities newly governed by the opposition. In Nampula, political scientists working on a report for USAID catalogued the sheer creativity of Frelimo's efforts to stymie the success of Renamo mayors, dubbing the approach "neopatrimonialism." As in Beira, municipal records were carted off to local Frelimo offices or the homes of party leaders, while Maputo withheld disbursements meant to fund salaries, erosion control, and road construction.

The Mapiko Lounge Bar, in Beira, was a municipal office until Daviz Simango won the mayoral election as a candidate for the opposition party Renamo.

Renamo-run towns had their boundaries changed abruptly, reducing the number of voters and taxpayers inside city limits.

A law stipulating a role for central government in municipal offices was selectively enforced in towns run by Renamo, as mayors were stripped of the power to levy taxes on market vendors or control public water fountains, and saw annual inspections by central government officials accelerate to three or four rounds a year. Civil servants working for the city of Ilha de Moçambique had their positions transferred to local offices of the provincial government. Nearly completed water-supply projects ground to a halt, only to become operational five years later—on the day Frelimo's candidate was announced as the winner of the mayoral race. Publicly funded community radio stations were shuttered on the grounds that they were functioning as "propaganda" for Renamo. In Angoche, a sleepy seaside town that was an important slave port under the Portuguese, the government withheld stipends for 120 unemployed elderly residents who volunteered in street-cleaning programs, with the argument that volunteering proved their ability to do real work. Renamo mayors responded in kind, expelling workers they saw as too loyal to Frelimo, only to have them reinstated by their provincial counterparts.

Seeing that endless turf wars with Frelimo were unlikely to produce results Beira's voters might reward with a second term, Simango took a more pragmatic approach. He won over career civil servants by making it a priority to pay them what they were owed, quickly ending the strike that threatened to paralyze the city government, and retained longtime administrators who were willing to stay and share their knowledge.

Faced as he was with an uncooperative central government, Simango's first task was to bolster the city's financial base so that he had some hope of turning the wheels of government without an influx of cash from Maputo. There were attempts to limit graft and self-dealing—"Nobody is allowed to send the cars or the trucks to the garage without [my] permission, nobody is allowed to go to any kind of shop or market to get an invoice without any permission," Simango told his staff as he explained a decision to funnel all municipal revenue through a single bank account—and to generate income where there had been none.[5] He cracked down on tax evasion at the port and introduced new taxes on fuel and on buildings, posting a ledger of the city's receipts and expenses in the lobby of city hall. Simango's deputies introduced competitive bidding for city contracts and required tax collectors to issue a stamped receipt for every payment. Simango appealed directly to foreign donors and nonprofits for project funding and leveraged it on high-visibility measures like improving trash collection and unclogging the drainage canals that flooded the city when it rained.

Beira is sometimes called the "cathedral of the opposition."[6] Historically, much of the city's power, like that of Lourenço Marques or Maputo, derived from links to colonial regimes in Rhodesia (now Zimbabwe) and South Africa. Before independence, some three-quarters of Zimbabwe's imports and exports passed through Beira and Maputo.[7] When, in the late 1970s, Frelimo blocked rail traffic from the apartheid government in Harare, Rhodesian goods had to travel nearly three times as far to port, to Durban, South Africa.

The political scientist Sergio Chichava has called Sofala Province a "thorn in the side" of Frelimo.[8] It was Sofala, along with neighboring Manica, where Afonso Dhlakama and many other key figures in Renamo were born, and where some of the strongest resentment to Frelimo's early policies of nationalization and collective farming crystallized.

One of the most powerful figures in late colonial Beira was Jorge Jardim, a Portuguese businessman and the publisher of the daily Notícias da Beira. Jardim, the godson of Portugal's longtime dictator, António Salazar, had already had a long career as a covert agent and a diplomat in Portugal's colonies.[9] During the war for independence in Mozambique, it was Jardim who spurred the formation of undercover units that staged brutal covert attacks against Frelimo soldiers and civilian supporters.[10] Two members of Jardim's so-called Special Groups would go on to play key roles in the founding of Renamo.[11]

As the war wore on and the Portuguese military strategy seemed less and less likely to prevail, writes Paul Fauvet, a British journalist who went on to edit Mozambique's state news service, Jardim and others began to seek out an alternative path to victory: "If FRELIMO could not be beaten on the battlefield, perhaps it could be cut down in the political arena. It had to be 'proved' that FRELIMO did not represent the majority of Mozambicans. That implied that, in a great hurry, alternative political organisations had to be created, and that a referendum should be held on the future of the country. This latter idea . . . never really got off the ground. But the first part of the plan worked. Mozambique was suddenly full of political parties."[12]

Several of these Portuguese-sponsored parties coalesced into a coalition led by Uria Simango, Daviz's father. Simango was a Protestant minister from Beira who had been a leader of Frelimo's early incursions against the Portuguese in the center of the country.[13] In 1970, when Daviz was six, his father was expelled from Frelimo during a power struggle following the death of Eduardo Mondlane, an early leader of Mozambique's independence movement.

Simango fled to Malawi and returned to Mozambique in 1974 to form the Partido da Coligação Nacional, or PCN, with a group of Frelimo dissidents and ties to Beira's Portuguese elites. Less than a year later, it would be outlawed in an independence treaty that made Frelimo Mozambique's sole political party.[14]

Both Daviz's parents would live out their last days in a reeducation camp in M'telela, in Mozambique's far north. When he was captured, Uria Simango was made to read a twenty-page confession of crimes against the country before an audience of hundreds of Frelimo fighters, journalists, and foreign dignitaries.[15] Later, Simango is said to have recited psalms while he was tortured. Uria Simango and his wife, Celina, were executed months apart in 1979 and 1980.

Daviz Simango and his siblings grew up with relatives in Beira. They wouldn't learn of their parents' executions until months, or perhaps years, after the fact. Lutero, Daviz's eldest brother, recalled writing a letter to the governor of Sofala as a boy in 1981, asking permission for himself and his two brothers to go visit their parents.[16]

When Lutero formed his own political party in Beira more than a decade later, he used the same acronym his father had—PCN—for Partido de Convenção Nacional.

Simango is now in his third term as Beira's mayor. His reputation for clean government has frayed, even among some of those who backed him enthusiastically in his first run. Critics will gladly take you on a tour of plum beachfront parcels developed by the mayor's friends and rattle off the places where Simango now owns large houses (South Africa, Maputo, Lisbon). Simango got his start in the party Lutero founded, PCN, or National Convention Party, ultimately joining a coalition with Renamo that produced his first run for mayor. In Beira, two of his cousins have become city councilmen, a brother-in-law served as his legal adviser, while another brother-in-law became his director of water and sanitation in 2015.[17] One cousin and city councilman, Obedias Simango, wound up in court in 2011 when it was revealed that he'd diverted loans made by the city into a personal account.[18] The money had been earmarked for ten local merchants to build warehouses so they could relocate in a less congested market than the one where they originally operated. At trial, a city employee testified that

Obedias Simango had pressed the merchants to make favorable statements to the judge. Obedias said he'd merely deposited the money in his account so that he could supervise the payments and repayments by the merchants.

Patronage is standard practice in Mozambican politics. In the late 1980s and early 1990s, as the IMF and the World Bank enforced the transition from Marxism to capitalism, the largest state-owned companies were sold to international investors, while hundreds of smaller firms passed into the hands of people connected to Frelimo party leadership.[19] Anxious to claim the wave of privatizations as a free market success, the World Bank and donor countries pushed loans to businesses owned by local elites, even when they knew there was little chance they'd be repaid.[20] Leading figures in Frelimo maneuvered to the center of the country's new capitalist economy. Armando Guebuza, who served as minister of transportation and communications from 1987 to 1994, grew a business empire out of the industries he'd overseen in government: logistics and port management, vehicles and vehicle inspections, public construction. Guebuza's partners, in turn, have included past ministers of the interior, of fisheries, and of tourism.[21] In the words of journalist Marcelo Mosse, musing on the vast web of connections traced through Guebuza's business network, "It seems as if everyone in the establishment is eventually linked to everyone else."[22]

Guebuza, who became president in 2004, spread the largesse among family members too, much as his predecessor Joaquim Chissano had done. One of Guebuza's daughters, Valentina, was one of the richest women in Mozambique by the time she died at thirty-six, thanks largely to her father's position.[23] Afonso Dhlakama, too, has rewarded people close to him—his niece, Ivone Soares, for instance, has risen quickly to lead Renamo's delegation in parliament. Alas, Renamo has never had quite the same opportunities for patronage as the party in power. A dominant theory of Dhlakama's return to war in recent years, in fact, has been that violence is a negotiating tactic to get a big enough pay-off that he can better reward those around him. Political scientists have argued that Simango's footprint in Beira presents a new pattern in Mozambican politics. If Frelimo puts the interests of the party first, and Dhlakama's main test is loyalty to himself, in Simango's movement, family ties rule.[24]

Simango has emerged as an exceptionally popular figure in Beira, with a reputation abroad as Mozambique's best mayor and a string of awards from a South African business magazine to match.[25] Yet at the end of Simango's first term, as he prepared to run for reelection in 2008, party leader Afonso Dhlakama passed him over for the mayoral ticket, claiming that Renamo's base didn't view him as a real member of the party.[26] Many observers saw a leader too insecure to allow a protégé to become popular in his own right. Simango "was just a good manager, but not a good politician," Dhlakama said later, a "kid" incapable of succeeding him as the leader of the party. Besides, Dhlakama himself had made Simango important by giving him a shot at mayor in the first place.[27] In a strange way, Dhlakama's paranoia was vindicated by the kid's response. Simango subsequently ran as an independent, and, after Dhlakama expelled him from Renamo for "breaking party rules," went on to win with 60 percent of the vote—a wider margin than his first victory.[28]

The following year, Simango formed his own political party, Movimento Democrático de Moçambique, known as MDM, and ran for president, winning 8 percent of the vote.[29] Almost immediately after MDM was created, it attracted, in the words of a man I spoke to in Maputo, "the thinkers of Renamo," including Daviz's brother Lutero and Maria Moreno, the head of Renamo's delegation in parliament.[30] After more than a decade with only one viable opposition party in Mozambique, the "thinkers of

Renamo" could finally choose their party affiliation on other grounds, and many chose to leave.

At times, MDM has seemed to surpass Renamo as the most credible threat to Frelimo's one-party rule. Simango hasn't improved on his first showing in national elections, but his party has ridden a wave of support from young urban voters to win mayoral races in Quelimane and Nampula. Today, three of MDM's seventeen deputies in parliament represent Maputo, where Renamo has never won a seat.[31]

In Simango's first term, he led a Renamo city council majority against Frelimo's very first experience of being an opposition party. The second time around, he was an independent candidate without a caucus: "It was Frelimo, Renamo, and GDB all against the mayor," he told me when I visited his office in 2016, referring to another small opposition party. Simango is now in his third term, and his own party, MDM, controls a majority of the seats on Beira's city council.

"If you get thrown into the water, you better know how to swim," he said, hunching over wearily in a navy blazer. It was eleven o'clock on a Tuesday morning, but Simango yawned repeatedly and said he hadn't slept. The day before, I'd read in the paper about a spat between the mayor's office and the district government over the renovation of a pair of elementary school classrooms in one of Beira's poor, outlying neighborhoods, on the road to the airport.[32] Simango had visited the school for a ribbon cutting a few days earlier, but neither the school principal nor any representative from the district education office—under Frelimo control—was there to take part.[33] "District government accuses city of usurping power," the headline read, "after Simango inaugurates infrastructure that doesn't belong to the city."

Decentralization of public services has been a halting, gradual undertaking in Beira. Agreements to transfer the machinery of

health, electricity, and transportation to the city have been marked
by similar disputes. Public education remains under the purview
of the central government. The schools are managed through a
district office that reports to Maputo. In this instance, both the
district government and the city of Beira claimed to have funded
the construction. No one disputed that additional classrooms
were an unequivocal good; the argument was about who should
be allowed to take credit.

Simango is a big, affable man with a gentle way of speaking
and a penchant for talking about himself in the third person. He
laughed out loud when I asked him if there had been other examples of this kind of friction over the optics of providing public
goods. Once, he said, he'd visited a school for a desk giveaway,
only to see the principal fired the next day. "We've given schools
desks and had the students shut in the classrooms so that they
wouldn't be shown with Daviz Simango giving away desks." When
top brass from city hall delivered ambulances paid for by the
European Union to the hospital, they found no staff downstairs
to accept them.[34] Then, looking up, Simango said, he'd seen nurses
watching from windows on the hospital's upper floors. "So we left
the ambulances with the neighborhood secretary," Simango said.
"As soon as I left, you heard an ambulance leaving the hospital,
sirens on, going to get a patient."

"There are lots of episodes," he muttered, shaking his head.
"Lots."

For twelve years, Frelimo—and later Renamo—had voted repeatedly against the municipal budgets he sent up, forging a compromise only when the law allowed for dissolution of the city
council if a budget failed to pass. Then, in his third term, things
shifted. "They knew that if the city council was dissolved, Daviz
Simango would be up for election again, and he'd win a majority on the council. So they would all be out of work. So . . . at
least once a year, they knew they had to approve the municipal

budget." He laughed. He said 2016 was the first time his annual budget was approved on the first vote.

One afternoon, I dropped by the offices of Beira's daily newspaper, *Diário de Moçambique*, to chat with the editor, Francisco Muiange, and flip through the paper's archives. Muiange was nonplussed by MDM's basic argument over the *sedes de bairros*—namely, that there was something wrong, prima facie, when property belonging to the government passed into private hands. Simango's election presented a novel case, but fundamentally, Muiange viewed the whole problem as another messy piece of Mozambique's transition from Marxism to multiparty democracy. "Lots of things are that way," he said. "The Frelimo headquarters in Maputo, wherever Frelimo meets elsewhere—they're all buildings that once belonged to the state. But in that period between 1974 and 1975"—when Mozambique became independent—"there was no documentation whatsoever.

"So Frelimo used the government's real estate as though it was always going to be a one-party state. And when there started to be multiple parties, they tried to register the buildings that had been used for public administration to show that they belonged to the party. As long as Frelimo ran the government, it stayed peaceful. It wasn't a problem for them to use the party's buildings for public administration. But as soon as someone else won the elections . . ."

Muiange shrugged. Even Frelimo had fallen prey to similar schemes. He told the story of a former provincial governor in Beira who discovered while in office that his official residence didn't have a plaque that said "Patrimonio do Estado" or a legal title saying the building belonged to the government. He registered the house in his own name, Muiange said, and when he left office, he kept it. Frelimo protested but, ultimately, the party lost out.

"There are lots of things that supposedly belong to the state that from a legal point of view *don't*," Muiange said coolly. "So Frelimo just says, 'Where's your documentation?'"

As the standoff over Beira's municipal buildings wore on, the case's long, contested timeline unspooled before a national audience. In the 1970s, the buildings that became Beira's *sedes de bairros* hosted Frelimo's local party cells, *grupos dinamizadores*, or "dynamizing groups."[35] By 1998, when Mozambique had transitioned to multiparty elections and passed a series of laws to strengthen municipal government, the *sedes de bairros* were being used to administer basic public services—leased, Frelimo would contend later, from the party by the Frelimo-run city government.[36] But it's unclear whether the buildings belonged to the party or to the state.

After independence, Frelimo's ascendant Marxist government nationalized Mozambican-owned rental properties alongside tens of thousands of houses and buildings that belonged to Portuguese settlers and the colonial state.[37] It later defined a process for divestiture to allow people to purchase the properties from the government at an affordable price. This is the process Frelimo claimed to have used to appropriate the *sedes* in Beira, except the dates didn't seem to line up. Records used in the court case point to four or five separate occasions on which the buildings were said to have passed from the state to the party.

The editorial page of Mozambique's leading independent paper, *Savana*, pointed out that Frelimo could not have legally leased the buildings to the city government in 1998, because the party itself was a tenant of the national government—it hadn't yet gone through the divestiture process.[38] What, then, of the back rent the court said the city of Beira owed to Frelimo? asked José Cruz, a leading MDM representative on the city council. "Let's say Frelimo was in fact a tenant of the Administração do Parque Imobiliário do Estado"—APIE, the agency that oversees government real estate holdings. "What is wrong is that [Frelimo] now wants to sublease these buildings to the [city], the entity that represents the state," Cruz said.

"Why should we have to rent state houses from a private entity, when we are the state?"[39]

Frelimo argued it had registered the buildings in the party's name in January 2003, well before Simango's election.[40] But Frelimo also made a request to the governor of Sofala to transfer the buildings to the party in June. The court ruled that the buildings passed into Frelimo ownership six weeks after that, on July 29. It wasn't until nearly a year and a half later that APIE published a notice in the *Diário* advising Beira of Frelimo's request for the transfer and giving citizens thirty days to object.

The city of Beira, meanwhile, produced documents showing that the *sedes* had been listed as municipal property at the time of the handover from Simango's predecessor—a Frelimo mayor—in 2004. Moreover, Simango argued, real estate records in the dispute listed addresses that didn't match the buildings Frelimo claimed. "[That's] an element that the court should consider," he said. In two cases, the buildings in question hadn't yet been built on the date Frelimo claimed its ownership began. They were constructed later, using municipal funds. In that case, observers asked, shouldn't the real question be how much else has Frelimo taken from the state?

A third layer of the dispute focused on judicial process: during the standoff, the parties couldn't agree which court had jurisdiction over the case. In December 2006, Sofala's provincial court ordered the city of Beira to cede the disputed buildings to Frelimo and pay the party a $30,000 penalty for lost rent.[41] Simango refused and swiftly appealed to the supreme court.[42] For three years, the case was in purgatory, while the city government continued to occupy the *sedes*. It finally landed in the high court in July of 2010. Two days later, the provincial court moved to execute its 2006 order and seize the buildings, five at a time, igniting the protests that brought the process, once again, to a standstill. "How strange," Simango told an independent weekly. "It was only . . . days ago that our case got to the Supreme Court."

The judge in the provincial court acknowledged that his order was provisory—should his ruling be struck down, the buildings would revert to the city of Beira—but the protesters would have none of it, continuing to cook over open fires in the street beside each *sede*, even as the police gathered around them in force. "We won't leave here," they sang, "come and kill us then."[43]

At the end of a week, the court had failed to hand Frelimo a single building.[44] The judge yielded to popular pressure, calling a meeting with Simango and Gilberto Correia, Frelimo's legal representative. At Simango's request, the court decided to commission an expert report on the property records in the case. Then, in a strange turn, suddenly it was Simango who wanted to let the provincial court handle the matter, while Correia accused the judge of "meddling with the case" when it was already in the hands of the supreme court.[45]

The mood remained tense for weeks. Then president Armando Guebuza met with Simango in Maputo, "to avoid bloodshed," as one paper put it.[46] By the end of July, even Renamo officials had joined cause with Frelimo in calling on Simango to give up and accusing him of using his supporters as pawns.[47] Manuel Joaquim, one of Simango's deputies, countered that Beirenses would protect the *sedes* until there was a "final verdict that we feel is just."[48]

Eventually, Dom Jaime Gonçalves, the archbishop of Beira, stepped gingerly into the fray. The archbishop, who spent years as the lead mediator in negotiations that brought an end to Mozambique's civil war in 1992, scrupulously avoided taking sides and simply encouraged the city to move on. The *sedes* were built more than sixteen years ago, he reasoned. "The city's needs have out-grown the buildings in question. The time has come to work to-gether and build anew." Dom Jaime was worried about "a situation where every one moves the coals to cook his own fish." That, he said, "isn't good for anybody."[49]

On November 16, 2010, the building that would become the Mapiko appeared on page two of the *Diário de Moçambique* along-side a forlorn-looking close-up of Daviz Simango before a micro-phone.[50] Without completing the property records report it had agreed to in July, the provincial court had abruptly issued a sec-ond order requiring the city of Beira to hand over the buildings later that week. Simango's appeal was still pending before the su-preme court, he protested. Yet twenty-four hours later, the trans-fers began in peace.[51] The handoff was completed by the end of the week; Simango said, grudgingly, that he'd accepted the idea of handing over the *sedes* to avoid getting people killed. At a rally in the MDM stronghold of Munhava, the mayor tried to glean some sense of victory and partisan pride from the setback. "The People see that Frelimo took over public buildings. We're not going to run after them because we know there will come a day when they'll be judged for it. . . . Don't be ashamed of what's hap-pening today," he urged Beirenses. "We're going to get new *sedes* built with our own hands."[52]

"Our challenge here in Beira is forever, even if we have to work beneath a cashew tree," he said.[53]

After meeting with Simango, in February 2016, I took a tour of Beira's Chiveve district, made up of eight neighborhoods that form the core of Beira's old "cement" city. The district's current *chefe do posto*, Manuel dos Santos Mussanema, was at the helm of a battered white pickup. Across the city, thirteen new *sedes de bairros* had been built to replace all but one of the fourteen lost in the court case. In Munhava, the city had built a new *sede de bairro* next door to the old one Frelimo won back in court, which now languished, unused, missing windows and doors. Chaimite's open-air *sede*, across the street from the Mapiko, was the only one left unbuilt—it was not under Simango's proverbial cashew tree, but shaded by a row of Indian almonds.

"We used to work in that building, and then it was turned into a discotheque," Mussanema said. He explained that he'd gotten to know the mayor a few years earlier, while he was trying to complete a philosophy degree at Beira's Universidade Pedagógica.[54] The department required him to submit five bound copies of his thesis, and he needed $100 to pay his last fees. "Out of desperation," he said, he got hold of Daviz Simango's number and sent him a pleading text message, hoping he would be able to give him a loan. Asked how a twenty-one-year-old stranger got the mayor's personal number, Mussanema said, "He's a very simple [mayor]: he gives his number to anyone."

In Bairro Quinto, we stopped at the newly constructed Posto Administrativo de Chiveve, formerly housed in the Mapiko. It was a simple cement bungalow where a group of cops waited in the shade of the courtyard next to a row of impounded *tchopelas*—three-wheeled covered mototaxis. Two benches stood against the wall of the front porch. Above them, it was easy to see the simple things Vicente missed at the *sede de bairro* in Chaimite: inside one window, a tidy row of lost ID cards was displayed so they would be visible from outside. On the wall, there were lists of eighteen-year-olds summoned to register for the draft, and marriage announcements and "household" notices that allow people to apply for employment benefits for their family members.

The furnishings inside were minimal, and dilapidated, yet they were enough to confer a basic dignity on the notion of administering public services. There were locking doors, a large wooden counter, and behind it, two employees sitting at desks absentmindedly watching a cooking show on TVM. There was a bathroom, a kitchen, and ancient, creaking filing cabinets.

Mussanema said that Beira's civil servants did include some Frelimo party members, despite oft-repeated critiques that the mayor was just as partisan as Frelimo.[55] "The [mayor] doesn't care that much. He doesn't like to, what? Get things mixed up. He wants to show how real democracy works. Political cohabitation," he said.

Later in the day, I returned to Chaimite and found Mr. Vicente and his colleagues doing a brisk business in declarations for school registration and bank accounts, with a line of people standing by the desk holding open passports, *bilhetes de identificação*, and ragged pieces of paper bearing names and addresses.

Periodically, Vicente reached into the lone drawer remaining in either desk and fished change out of a small plastic bag. The all-important *carimbo*, a wooden stamp marked "Conselho Municipal de Beira," sat on the desk as he worked, the thump of ink against paper punctuating each transaction.

When the office closed at three thirty, I sat beside Vicente, who leaned back in a cream-colored guayabera and black loafers, a pen clasped between long, slender fingers. The Mapiko, resplendent pink in bright sun, loomed over his right shoulder. "As long as Frelimo was in power, the neighborhoods had no problems finding offices," Vicente complained. There were lots of houses that had no plaque saying "Patrimonio do Estado." "How is it that this idea came up just now?"

At three forty-five, two young men approached in tank tops and shorts, hoping to get declarations. Mr. Vicente grabbed at his own embroidered collared shirt and gave the men a disappointed, quizzical look. "Come back tomorrow with shirts!" he scolded them. "*Assim?*" he asked, gesturing at their outfits, incredulous. Like this?

The people of Chaimite, Vicente explained, continue to complain about the lack of an actual, physical *sede de bairro*. "When it's raining," he said, "they come here and find no one. 'Where are the civil servants who work here?' They come to a public agency expecting to be served. But when it's raining, no one stays here getting wet just to give out information!

"Some ask, 'When will you get offices?' 'What do you do when it rains?' 'Why are you working like this?'" Vicente said. "Our answer is always the same: 'The day will come when we will get offices.'"

Vicente is a veteran of the colonial civil service. After the civil war, in the 1990s, he rose to the top of the city administration, becoming chief of staff under a Frelimo mayor. When it changed to Renamo, he said, "I got kicked out." Vicente struck me as a consummate bureaucrat in the best sense of the word. He saw his post as a civil servant, however humble it might be, as a vocation, a calling. By sheer will and respect for the office, after all, Vicente managed to enforce a dress code in the midst of Chaimite's outdoor market, even if the only perimeter he could erect around the *sede de bairro* was a psychological one.

"Frelimo is in the minority now," Vicente said. "They don't take a liking to anything MDM does. I'll try to explain," he said, a glint in his eye. "Here in Mozambique, in any part of the public administration, the bosses are from Frelimo: those are what you call *lugares de confiança*"—positions of trust. "When I'm in public administration, I put political parties to the side," he said resolutely. "To the point that people have doubts—'Is he from Frelimo? Is he from MDM? PDD?' That's what all civil servants should do."

"These complaints [about the *sede* being outside]," Vicente went on, "it doesn't just hurt the city; it hurts us, because when it rains, we suffer. When it's hot and there's lots of dust, we suffer! And we write it in our reports: please, accelerate the construction of . . ."

He trailed off. "If we had a house, we could have chairs. As it is, three, four, five people show up, and they all have to stand. It doesn't work."

Vicente packed up the stamp along with the plastic bag holding the day's receipts, slung his chair over his shoulder and carried it to the soda distributor to store overnight, and headed home.

9

The Selling Life

MAPUTO

I met Bento because he wanted to buy my bicycle. I was wrestling with my bike lock on a corner of Avenida 24 de Julho, in Maputo, when Bento appeared, sauntering down the sidewalk, oblivious to the heat. Bento was on the younger, charming end of fourteen. He wore flip-flops and a gray T-shirt that came nearly to his knees and carried several dozen corn muffins in the bottom of a clear plastic sack, which he swung about with abandon as though it were full of dead leaves. Reaching the corner, he stopped to greet a boy a couple of years his senior who sold phone credit. Bento nodded at me with his chin, grinning.

"*Amigo*, I like your bike," he said. "Why don't you sell me your bicycle and buy a car?" Bento said *amigo* with unsettling authority—pleadingly, as the best vendors and minibus touts do—as if to win me over with willful camaraderie.

"I'm not selling it."

"How much will you sell me that bicycle for?" he repeated.

"How many muffins have you got?"

"Fifty." I made what I thought was an obvious joke and told Bento I would only sell my bicycle for at least seventy corn muffins. He was unfazed: "I'll give you money to top it off."

"I only accept muffins," I said.

"Then give it to me. Your race should have cars, anyway."

"You know, not all white people have enough money to buy cars as they please."

"Yeah, I know that not every *branco* can just buy cars, but it's the right of your race to have a car. Only we *negros* go around on foot. It's our right to suffer."

"Why is that?" I asked.

"It's the law of our race."

I was speechless. Bento gave me his phone number, asked me to "beep" him with a missed call so that he'd have mine, and continued on his daily route. "We'll talk," he assured me. He saved my phone number as "Branco"—"White." I rode away in wonder. He was like a fourteen-year-old prophet, frankly laying out a worldview that had been imposed upon him by a childhood on the streets of Maputo. There was plenty of truth in it, too. Other than the occasional backpacker, you rarely saw *brancos* outside of their cars unless it was on the terrace of a sidewalk café or on the brief walk from a parking spot to an apartment building.

Mozambique's postwar prosperity has paid for renovations at Maputo's most famous colonial hotel and erected a state-of-the-art office tower for the cell phone provider Vodacom. Chauffeurs in Mercedes SUVs and luxury sedans cruise downtown displaying an aggression toward pedestrians that borders on the pathological. Real estate prices in neighborhoods like Sommerschield approach those in Brooklyn and San Francisco, with houses selling for upward of $1 million. Yet Bento didn't seem to dwell on any of this. He was just stating the facts.

Two days later I ran into Bento early in the morning on Avenida Eduardo Mondlane, his sack twice as full as it had been

Shoppers and vendors cross the street near the Mercado Central in Baixa, Maputo's bustling downtown shopping district.

when we met. We stood chatting by the tailgate of a parked jeep, and I invited him across the street to have an egg sandwich. "*Deixa lá,*" he said. Let it be. "Now is the time to sell." He gestured bashfully at his clothes—another ragged T-shirt and shorts—as if to say, "I can't be seen in this." "I don't work Sundays," he said. "One Sunday we'll get together, when I have a long, free afternoon. We can go *passear.*"

Bento was born in 1997, in the bush outside Pambara, a crossroads about ten hours north of Maputo, in Inhambane Province. He was raised by his father's mother. His older brother, charged with looking after him while his grandmother farmed during the day, simply brought him along to class beginning at age three; before he turned ten, Bento had already gone as far as he could go in the primary school closest to home. After sixth grade, a few of his brothers' peers went on to work as porters and haulers for Chinese logging operations. Most started families young and farmed dry patches of cassava and beans. Bento wasn't old enough to haul logs, and he didn't feel like farming, so he decided to come to Maputo.

According to the national census, along with Gaza, to the west, Inhambane supplies more migrants to Maputo than anywhere else in the country. On the whole, the southern half of Mozambique, which includes both provinces, is vastly more developed than the north: taking a bus from one end of the country to the other, you can track the growth of corrugated steel roofs, stereos, and shops for motorcycle parts as you move closer to the capital. But most of Inhambane is still remote and underdeveloped. As recently as 2012, there were whole *distritos*, or counties, without a doctor. Until you reach Inchope, more than six hundred miles from Maputo, a single paved road cuts a path through the countryside. Gray scrub and coconut plantations are interspersed here and there with houses made of reeds and gnarled cashew trees, plumes of smoke rising from barely tended fires. Sacks of charcoal and stacks of cut firewood line the roadside. It is a form of commerce that requires no signs and no immediate oversight. If a car stops, a child or a woman will come running from the nearest house to make a sale. Gathering firewood, sold in bales of 5 or 10 meticais (15 to 30 cents) over the better part of a year, is how Bento saved enough money to come to Maputo. He had a total of 800 mets ($30) when he started his trip.

Half Bento's savings went immediately to bus fare. While the bus idled in Pambara, the other passengers reached out the windows to buy sodas and cookies and cashews from teenagers holding their merchandise over their heads. Bento peeled off another 100 mets to treat himself. "In the spirit of going along with other people," he explained. "You won't manage to make the whole trip sitting like that"—he crossed his arms—"while everybody else is eating. You just won't." Bento bought bread, Coca-Cola, and cashews.

The bus from Pambara stopped at the Junta, a swarming open-air depot on the northern edge of the capital. Bento stepped down into a parking lot filled with tractor trailers hauling produce from South Africa, fifty-pound sacks of potatoes and onions testament to the difficulty Mozambican farmers face in competing with agribusiness from their neighbor to the south. Bento had already spent more than half his savings, which left him just under $15. He wandered back to the main road and watched minibuses heading into the city. Touts leaned out and rapped on the sliding doors, shouting their destinations impatiently. Crowds of people pushed past him to board. "They were saying 'Xikelene, Xikelene'— I didn't know what Xikelene was," Bento said, laughing at his younger self. He got on one bound for Xipamanine, then walked around the neighborhood's endless market asking for work. Before long, a boy selling bean fritters from a bucket brought him to the house of a surly fat woman—*minha senhora*, he called her— who agreed to take him in. The job interview went something like this:

"Where are you from?"

"Pambara."

"I only want someone who doesn't rob or steal."

"I don't steal."

In this way, Bento joined the ranks of Maputo's ubiquitous hard-boiled-egg vendors, nearly all of whom are school-age boys. In the mornings, he went and bought charcoal and four dozen eggs at the market and rounded up some cardboard to start a fire. He sold each egg for 6 meticais, so that the last dozen was sold for profit. If he managed to sell quickly, he repeated the exercise in the afternoons. In the best-case scenario, Bento could make 44 meticais, about $1.50, after selling eight dozen eggs and turning over the first 100 mets in profit to his madam. But he often finished the day out with a dozen or eighteen eggs left over and went home with not even 100 mets for *minha senhora*. There were nonpaying customers and other occupational hazards.

Mashangaan, or people from Gaza Province, Bento says, think that Manhambane—people from Inhambane—are stupid. Though they aren't from the capital themselves, the Mashangaan have become a sort of elite among migrants to Maputo. They have a longer history in the city, dating back to its colonial days, and their language, Tsonga, has displaced the local Ronga as Maputo's lingua franca. "In Xipamanine, I suffered, because I'd just gotten here: a guy might eat your egg and get short with you if you ask for your money before he's finished. He'll say, 'Hey, do you work for the government or something?'" In Maputo, Bento quickly fell victim to his own naïveté.

On one occasion, early in the morning when the eggs were fresh, Bento was making his rounds downtown in Maputo's Central Market, a cavernous colonial pavilion with a rusty corrugated roof and mounds of produce displayed on tables fashioned from shipping pallets. Near the entrance, Bento stood by and watched as two older boys ate four eggs each in quick succession. They were fifteen or sixteen, Bento figured, in retrospect. "Hey! These eggs are big!" one gushed. "They're hot too," his friend added. "Ya! How much have we eaten?" Twenty-four meticais each, Bento told them. They wanted to eat more eggs, they said, but they wanted bread to go with them. Could Bento go get them bread? It's not uncommon for a stranger to ask a small boy to run an errand, even in the city, or for customers to make this sort of above-and-beyond demand of vendors in the informal sector—often, it's the price of doing business.

One of the boys produced a purple 20 meticais note and gave it to Bento. "I took two steps, and then one of them said, 'Hey, wait—how do we know you're going to get the bread? We're giving you our money and you're not giving us anything in return. Either you need to give us your eggs or give us your money.'" Incredulous at his former self, Bento said he'd given them the eggs—three dozen of them—though they hadn't yet paid for those they'd eaten. "I didn't know!" He laughed raucously. "I didn't know!" When he came back with the bread, of course, the boys were nowhere to be found, and Bento sat down and cried, realizing he'd been had. Several matronly produce vendors came and asked him what happened, and Bento told his story. "Here in Maputo," one of the women said, "you need to open your eyes."

Besides his daily pay, the terms of Bento's employment allowed him room and board and 500 mets, or $16, at the end of each

Bento is one of an army of thousands of boys selling goods on the streets of Maputo and most other Mozambican towns. Here, two teenagers from Gaza Province sell used clothing, called *calamidades*, or "calamities," shorthand for the government office—the Department for the Prevention and Combat of Natural Calamities—that distributed them, along with food aid, during the civil war.[1]

month. The problem was that his madam and he didn't see these conditions in quite the same way. Room meant cardboard on the floor of his madam's kitchen, and board meant dinner. If Bento failed to produce 100 mets at the end of each day, which he invariably did at least once a week, his madam considered that he'd been "looking after his own business," which meant that she didn't pay him his monthly wage.

In the end, his *senhora*'s miserly suspicion amounted to a self-fulfilling prophecy. Because he couldn't expect to eat before the end of the day, or to receive his pay at the end of the month, Bento ended up doing as much of his "own business" as he could. With one batch of eggs safely behind him at noon, he began to hang out at the Central Market, where he could earn enough for lunch by toting around shoppers' parcels. Whatever clothes and possessions he accumulated, he hid with peers whose madams were a bit more lenient.

Telling all this with four years' hindsight, Bento was remarkably even-keeled. He possessed something like the opposite of entitlement, a fatalism that ran far deeper than the portraits of teenage nihilists we see on television. His was the only path Bento knew for boys in a similar situation, and he didn't seem to preoccupy himself with its injustice. Contentment was clearly his survival mechanism, yet somehow, I still wanted him to feel the outrage that came so easily to me, the indignation of the rich on behalf of the poor.

Most of the circumstances that defined Bento's life on arrival in Maputo were actually illegal: he was too young to work, and he was paid less than half the minimum wage. His whole industry of sidewalk vending was outlawed, and he had a "right," as a minor, to a battery of things he did not, in fact, have. The norms were so far outside the law that it made you wonder whether the law did any good at all. Didn't such a state of affairs simply undermine the government's credibility on the issues where it did have some traction?

Traffic safety offers a good example of the problem. Thorough enforcement of the rules would require police to issue violations to almost every passing vehicle. The law calls for all sorts of things that you do not commonly find on the road in Mozambique: seat belts, no more than three people per row in back seats, emissions control, functional headlights. In 2011, a law was passed requiring safety vests and triangles for every vehicle. Strangely, given that so much was wrong with the average car on the road, the law on safety vests was strictly and immediately enforced. Many people saw this simply as a ploy used by traffic cops to collect more bribes. In Mocuba, a small town in the north, I remember seeing something similar occur with motorcycle helmets. Overnight and without explanation, helmets were in great demand: clusters of three and four *taxistas*—motorcycle taxi drivers—would share a single one, trading off between fares. They did this, they said, to avoid a fine that had suddenly become the police's top priority. Still, not a single passenger wore one, so that you might see a helmeted *taxista* ferrying a helmetless mother and her two children on the back of his bike, the hair of all three passengers blowing in the wind. To enforce that requirement uniformly would have brought Mocuba to a halt. No one would have been able to do their errands, to get a ride when they were late for work. Corruption served as a sort of compromise between reality and the law.

More broadly, you might say that the same was true of other forms of opportunism like the ones that weighed on Bento in Xipamanine. With so much reality in supply, the force of the law's demand was next to nil. "The problem here is that no one respects the minimum wages," I heard my landlord in Maputo say one Saturday afternoon, looking up from a newspaper. "In the informal sector, no one makes that."

"Ah—yes," his wife answered knowingly. "But who will pay it?"

Bento continued to sell eggs for seven months, until he couldn't tolerate his *senhora*'s stinginess any longer. Then he found another house, in the neighborhood of Mafalala, where he sold *bajia*, or bean fritters, typically served on a long white roll, as the filling in a greasy, dry sandwich. Selling *bajias*, things were not nearly as bad as they had been in the egg house, but Bento often had to stay out until eleven or midnight to sell out, and his unconventional education continued apace. "At that hour, there's no one in the streets. Only police and *molwenes*"—thugs.

"How can you tell if someone is a *molwene*?" I asked.

"You can't—that's the problem. There are some *molwenes* who wear shirts and ties. You'd never think they were *molwenes*. It's the truth!" By now, Bento knows the demographic well: playboys, well dressed, a few years older than he is. *Molwenes* are suave, arrogant, insistent. They call you *amigo*, "my friend," or John—a bit of slang that has crept over the border from South Africa. Their most common ploy is to present themselves as customers.

Bento told me the story of three *molwenes* he'd run into down on Maputo's seaside promenade, the *marginal*. The *marginal* is that strange brand of urban property that seems to defy the laws of real estate. It's the most picturesque, and also the most dangerous, stretch of land in downtown Maputo, a meandering stone-walled road by the ocean with rows of coconut palms overlooking the whitecaps. *Molwenes* abound. These particular *molwenes* beckoned Bento and ate three breads with five *bajias* each. They told him to sit down and insisted when he refused. When he asked to be paid, they only teased him: "Man, you've got some fancy clothes, kid. What do you need our money for?" They grabbed at his collar and at his pants, and then one found the thick knot of change in Bento's second pair of pants. Your second pair of pants? I asked. "I always walk with two pairs of pants," Bento explained, with just this sort of situation in mind. He was beginning to "open his eyes," as the woman at the Central Market had advised. When the *molwene* got ahold of his cash, Bento tried to flee, only to be slapped and held back by the collar. He bit the arm that held him and received a kick in the shin, at which point a group of police officers showed up.

Police: "What's happening here?"

Molwene: "Nothing. This is my little brother; we're just playing around."

Police, to Bento: "What's happening?"

Bento: "Yeah, this is my brother. Everything's cool." You won't really have trouble with a *molwene* until you try to get them arrested, Bento says. "It's better to let them be, because you know you're going to see them again. If you get a *molwene* arrested, the next thing your friends will hear about you is that you're dead." Instead, covering up for the *molwene* earned Bento a kind of begrudging truce, though he never got paid for those three sandwiches. Bento saw the *molwene* once, soon after their scuffle, and greeted him as kind of a peace offering. He got no response. The second time he saw him, he tried again. "Now he knows me," Bento concluded, with a funny kind of pride.

Even after five years on the street, Bento still has problems with *molwenes*. Sometimes the ruses are complex, seemingly improvised among several different people: "You sell one muffin on the sidewalk, and a *molwene* says he has friends who want to buy them too. So they take you into a bar or to a stoop where a bunch of them are hanging out together. They eat their fill, *a vontade*"—to their satisfaction. "Then you ask for your money, and they tell you to relax. Then they get up and leave, one by one. But they always choose someone else who will pay their portion of the bill. By the end, only one is left, and he offers you 20 meticais. You say, what about all the rest? And he says 'I only ate four.' You get mad, and another older boy comes along, a friendly stranger. '*Moço*,' he says. 'Boy, what happened?' You tell him. The stranger gets angry with the last person from the group. They argue, and maybe they'll even start to tussle, and then the guy runs. 'Catch him! Catch him!' the other one says, and no one does anything. So you're left with no money and no muffins, and the stranger still pretends he's your friend: 'Sorry, kid. You've been conned.'

"The story's over," Bento concluded. "That's life here."

One day in December 2007, Bento and a few friends in his line of work took off early and went exploring. Riding on the back of a truck, they got as far as Ressano Garcia, Mozambique's main border crossing with South Africa, which lies 60 miles northwest of Maputo. They goofed off and ate snacks while watching cars laden with goods trickle out of customs back toward Mozambique. On the side of the road, men approached Mozambicans headed the other way: "Do you want to go South Africa? You want to go to South Africa?" Bento was intrigued.

The following week, shortly before Christmas, Bento informed his *senhora* that he needed to go home to Inhambane—"when in fact, no! I wanted to go to South Africa!" Perhaps Manhambane aren't so stupid after all. He went to Ressano Garcia once more and began shopping around. "When you go without documents, it's not expensive [to go to South Africa]," Bento says. "Five hundred meticais! I told a man that I only had two hundred. I told him that I had come with my father, but that my father had disappeared and left me behind. 'But, the place where you are going, you know it?' 'Yeah, I know it,' I told him. Pronto. From South Africa to Durban, it's 100 mets, converted to rand."

Bento's self-assurance was disarming. Even as he told me this story, four years later, he was barely five feet tall, with a high, raspy voice. His skin had the soft, pliant glow that we leave behind in puberty and never recover.

From Nelspruit, on the South African side of the border, Bento got on a *combi* (South Africa's name for the minibus) to "Deh-bahn"—Durban—where he repeated his first day in Maputo, walking around in search of work. "I don't have work," a woman told him, "but come to my house and sleep, and then tomorrow you can go out looking." "I took a bath, I had some food, and I slept there." The house was grand: tile, carpeting, hot water, plusher beds than he'd ever slept on. He never found work. Instead, he stayed for three months, doing odd jobs around the house until the woman gave him money to come back to Maputo.

In Mafalala, Bento's *senhora* took him back in without asking questions, and he returned to selling *bajia* and dodging the *molwenes* downtown. If he sold out early, Bento hung out near the Central Market until dinnertime, to avoid being given extra work at home, and to avoid being told, when business was slow, that he ought be working harder. The following Christmas, Bento again told his *senhora* that he needed to go home to Inhambane. This time, he did. It was the first time he'd been back since coming to Maputo.

"When I go home, I'm famous," Bento says. "People say 'Hey, John, we want to drink something, come on, pay a round.' They don't know anything about Maputo. They even ask, 'Is there sand in Maputo?' as if the whole city was paved with asphalt and bricks." Bento seemed to revel in the absurdity of the question. He laughed vigorously. Outside the old colonial streets and the city's main corridors, Maputo is filled with sand, just like Pambara. "They think things are nice like that, and when I tell them, 'You don't know how we suffer there,' they say, 'Ah, we knew you were you going to say that.'"

"I tell them, 'You think it's easy, but in the minibuses in Maputo, you can't even get a seat. People are sticking their little heads out.'" Bento mimed limbs and heads coming out of minibus windows. "'You can get in as clean as can be, and when you get out, you're already dirty.'" Bento was aghast, and he changed the subject.

"In your country, are there people who don't speak Portuguese?" Earlier, he had asked me if the United States spoke Portuguese or English, but here, the assumption was that if they spoke English, then perhaps they *also* spoke Portuguese. Very few people in my country speak Portuguese, I told him. Bento pondered this for a second, then asked a question that had been on his mind for some time. "Myfriend," he said, pronouncing it as one word, "what does it mean, after all?"

It means *meu amigo*, I told Bento, and watched his eyes widen with wonder.

Bento had grown up saying "myfriend" as a matter of course. In Pambara, it was what you said to the Chinese contractors building the road, and nearby, in Vilanculos, chockablock with South African vacationers, it was what you said to the tourists walking down the beach, to ask them for money or to sell them seashells. It was also what you said to your Mozambican friends, but no one knew what it meant. "Once, I said 'myfriend' to a Boer"—a white South African ("they're all big and tall," Bento promised me)—"and he answered me in my language, Tswa: 'Who's *myfriend*? Am I *myfriend*? I'll beat you up!'" Bento fled the Boer's threat without responding. "All the other English I know—'howareyou I'm fine,' 'where you go'—I learned here in Maputo."

"Knowing" other snatches of English did not mean that Bento had any idea what they meant—only, like "myfriend," that he could mimic them convincingly. Most of his education in the capital must have occurred in a similar fashion: learning to ingratiate himself with the *molwenes*, to hustle after a sale, to dodge the suspicions of a mistrustful *senhora*. All of these skills relied on nothing so much as a knack for acting.

*   *   *

At two p.m., when I called Bento to go *passear*, as we'd planned, he'd already sold all but two of the day's muffins. I met him in front of a KFC restaurant—there are three in Maputo—at a street corner downtown known as *punto final*, "the last stop," where hordes of people jostle for seats in *xapas* to the outskirts of the city. Bento sidled up nonchalantly amid the confusion, muffins draped over his shoulder. *"Amigo! Como vai?"* Bento shrugged off the last two muffins and said he'd buy them from his *senhora* himself. *"Não faz caso,"* he said—don't worry about it. He still had outstanding debts to collect from customers he'd seen that morning, but he would come back for those later. In the meantime, Bento wanted to show me his house. His *senhora*'s daughter wanted to meet me. A few days earlier, Bento said he'd used me as an alibi when he came home with a suitcase to keep his clothes in. "My friend the *branco* bought it for me," he told his madam. Having any savings of his own would rouse her suspicions.

As we walked, Bento asked me about my bicycle again. Most of our route was taken up with my attempt to explain to him why it is that although bicycles are just as expensive in the United States as in Maputo, most everyone has one, or could afford one if they wanted to.

"Have you ever heard the word *economia*?"

"No. What's that?"

I tried to explain what an economy is: "An economy is . . . an economy is . . . when you add up all the people in the whole country working, buying, selling . . ." I had no idea whether I was making any sense at all, but he took it in eagerly.

"Ya," he said. *"É complicado."* On our way, Bento got a phone call from his older brother, who works as a logger in Inhambane. This was the first I'd heard of Bento's immediate family.

He chattered in Tswa and laughed infectiously. His brother was calling from high up in a tree, which was the only place he could get service.

We entered his neighborhood through a narrow alley bisected by a gutter that opened up onto a ring of dirt road with houses on all sides. There is a rural aspect to most slums in Maputo, with their meandering sand alleyways and corrugated roofs separated by tiny stands of papaya and moringa trees. This may explain why Bento found it so funny that his friends in Inhambane wanted to know whether there was any sand in the capital: his living situation more closely resembles the village he'd grown up in than it does Maputo's downtown. In the colonial era, these parts of the city were called the *cidade de caniço*, or the "city of reeds," for the most common building material used by poor Mozambicans. The use of concrete and flush toilets was outlawed in the reed city. The Portuguese lived in the *cidade de cimento*, with piped sewage and streets laid out on a grid. Now, nearly all of Maputo is built with *cimento*, or cement, but the old cane city still retains the same outlines of one-story shacks and doglegged streets. Whole neighborhoods are built like improvised mazes, cut off from most car traffic and passers-through by the labyrinthine trajectories of their walls and streets. Houses are built on continually subdivided, lumpen lots, and there is so little space in each yard that people hang out directly in the street, doing their hair, playing soccer, selling vegetables and water bottles filled with soybean oil.

Bento was received with waves and warm shouts from the kids before he stopped to open a rusty gate on our right. Stepping through it, we turned three corners between high cement walls and emerged in a shabby backyard. The ground was like silt, puddled muck in some places and devoid of plant life. Against the rear wall was a spigot with an attached water meter, an avocado tree, and a large, teetering papaya plant, shooting up in a single stalk. In the middle, two enamel-wrapped steel wires crossed and sagged with incongruously clean clothing.

Bento lives with his *senhora*, whom he calls Vovó, or Grandma, as well as her daughter and granddaughter. None of them was there when we arrived, so Bento took me to his room. He sleeps in an alcove by the front of the house—originally intended for cases of empty beer bottles—next to a now-defunct front-yard bar that the *senhora*'s husband ran until he died. There was a blanket on the floor and a sheet draped over an open window. His clothes and few possessions were stashed behind the concrete bar, where Bento stood, holding court, and told me about his life there: "My *senhora*, she treats me well. *Bem mesmo.* She treats me like—like a son. There are many people in the neighborhood who don't know that I work. They don't know that I'm not in school. They just think I'm her grandson or something. Many people don't know that I'm from Inhambane."

He leaves the house at seven o'clock each morning. "And it's not that she tells me to leave at seven," he added. The distinction was of great importance: "Sometimes, if I'm out late playing around I'll get up at seven forty-five and run out the door at eight, and she doesn't say anything; you could talk to her, if she were here, and she'd tell you, 'That boy plays, but he doesn't play at work. He sells.'" Bento usually finishes selling by three or four in the afternoon, then stops off at home and goes out to buy eggs, butter, or whatever else that day's money will get the house. He returns home to dinner "with the table already set. We eat together. And then, my *senhora*, she washes the dishes, even as I'm seated at the table. You see? And that's it, I don't have to sweep or do laundry or anything." The perks that thrilled Bento were strikingly ordinary— not to be made to wash the dishes every night, to be allowed a moment's rest while someone else is working—but they gave a clear picture of the kind of indentured servitude he'd grown accustomed to selling eggs and *bajia*.

Bento found his current *senhora* when he returned from his Christmas trip to Inhambane, in January of 2009. He was intent on avoiding a return to his previous madams, and he found the gig selling muffins without too much trouble, which he considered a stroke of good fortune. Of his friends, Bento has by far the best situation. Others get up at four to pound the beans for the *bajia* they sell until ten or eleven at night, or they are expected to wash dishes and do other domestic chores as well. They have madams who scold them and dock their pay when they don't sell out, as it had been for Bento when he sold eggs, so that some never manage to get together the cash to go home to Inhambane or Gaza.

I asked if there were girls his age who made the same trip he did, and he said they were more likely to go to Inhambane and Maxixe, or other towns closer to home, where they worked as domestic servants. Bento was sure they had it easy: "It's a little bit easy, for girls. Everyone wants a girl to bathe their baby, to do the laundry, to sweep." I doubted whether he was right, but I was glad that he was ignorant of the realities of prostitution and sexual abuse that likely afflicted the other half of his demographic. The thought of girls seemed to bring Bento back home.

His father, he said, is mentally ill. He has been that way long enough that Bento does not remember him another way. He is told that his father used to work in the mines in South Africa, but now he sits on the porch of Bento's grandparents' house and "talks about things that aren't there." Bento's mother died when he was four or five. He remembers her, he says, "but her face, it doesn't come." Bento scanned the wall behind me, and I felt silly for having asked him. "You think I'd be here if my mother were still alive? That she would just let me get up and leave to Maputo? Ahhh! *Nada*." No way. He laughed at the thought of it; kids with mothers stayed home!

The same was true of all his friends who made a living vending: death, mental illness, addiction, or infirmity had robbed each of them of one parent, or both, in practical terms. How clueless I must have seemed to Bento for asking about his mother. Though he hadn't mentioned it, her death must have stood out as the defining fact of his strange, grown-up childhood. How else was it that a nine-year-old would muster up the courage and desperation to come to the capital?

"In November, I want to go home and stay a while," Bento said, suddenly seeming like a kid again. "Go there and play, rest up. I've already seen the city. *Ehhh pa*. I've seen it—that's enough." Bento peppered his speech with the sliding onomatopoeias of distaste and exhaustion: *"Ahhhhh*—I'm already exhausted with the city," he said. This time, when he goes home, he wants to see "if it makes sense to come back or stay home. Things are changing there." I asked which things. "Many people have moved and now live close to the road. There is a project to install electricity there." He pondered this for a moment. Though few migrants return home to stay, those who remain in Maputo often end up disenchanted: the daily grind is exhausting, and even demeaning, but it is hard to desert the material comforts of urban life like electricity and running water.

"If I manage to buy a bicycle, I'll go home, to Inhambane," Bento concluded. He was kneeling on a stool, hands clasped, elbows resting on the bar. "This selling life? It's not worth a damn. I need to study, you know? Just study. That way I can become a security guard or something." He paused. "Life here in Maputo, it costs." Bento used the word *custa*, which, in Mozambique, often refers to something more than money. "It costs" may mean that something is expensive, but also that something is taxing, draining, nearly impossible—physically, emotionally, mentally. "Maputo *custa*," Bento repeated. "People have cars and things, but to *live* here is rare. Very rare. They've gotta have a store or a bank or something to back it up. Here, every little tomato and onion is money. Firewood, money. You see, there, in Inhambane, if you need firewood, you go cut it. We've got mangos. We've got coconut trees. To make *xima*, we have corn, and we grind it. Here, it's all money."

When he returns home, Bento says he wants to try to attend eighth grade in Vilanculos, about fifteen miles from his house. When he was younger, the prospect of coming up with the money or the means of transport to get to school there intimidated him. Now, he says, if he had a bicycle, the school fees wouldn't be a problem. He'd sell firewood, or anything at all, he said, to pay for school; any decent job requires a high school diploma.

On that note, Bento led me out into the dirt courtyard, through the narrow concrete alley that bounded the house, and back into the street. It was nearing five o'clock, and he needed to collect from his delinquent customers before they went home for the night.

The following week, I asked Bento if I could come along on part of his sales route to see how the business worked. He agreed to call me when he reached Baixa (pronounced *BYE-sha*), Maputo's central shopping district. Each day, he traces a grand rectangle that runs from Mafalala down to Maputo's port, through Baixa, and back out to Mafalala along a different route. It seemed like an awful lot of ground to cover to sell fifty muffins over the course of an entire day, somewhere in the neighborhood of eight or ten miles. I wondered why Bento didn't sell something else as well. Throughout the city, the sidewalks teemed with itinerant men and women selling a single item—cigarettes, phone credit, shoelaces, sunglasses, peanuts, ice pops, bananas, pens. It seemed like a lost opportunity. How could you "upsell" your customers, or attract new ones? Not everyone wanted a muffin; why not sell cigarettes?

Every economy has its riddles: a Mozambican in the United States would surely gape at the working televisions that line the sidewalk on trash day, or drinks that cost the price of dinner. Bento said he had sold phone credit in the past but that it had created problems with his *senhora*; he didn't want to be accused of taking care of his "own business," and risk ending up on the street again.

The informal economy in Maputo is long on labor, short on trust, and short on capital. Risk aversion—be it fear of unemployment or fear of loss—is a powerful force in the milieu that Bento inhabits. Those like him who spend their days working for someone else must constantly guard against giving off the impression of disloyalty lest they end up without a place to sleep. Even those who use their own capital for sidewalk vending generally live hand-to-mouth. Most vendors in Maputo participate in informal credit groups called *xtik* (pronounced *shteek*) to put aside whatever savings they can. Bento contributes 10 meticais every day to receive 300 in a lump sum at the end of the month. It is a challenge to keep enough money around to accumulate any kind of a diversified inventory: today's profits must always go to tonight's dinner and tomorrow's supply. Everyone stands to lose by theft, getting duped out of four dozen eggs, having phone credit snatched out of your hand, or seeing the police confiscate your goods altogether.

All of which converges on a bizarre sort of efficiency in sidewalk commerce, akin to the uniformity of gas stations or fast-food chains at the other end of the spectrum. When competition is tight, change and innovation are often too costly to consider. Instead, everyone ends up with a business that looks much the same as their competitors'. On the sidewalks of Baixa, it's often the simplest rig you could imagine for the task at hand: the hard-boiled-egg vendors carry eggs, plastic bags, and small reused gin bottles of salt, chili powder, and vinegar, all arranged on a square of egg carton; peanut vendors have flat, circular baskets piled with peanuts, a stack of newspaper wrappers, and different-sized plastic caps to measure out their sales; muffin vendors carry muffins. In the little portion of Baixa where I lived, shoes and clothes dominated

the sidewalk, and you could often chart the time elapsed since the
last passage of the municipal police by looking at the shoes for sale
on the pavement. If it had been more than an hour since the cops
came by and told the men to clean up, ladies' heels were lined up in
rows, sorted by size and style. If the cops had come more recently,
the shoes were piled high and haphazardly. Every time the police
came, the vendors hightailed it around the corner, carrying
their merchandise on their backs, only to return a few minutes
later.

Bento beeped me with a missed call at ten thirty the next morning. By the time I went out to meet him a half hour later, I was
surprised to see that he had already sold every last muffin. Before
him on the sidewalk stood a shiny see-through octagonal bucket.
"Amigo!" he said warmly, offering me a firm grip. What's with
the bucket? "My *senhora* got it for me. I kept telling her that the
customers couldn't see what I'm selling." Bento had noticed the
buckets months earlier, swinging in the hands of some of his
peers. In the few days since he'd had it, his muffins had been
selling more than twice as fast, and he sometimes finished before
ten a.m. Innovation had paid off.

Around this time, I decided to buy Bento a bicycle. Only part of
me believed that it would help him go back to school. It just
seemed like he could use a break. We met up on a Saturday, and I
walked with him on the last part of his route, which had been
seriously curtailed since he began selling from a clear bucket. He
introduced me to two of his regulars, young women working at a
cosmetics store, and turned bright red when they began to tell me
what a good boy he was. Two blocks later, Bento tried to collect
from a man washing cars on the side of the road who had eaten a
muffin early in the morning. "I told you to come at noon," he bel-
lowed, rag in hand. "There's no work! How am I supposed to pay
you when there's no work?" Bento reasoned with him.

"Ya, it's not that, John. . . . It's just—I'm finishing early." The man reluctantly dug up a coin, which Bento secured inside his second pair of pants.

At the store, Bento fell immediately in love with a BMX bike, which, he said, was like those of the "filhos de ma-John-John," the sons of ma-John-John. He gripped the handlebars approvingly. Ma-John-John are the Mozambican miners who work across the border in South Africa. Historically, miners' repatriated wages have been of huge importance to the Mozambican economy, and they are (rightly) seen as rich men in the poor rural areas where their families live. There's a chain retailer called Kangela (it has an outlet in Vilanculos, near Bento's home) that caters specifically to miners and their families. The men make orders and pay at kiosks set up at the mines in South Africa and pick up the goods when they come home on leave, using a green slip of paper redeemable at warehouses throughout the southern half of Mozambique. As if the status conferred upon the miners by their purchases were not enough, they often visit the warehouse to make the pickups with the whole family decked out in their Sunday best.

The storekeeper did not want to sell us the BMX bike. "It's too small," he insisted. "Tomorrow, you'll come back and say, 'The bike broke, the bike broke.' No good. He needs a bigger bike." I worried about finding spare parts, and for a moment, I tried to nudge Bento toward a more conventional choice. A single model of bicycle prevails on the roads outside Maputo—a full-size Indian-made gentleman's bike with a spring-loaded baggage rack and longhorn-like handlebars. Hero was the brand. I knew, from observation, that they could be made to last nearly forever. At a national park, I'd seen a cache of fifty or sixty Heros confiscated from poachers who rode them through the woods to go after warthog and antelope. Elsewhere, in the countryside, you can commonly see three people teetering over gravel on a single bicycle. Heros haul sacks of charcoal and goats to market. They continue to roll long after the plastic pedals have begun to disintegrate and the seats have worn through. If Bento managed to keep from getting his bicycle stolen, it seemed like Hero might be a good choice in the long term.

The storekeeper was a tall, grizzled Pakistani man in his sixties. His wife, standing by him peering out from behind a head scarf and a pair of soda-bottle spectacles, reached the middle of his chest. Impassively, the two of them watched us deliberate with their hands folded on the glass counter. Bento wasn't interested in the Hero. Again, the man refused to sell the BMX. He shook his head adamantly and shuffled papers by the register.

In the end, money prevailed, and the storekeeper relented. "You promise you won't come back?" he asked as he filled out my receipt.

"Today, I am happy," Bento said. We rode back to Mafalala, and he vowed, unprompted, not to take the bike out of his house.

Bento poses with a cell phone and his new bicycle in the courtyard of his *senhora*'s, or madam's, home in Mafalala, a neighborhood on the periphery of Maputo.

He would wash the wheels and take the air out of the tires and leave it in the closet, he promised, so that it didn't get picked up by any *molwenes* before he got it back to Pambara.

The month before I met Bento, UNICEF released a major report on the state of child welfare in Mozambique, based on a "deprivations" approach, which considers the various "deprivations" that can interfere with a child's healthy development. The overall picture was better, the report said, than it had been several years before, but on the whole, the findings were dismal. Half of Mozambican children suffer from chronic malnutrition, and more than two-thirds of schoolgirls said that some teachers require sex in order to pass their classes. Only a small portion of the report deals with child labor, which is prohibited outright in Mozambique. It found that 15 percent of urban children and 25 percent of rural children worked, and that most working children also attended school.

From the perspective of a casual observer, these figures were optimistic. It seemed to me that far more children worked and far fewer attended school than the report let on. But interestingly, the report showed similar levels of school attendance among children who work and the population at large. I wondered whether this would be true if the same children didn't work: Would they still be able to go to school? Who would pay for their books and uniforms? While I hung out with Bento, I returned again and again to the assumption underlying the report's discussion of child labor: would he be better off if he hadn't been able to sell muffins? Certainly, Bento would be better off in a world where his best option wasn't selling muffins, but that world seems a long way off. I wondered whether he'd ever considered it. It was obvious that Bento's stint in Maputo had included moments of trauma. He'd lost a good chunk of his childhood and been through experiences that would be best avoided by adults and children alike. By the time I met him, he was a veteran of difficult circumstances. But with his pluck and determination, it seemed that he might turn out all right.

In the last week of September, I left Maputo by train and took a roundabout route to Tete, in the western reaches of the country, where there is a multibillion-dollar coal-mining industry taking root. Bento and I stayed in touch sporadically by phone. In the Mozambican way, our calls never lasted more than thirty seconds or a minute, out of tacit concern for running out of credit. In November, he said he would be in Pambara for Christmas and that I should call if I passed by on my way back south. I did, but I got a robotic recording instead, known, colloquially, as a *liga-mais-tarde*, or "call back later." Call-back-laters are not very specific. The same message may mean that someone's phone is off, that it's in an area without service, that the line has been disconnected, or simply that the network is having technical problems, which it often does. I continued getting call-back-laters every time I tried him for the next month, when I left Mozambique, and each time I've tried him since.

The last time I saw him was in the afternoon, a few days after we got his bike. Once I met Bento, I seemed to run into him everywhere, and on this day, he got my attention from the other side of a highway that cuts into the center of Maputo on a long, steady incline, its two sides separated by a wide drainage canal. *"Aaaamiiiigo!"* Bento shouted from the opposite embankment. I looked over and he waved with his whole body. We stopped to chat on either side of the canal, crouched halfway down the sloping concrete banks. Bento was running some errands. Sales were good; his *senhora* was impressed with the bike. He assured me he hadn't taken it out of the house. "Ya, okay," he said. "We'll talk."

I didn't find out whether Bento made it back to Pambara for Christmas until years later. I'd held on to a phone number for his *senhora*'s daughter, Bemvinda, though, and she was one of the first people I called when I was back in Maputo at the start of 2016. One morning, I made my way from meeting a friend in Sommerschield, a leafy neighborhood of ambassadors' residences and tall cement walls, to the house she shared with her mother in Mafalala, along a narrow sand street by the airport. You can chart the wealth of each neighborhood in Maputo by the produce on offer in the street, from Sommerschield's welded steel carts heaped high with butternut squash, pineapple, and imported grapes, to Mafalala's meager displays of green peppers and pale cabbage laid on crude tables made of pallet wood.

Bemvinda was waiting outside, cell phone in hand. The home was just as I remembered it. Midday sun poured in through a window onto pink walls stained with soot. Bento's *senhora*, Essina João Chambe, sat on an overstuffed armchair patched with bits of woven plastic rice sacks. The television sat on a tall mahogany shelf next to a carved wooden cat; a refrigerator stood on a pallet in the corner. Chambe is a slight woman with a proud bearing and a soft smile. She had come to Maputo in 1989 after her husband died, leaving her with three small children to raise and feed in the midst of the war. A few brothers and sisters had already followed fortune into the capital, so Chambe came too. She quickly found work as a maid, first with a Portuguese family, then for Swiss, and then for Italians. For a time, in the early 1990s, she'd left her kids with relatives and followed her employers back to Italy. They wanted her to stay, but she couldn't stand being apart from her children, and she returned within months.

When I asked how she'd gotten started hiring boys like Bento, Chambe replied, "Life." By the late nineties, bills for groceries, books, and school clothes gradually outstripped her maid's salary, and she began to bake muffins at night after she returned from work. Bento—the family called him Dino—was among the last of ten or fifteen boys who have stayed with her since 2000, selling her muffins by day. "I tried to treat them like my own kids, because I already knew what suffering is." By Bento's account, at least, she did cook good meals for them. The kids spent their evenings watching TV or playing soccer in the street, as her own children would have done, and yet, they also slept outside on a small mat.

Bento had come to the house for the first time with another boy who was already living there. He said he'd been mistreated with a previous madam, Chambe recalled, so he moved in, and the two of them sold together for a time. In Chambe's memory, he'd stayed for only two years. By my count, he was there for more than three. He left for South Africa at the end of 2014, after going home to Pambara for the holidays, to live with an older brother near Johannesburg. Bento, I thought, was finally old enough to become a ma-John-John. When he left, I was glad to hear, he still had his bicycle. "He tied it up so neatly!" she said, a glint in her eye. "That boy has judgment!" Bento had earned less than $40 a month for his work. And yet, Chambe said, with the pride of someone all too familiar with the juggling such a tight salary required, "With the little I gave him, he managed to buy things."

Bento had fallen out of touch with the family since he left the country, but he'd stopped by the house just a few weeks before I did, Chambe said. He was on his way home for Christmas. "He's already grown!" She beamed: a broad-shouldered nineteen-year-old with a deep voice striding through the doorway a boy had left less than two years before. He called her Vóvó, or Grandma. He seemed happy, energized, she said. "I said, 'You, here?'" Chambe recalled, giddy. "'*E pa*! *You* remember *me*?' He said, 'How could I forget, Vóvó?'"

Acknowledgments

This book owes a great deal to the generosity and goodwill of the Mozambicans whose lives are recorded in its pages. They gave freely of their time, their insight, and their convictions, a debt that no amount of writing could repay.

I hope my endnotes, too, serve as acknowledgments unto themselves, of the scholars, journalists, and others whose work has shaped my understanding of Mozambique's place in the world. I am grateful to the Fulbright Program for making my travel possible, and to Jermaine Jones, at the Institute of International Education, for graciously allowing me to veer off course without reproach.

In Mozambique, I relied on the companionship, guidance, and hospitality of countless friends and strangers alike. In particular, I wish to thank Paulo, Julio Khonamumba, Beto Vasco Vares, and the other Woodcarvers of the June 16th Collective; Casimiro, Muanhua, and Fernanda, in Quarterão 16; Ahmed and Ali, in Bombeiros; and Father Marcelo Anggo in Liupo, each of whom helped me begin to understand a different piece of Nampula. Many thanks to Osório, whose warm welcome, creativity, and book recommendations enriched my time in Tete immeasurably; to Silvia Cheia, for her help in navigating MDM; and to Lídia Lópes, whose good cheer brightened many a day in Maputo.

Emiliano and Lúcia da Silva let me into their family and shared their lust for life (and love of *kizomba*) over the course of many feasts on the terrace behind their apartment in Baixa. Conversations in their living room jolted my curiosity and offered a taste of Maputo I will not soon forget.

My fellow students and researchers at Universidade Eduardo Mondlane all made the Centro de Estudos Africanos a truly welcoming and inspiring environment for a newcomer; most of all, Elisio Jossias, who humored me through constant tweaks to the focus of my research and helped me make valuable connections to scholars throughout the university. Roberta Pegoraro, David Morton, João Feijó, and Nadia Esteves each sharpened my Portuguese and curiosity for Mozambique with valuable feedback and encouragement early on. Kory Russell, Emily van Houweling, and Wouter Rhebergen became fast friends and opened their doors on my arrival in Nampula. Thanks also to John Haas, for picking up the first story I filed there.

Gideon Yago convinced me that writing a book was easier than it seemed. As grateful as I am that I believed him, let the record show that he was wrong. My agent, Valerie Borchardt, lent her talent and support to an early vision for this project when I had only begun to piece it together. Marc Favreau's quick reading and deft touch made revising the manuscript far easier than writing it; Emily Albarillo and the whole team at The New Press pitched in with enthusiasm and expertise to turn it into something that can be pulled down off the shelf.

Portions of this manuscript benefited from early readings by Laura Silver, Lis Harris, and Bill Finnegan, and from tidbits of wisdom on publishing, besides, from Mark Krotov, Edward Orloff, Carole Sargent, and my aunt Honor Moore.

No writer could ask for better friends and sounding boards than Will Benét, Gabriel Louis, and Oliver Munday—I hear his book covers are pretty good, too.

Lastly, I have a deep well of affection for my family, who kept me focused and upbeat throughout. My parents, Tom and Adelia, were some of my earliest readers, as was my brother Carrick, who gave me a place to lay my head when I started writing. Most of all, I am grateful for my wife, Lena Jackson, who read, and lived with, more versions of this manuscript than anyone should have to, and without whose support I might never have finished it.

Notes

All translations from Portuguese-language sources are the author's unless otherwise indicated. Most interviews were conducted in Portuguese.

Introduction: It All Happens on the Margins

1. "'Quinhões da riqueza' de Moçambique disputados entre governo e RENAMO," interview with Carlos Nuno Castel-Branco, AfricaMonitor Intelligence, March 7, 2017, www.africamonitor.net/pt/politica/castelbranco -ec017.

2. William Finnegan, *A Complicated War: The Harrowing of Mozambique* (Berkeley: University of California Press, 1992), 94.

3. Joe Brock, "Mozambique's Tuna Fleet Rusts as an African Success Story Fades," Reuters, May 7, 2016.

4. "Frelimo reunida na Matola," *RFI Português*, February 5, 2016.

5. Henry Stanley, *The Three Voyages of Vasco da Gama, and His Viceroyalty: From the Lendas da India of Gaspar Correa. Accompanied by Original Documents* (New York: Hakluyt Society / Burt Franklin, 1869).

6. Ibid., 81.

7. See Allen F. Isaacman, *Mozambique: The Africanization of a European Institution: The Zambesi Prazos, 1750–1902* (Madison: University of Wisconsin Press, 1972).

8. Simon Katzenellenbogen, *South Africa and Southern Mozambique: Labour, Railways, and Trade in the Making of a Relationship* (Manchester, UK: Manchester University Press, 1982).

9. David Morton, "Age of Concrete: Housing and the Imagination in Mozambique's Capital, c. 1950 to Recent Times" (doctoral diss., University of Minnesota, 2015), 61–62.

10. John Saul, "Inside from the Outside? Mozambique's Un/Civil War," in *Civil Wars in Africa: Roots and Resolution*, ed. Taisier M. Ali and Robert O. Matthews (Montreal: McGill-Queen's Press, 1999), 131.

11. Caroline A. Gross, "War-Stopping and Peacemaking in Mozambique," in *Stopping Wars and Making Peace: Studies in International Intervention*, ed. Kristen E. Eichensehr and W. Michael Reisman (Leiden: Martinus Nijhoff, 2009), 185–212.

12. Joseph Hanlon, "Success Story? Bretton Woods Backlash in Mozambique," *Southern Africa Report* 13, no. 1 (November 1997).

13. Robert Naiman and Neil Watkins, *A Survey of the Impacts of IMF Structural Adjustment in Africa: Growth, Social Spending, and Debt Relief* (Washington, D.C.: Center for Economic and Policy Research, April 1999).

14. *Mozambique Rising: Building a New Tomorrow* (Washington, D.C.: International Monetary Fund, African Department, 2014), 8.

15. Paul Biya, Cameroon; Teodoro Obiang, Equatorial Guinea; José Eduardo dos Santos, Angola; Yoweri Museveni, Uganda; Omar al-Bashir, Sudan; Idriss Déby, Chad; Isaias Afwerki, Eritrea; Paul Kagame, Rwanda; Blaise Compaoré, Burkina Faso; Hosni Mubarak, Egypt; Omar Bongo, Gabon; Lansana Conté, Guinea; Yahya Jammeh, Gambia; Muammar Gadhafi, Libya; Maauya Ould Sid'Ahmed Taya, Mauritania; Gnassingbé Eyadéma, Togo; Zine El Abidine Ben Ali, Tunisia; Abdelaziz Bouteflika, Algeria; Ismaïl Omar Guelleh, Djibouti; and Joseph Kabila, Democratic Republic of the Congo, for example.

16. European Union Election Observation Mission, *Mozambique—Final Report: General Elections, 15 October 2014*, eeas.europa.eu/sites/eeas/files/eueom_mozambique_2014_finalreport_en.pdf.

17. Jeremy Weinstein, "Mozambique: A Fading UN Success Story," *Journal of Democracy* 13, no. 1 (January 2002).

18. International Monetary Fund, *World Economic and Financial Surveys—Regional Economic Outlook: Sub-Saharan Africa: Keeping the Pace* (Washington, D.C.: International Monetary Fund, 2013), 45.

19. Hanlon, "Success Story?"

20. Weinstein, "Mozambique."

21. Joseph Hanlon, "Following the Donor-Designed Path to Mozambique's $2.2 Billion Secret Debt Deal," *Third World Quarterly* 38, no. 3 (October 2016), www.open.ac.uk/technology/mozambique/sites/www.open.ac.uk.technology .mozambique/files/files/Hanlon-Mozambique-3WQ-Final-Accepted.pdf.

22. "About Mozambique," USAID, www.usaid.gov/mozambique.

23. Antoinette Sayeh, "Africa's Success: More Than a Resource Story," October 31, 2013, blogs.imf.org/2013/10/31/africas-success-more-than-a -resource-story.

24. Mark Tran, "Mozambique Smelting Profits Should Not Fill Foreign Coffers, Say Campaigners," *The Guardian*, January 8, 2013, www.theguardian .com/global-development/2013/jan/08/mozambique-smelting-profits -foreign-coffers.

25. E.g., Spokesperson on the General Elections in Mozambique, "Statement," European Union Brussels, October 17, 2014, eeas.europa.eu/archives /docs/statements/docs/2014/141017_03_en.pdf.

26. "Prosecutors Close Investigation into the Murder of Judge Silica," Club of Mozambique, February 10, 2017, clubofmozambique.com/news /prosecutors-close-investigation-murder-judge-silica; "Mozambique: Suspect in Murder of Prosecutor Escapes," AllAfrica.com, November 2, 2016, allafrica.com/stories/201611030143.html.

27. Joseph Hanlon, ed., *Mozambique News Reports & Clippings*, no. 342, October 24, 2016, www.bit.ly/mozamb; Joseph Hanlon, ed., *Mozambique News Reports & Clippings*, no. 345, November 5, 2016, www.bit.ly/mozamb.

28. In August 2017, President Filipe Nyusi finally agreed to meet Dhlakama on his terms, traveling to Gorongosa to talk with him in the bush. "Mozambique: Nyusi Meets with Dhlakama in Gorongosa," AllAfrica.com via Agência de Informação de Moçambique, August 6, 2017, allafrica.com /stories/201708070627.html.

29. Paul Fauvet and Marcelo Mosse, *Carlos Cardoso: Telling the Truth in Mozambique* (Cape Town, South Africa: 2002), 296–300; Luis Nhachote, "Mozambique's 'Mr Guebusiness,'" *Mail & Guardian*, January 6, 2012, mg.co .za/article/2012-01-06-mozambiques-mr-guebusiness; Rachel L. Swarns, "'Trial of the Century' Enthralls Mozambique," *New York Times*, January 8, 2003, www.nytimes.com/2003/01/08/world/trial-of-the-century-enthralls -mozambique.html.

30. "O cabrito come onde está amarrado." See, for instance, Danúbio Mondlane, "Polícia da Guarda Fronteira ainda vive de cabritismo," *A Verdade*, January 25, 2011, www.verdade.co.mz/nacional/16973-policia-da-guarda -fronteira-ainda-vive-de-cabritismo; Gabriel Mithá Ribeiro, "Chissano contra Machel e o colono: representações sociais do estado em Moçambique," *Cadernos de estudos africanos*, nos. 13–14 (2007), cea.revues.org/484.

31. Hanlon, "Following the Donor-Designed Path."

32. Ibid.

33. "'Quinhões da riqueza' de Moçambique."

34. Ibid.

35. Jeffrey Barbee, "'Who Knows What We'll Find Next?' Journey to the Heart of Mozambique's Hidden Forest," *The Guardian*, March 25, 2017, www.theguardian.com/world/2017/mar/25/journey-mozambique-mabu -forest-julian-bayliss-google-earth.

1. Small-Town Hustle—Zambezia

1. Mozambican dancer, as told to João Feijó. Cited in "Eles fingem que nos págan, e nós fingimos que trabalhamos—resistência e adaptação de trabalhadores Moçambicanos em Maputo," *Estudos moçambicanos* 22, no. 1 (December, 2011): 122.

2. Recording Industry Association of America, U.S. Sales Database. Data available at: riaa.com/u-s-sales-database.

3. Alan Murphy, Kate Armstrong, James Bainbridge, Matthew D. Firestone, Mary Fitzpatrick, Nana Luckham, and Nicola Simmonds, *Lonely Planet Southern Africa* (Melbourne: Lonely Planet, 2010), 259.

4. Sam Cowie, "Few Jobs Despite Booming Mozambique Economy," *Al Jazeera*, December 2, 2014.

5. "Unemployment, Youth Total (% of Total Labor Force Ages 15–24)," International Labour Organization, ILOSTAT Database, data.worldbank.org /indicator/SL.UEM.1524.ZS.

6. Keith Hart, "Informal Income Opportunities and Urban Employment in Ghana," *Journal of Modern African Studies* 11, no. 1 (March 1973): 61–89.

7. James Heintz, "Informality, Inclusiveness, and Economic Growth: An Overview of Key Issues" (SIG working paper 2012/2, International Development Research Centre, 2012), 8; Ravi Kanbur, "Conceptualising Infor-

mality: Regulation and Enforcement," *Indian Journal of Labour Economics* 52, no. 1 (January 2009): 5.

8. To the extent that "formal" and "informal" are defined by a relationship to regulation, much depends on how well the government enforces its own rules (Kanbur, "Conceptualising Informality"). Is it still formal work if low wages or months-long pay interruptions prompt workers to earn their keep through *biscatos* and *boladas*—"side hustles" and "scams"? The government's zeal and capacity for enforcement can vary dramatically over time and from place to place. Organized corruption among formal businesses— bribes paid to avoid fishing inspections, say—may upend the rule of law far more efficiently than workers in informal businesses, like small-scale fishermen who use illegal nets.

9. Firms that start out as informal almost never become formal: according to one estimate, 91 percent of registered firms start out that way. See Rafael La Porta and Andrei Shleifer, "Informality and Development," *Journal of Economic Perspectives* 28, no. 3 (Summer 2014): 109–26.

10. Sam Jones and Finn Tarp, "Jobs and Welfare in Mozambique" (WIDER working paper 2013/045, UNU-WIDER, Helsinki, 2013). The paper is based on three successive Household Budget Surveys (*Inquérito ao Orçamento Familiar*) carried out by INE (Instituto Nacional de *Estatística*). Any concept of the informal also captures unpaid work or businesses whose finances are indistinguishable from those of the families who run them, like the members of a household who help bring in the harvest, or the mothers who sell rice by the cupful outside their homes each time they can afford a new sack. How many hours of labor are required to call this employment? And how can you sort profits from losses? Roughly 80 percent of the workforce is in small-scale agriculture.

11. Ibid.

12. The Mozambican government defines part-time work as anything less than forty hours a week (Jones and Tarp, "Jobs and Welfare in Mozambique").

13. Ibid.

14. Michael Lipton, "Family, Fungibility and Formality: Rural Advantages of Informal Non-Farm Enterprise versus the Urban-Formal State," in *Human Resources, Employment and Development*, vol. 5, *Developing Countries*, ed., International Economic Association series (London: Palgrave Macmillan, 1984), 198–201, as quoted in Kanbur, "Conceptualising Informality."

15. W.A. Lewis, "Economic Development with Unlimited Supplies of Labour," *Manchester School* 22 (1954): 141, doi: 10.1111/j.1467-9957.1954.tb00021.x.

16. Sam Jones, "Growth Is Not Enough for Mozambique's Informal Workers," *Jobs: Jobs and Development Blog*, World Bank, May 24, 2016.

17. António Cabral, *Dicionário de nomes geográficos de Moçambique—sua origem* (Lourenço Marques: Empresa Moderna, 1975), www.malhanga.com/flipbook/dicionario.nomes/index.html?pageNumber=1 pp101-102.

18. Nelson Belarmino and Agência de Informação de Moçambique, "Mussa Bin Bique encerra duas faculdades na Zambézia," *O País*, June 16, 2011, opais.sapo.mz/index.php/sociedade/45-sociedade/14652-mussa-bin-bique-encerra-duas-faculdades-na-zambezia.html.

19. "Mozambique—Telecoms, Mobile, Broadband and Digital Media—Statistics and Analyses," BuddeComm, October 10, 2016, www.budde.com.au/Research/Mozambique-Telecoms-Mobile-Broadband-and-Digital-Media-Statistics-and-Analyses.

20. Ibid.

2. What Can You Do with an Aging Warlord?—Zambezia

1. Joseph Hanlon, ed., *2014 National Elections: Mozambique Political Process Bulletin*, NE-37, CIP, Centro de Integridade Pública and AWEPA, European Parliamentarians for Africa, September 2, 2014, www.open.ac.uk/technology/mozambique/sites/www.open.ac.uk.technology.mozambique/files/files/National_Elections_37-2September2014-Campaign_starts-EU_to_observe(1).pdf.

2. Joseph Hanlon, ed., *2014 National Elections: Mozambique Political Process Bulletin*, NE-72, CIP, Centro de Integridade Pública and AWEPA, European Parliamentarians for Africa, October 24, 2014, www.open.ac.uk/technology/mozambique/sites/www.open.ac.uk.technology.mozambique/files/files/National_Elections_72-24october2014_turnout_and_ballot-box_stuffing.pdf.

3. "Dhlakama threatens bloodshed in Mozambique," *IOL*, November 13, 2012. www.iol.co.za/news/africa/dhlakama-threatens-bloodshed-in-mozambique-1422015.

4. Joseph Hanlon, ed., *Mozambique News Reports & Clippings*, no. 329, June 26, 2016, www.bit.ly/mozamb.

5. Joseph Hanlon, ed., *Mozambique News Reports & Clippings*, no. 330, July 11, 2016, www.bit.ly/mozamb.

6. Joseph Hanlon, *Mozambique News Reports & Clippings*, no. 334, August 1, 2016, www.bit.ly/mozamb.

7. Tom Bowker, Simon Kamm, and Aurelio Sambo, "Mozambique's Invisible Civil War," *Foreign Policy*, May 6, 2016, foreignpolicy.com/2016/05/06/mozambiques-invisible-civil-war-renamo-frelimo-dhlakama-nyusi.

8. "Dhlakama Shouldn't Evoke Memories of Past Atrocities?" *The Herald*, October 30, 2012, www.herald.co.zw/dhlakama-shouldnt-evoke-memories-of-past-atrocities; "Dhlakama Threatens to Destroy the Country," Agencia de Informação via Club of Mozambique, November 15, 2012.

9. Joseph Hanlon, "Mozambique," in *Africa Yearbook*, vol. 11, *Politics, Economy and Society South of the Sahara in 2014*, ed. Andreas Mehler, Henning Melber, and Klaas van Walraven (Leiden: Koninklijke Brill, 2015), excerpt available at www.open.ac.uk/technology/mozambique/sites/www.open.ac.uk.technology.mozambique/files/files/Africa%20yearbook%202014%20Mozambique%20final.pdf; "Renamo quer declaração de cessar-fogo antes de aperto de mão," *Savana*, August 15, 2014, 2–3, www.open.ac.uk/technology/mozambique/sites/www.open.ac.uk.technology.mozambique/files/files/Documentos_do_acordo_Renamo-governo_Savana-1075_augusto-2014.pdf.

10. Deloitte, *Mozambique's Economic Outlook: Governance Challenges Holding Back Economic Potential*, Deloitte, December 2016, 23.

11. Gustavo Mavie, "Renamo exige mais dinheiro como condição para se manter como partido," *Sapo Notícias*, April 29, 2013, noticias.sapo.mz/aim/artigo/764629042013191455.html.

12. De Brito is the director of research at the Instituto de Estudos Sociais e Econômicos (IESE), a prominent Maputo think tank.

13. Simon Allison, "Think Again: Renamo's Renaissance, and Civil War as Election Strategy," Institute for Security Studies, October 21, 2014, issafrica.org/iss-today/think-again-renamos-renaissance-and-civil-war-as-election-strategy.

14. Sam Jones and Finn Tarp, "Jobs and Welfare in Mozambique" (WIDER working paper 2013/045, UNU-WIDER, Helsinki, 2013).

15. "Dhlakama Threatens Bloodshed in Mozambique," *Agence France Presse*, November 13, 2012.

16. See, for example, Antoinette Lazaruz, "Mozambique Elections 'Peaceful, Free and Fair': SADC," *SABC News*, October 17, 2014. Observers from the United States and Europe have stopped short of using the term "free and fair" but have nevertheless tended to couch their critiques of Mozambican elections in terms of continued progress and have never recommended that an electoral result be invalidated. As the Carter Center wrote, summarizing its report on the 2014 elections, "The elections were overall more competitive, peaceful, and transparent than previous elections The Carter Center has observed in Mozambique." (Summary of "Final Report: 2014 Presidential, Legislative, and Provincial Assembly Elections in Mozambique," available at https://www.cartercenter.org/news/publications /election_reports.html.)

17. William Finnegan, *A Complicated War: The Harrowing of Mozambique* (Berkeley: University of California Press, 1992), 54.

18. Ibid., 15.

19. Ibid., 67.

20. "Mozambique: Assembly Passes Statute of Veterans." All Africa, May 18, 2011. http://allafrica.com/stories/201105190241.html. See also Nerea Atieno Thigo, "The Impact of Disarmament and Demobilization of Child Soldiers on Peace Agreement: A Case Study of Mozambique" (master's diss., University of Nairobi, November 2011), 81.

21. "Afonso Dhlakama, o intocável guerrilheiro da Renamo," *Publico*, December 1, 2004, macua.blogs.com/moambique_para_todos/2004/12/afonso _dhlakama.html.

22. Stephen A. Emerson, *The Battle for Mozambique: The Frelimo–Renamo Struggle, 1977–1992* (Solihull, UK: Helion and Company, 2014), 49.

23. Zimbabwe African National Union—Patriotic Front.

24. Mozambique National Resistance.

25. www.clubofmozambique.com/pt/print_current.php?secao=news&id =19889.

26. He was sixty-four at the time of this writing.

27. Nelson Bellarmino and José Belmiro, "Aires Ali diz que o país está estável e não precisa da cesta básica," *O País*, June 16, 2011.

28. Joseph Hanlon, "Mozambique: A Masque of Success," in *Postconflict Development*, ed. Gerd Junne and Willemijn Verkoren (Boulder, CO: Lynne Rienner, 2004).

29. "'Quinhões da riqueza' de Moçambique."

30. Michel Cahen, "Dhlakama é Maningue Nice! An Atypical Former Guerrilla in the Mozambican Electoral Campaign." *Transformation* 35 (1998). Translation of "'Dhlakama é maningue nice!' Une guérilla atypique dans la campagne electorale au Mozambique," originally published in *L'Afrique politique* (Paris: Karthala, 1995), 27.

31. Prexy Nesbitt, "Renamo: Externally Funded Bandits Terrorize Mozambique," *Renamo Watch*, February 1990.

32. Steve Askin, "Mission to Renamo: The Militarization of the Religious Right," *Issue: A Journal of Opinion* 18, no. 2 (Summer 1990): 32.

33. "Mozambique Revisited," *Frontline Fellowship*, www.frontline.org .za/index.php?option=com_content&view=article&id=1201:mozambique -revisited&catid=67:mozambique-and-malawi&Itemid=268.

34. Bill Bathman, "Understanding the attacks on Peter Hammond," *Frontline Fellowship*, frontline.org.za/index.php?option=com_content&view =category&layout=blog&id=65&limitstart=45.

35. Don Shannon and Norman Kempster. "2 Key GOP Senators Challenge U.S. Backing for Mozambique," *Los Angeles Times*, July 15, 1987.

36. Joseph Hanlon, *A Decade of Mozambique: Politics, Economics, and Society 2004–2013* (Leiden: Brill, 2015), 46.

37. Development Assistance Committee of the Organisation for Economic Co-operation and Development, Geographical Distribution of Financial Flows to Developing Countries, Development Co-operation Report, and International Development Statistics database. Available at data.world bank.org/indicator/DT.ODA.ALLD.CD?year_high_desc=true.

38. By one measure, Transparency International's global Corruption Perceptions Index, based on an annual survey of perception of public sector corruption, Mozambique fell from 99th to 142nd from 2006 to 2016, out of more than 170 countries. Data available at www.transparency.org/research/cpi/overview.

39. See, for example, Michael Gersovitz and Norma Kriger, "What Is a Civil War? A Critical Review of Its Definition and (Econometric) Consequences," *World Bank Research Observer* 28 (2013): 159–90; Luís Madureira, "Cahen, Michel. Les Bandits: Un historien au Mozambique, 1994. Paris: Fundação Calouste Gulbenkian, 2002. 351 pp.," *Luso-Brazilian Review* 40, no. 2 (2003): 157–61.

40. Askin, "Mission to Renamo," 30.

41. Carrie Manning, "Constructing Opposition in Mozambique: Renamo as Political Party," in "Special Issue on Mozambique," special issue, *Journal of Southern African Studies* 24, no. 1 (March 1998): 178.

42. Stephen C. Lubkemann, "Migratory Coping in Wartime Mozambique: An Anthropology of Violence and Displacement in 'Fragmented Wars,'" in "The Demography of Conflict and Violence," special issue, *Journal of Peace Research* 42, no. 4 (July 2005): 493–508

43. Suzanne Daley, "In Mozambique, Guns for Plowshares and Bicycles," *New York Times*, March 2, 1997.

44. Stephen C. Lubkemann, "Migratory Coping in Wartime Mozambique," 498.

45. In 1988, Neil Boothby, a child psychologist at Duke University, traveled to Maputo to work for Save the Children at the Lhanguene Rehabilitation Center for former child soldiers. On research trips over the next sixteen years, Boothby followed the lives of thirty-nine boys, aged six to sixteen in 1988, who had escaped or been liberated from Renamo camps around Mozambique. It was the first ever longitudinal study of "life outcomes" for former child soldiers. Published in 2006, the findings showed, optimistically, that the vast majority of Dhlakama's former acolytes had become "productive, capable and caring adults." In many cases, they'd become unusually active role models and members of their community, "paying back others," one said, "for the bad things I did with Renamo."

The Renamo years haunted them. As grown men, some steered clear of farm tools, like machetes and hoes, which they'd grown to think of as weapons, and of butchering animals, which reminded them of the violence of their training. "In the first phase of indoctrination," Boothby writes, "a progressive series of tasks—taking the gun apart and putting it back together, shooting rifles next to their ears to get use to the sound, killing cows—culminated in requests to kill unarmed human beings. Children were expected to assist adult soldiers without question, or emotion. Those that resisted were often killed. Those that did well became junior 'chiefs' or garnered other rewards such as extra food or more comfortable housing."

The thirty-nine boys who left Renamo and ended up at Lhanguene had the opportunity to make as clean a break as possible with their lives under Dhlakama. They could try, once again, to meld into mainstream society. But thirty-nine is a very small number—much smaller than the number of former soldiers, porters, cooks, cleaners, and spies who continued to rally around Dhlakama as lay supporters, party officers, or members of the Presidential Guard twenty years later. See Neil Boothby, "What Happens When Child Soldiers Grow Up? The Mozambique Case Study," *Intervention* 4, no. 3 (2006): 244–48.

46. Cahen, "Dhlakama é Maningue Nice," 27.

47. Obede Baloi, "Electoral Choice and Practice and the Democratic Process in Mozambique," *Journal of African Elections* 2, no. 1 (2003): 63–70.

48. Five hundred meticais.

49. Hanlon, "Mozambique: A Masque of Success," 481.

50. Fátima Mimbire, "Guebuza conferência com Dhlakama em Nampula," Agência de Informação de Moçambique, December 8, 2011, noticias .sapo.mz/aim/artigo/323108122011180904.html.

51. Francisco Chuquela, "Ex-guerreiros da Renamo revoltam-se contra Dhlakama exigindo manifestações para destituir a Frelimo," *A Verdade*, January 17, 2012.

52. "Ex-guerrilheiros da Renamo insurgem-se com Dhlakama," *Wamphula Fax*, January 16, 2012, macua.blogs.com/moambique_para_todos/2012 /01/ex-guerrilheiros-da-renamo-insurgem-se-com-dhlakama.html.

53. "Renamo ensaia 'revolução' prometida," *Mediafax*, no. 4963, December 23, 2011. See also Carlos Serra, "Afinal Dhlakama está em Tete," *Diário de um sociólogo* (blog), December 23, 2011, oficinadesociologia.blogspot.com/2011 /12/afinal-dhlakama-esta-em-tete.html.

54. Chuquela, "Ex-guerreiros da Renamo revoltam-se contra Dhlakama."

55. "Mozambique: Dhlakama Insulted by Renamo Demobilised," Agencia de Informação de Moçambique via Allafrica.com, January 16, 2012, allafrica .com/stories/201201162163.html.

56. "Renamo desmente ter feito um homem refém em Nampula," Lusa via *Sapo Notícias*, March 1, 2012, noticias.sapo.mz/lusa/artigo/13911185.html.

57. "Renamo desmente a polícia e diz que matou vários polícias em Nampula," Rádio Moçambique, March 14, 2012.

58. Henri Cauvin, "Strife in the North Rattles Stable Mozambique," *New York Times*, December 8, 2000; "Mozambique: Chissano Defends Police Action in Deadly Riots," Panafrican News Agency (Dakar) via Allafrica. com, November 11, 2000, allafrica.com/stories/200011110102.html. For a brief chronology of political instability in Mozambique since independence, see "Momentos de instabilidade política em Moçambique—uma cronologia," Deutsche Welle (Portuguese), August 6, 2014.

59. "Renamo diz que partido não tem medo da guerra," Lusa via *Diário Notícias*, March 8, 2012; "Frelimo responsabiliza Renamo pelos tiroteios de Nampula, mas oposição diz-se inocente," Lusa via *Sapo Notícias*, March 12, 2012, http://noticias.sapo.ao/lusa/artigo/13969242.html; "Dois mortos, vários feridos ligeiros e 33 homens da Renamo detidos é o último balanço dos confrontos em Nampula," *A Verdade*, March 8, 2012, www. verdade.co.mz/tema-de-fundo/35-themadefundo/25580-tiros-na-rua-dos -sem-medo-homens-da-renamo-tentam-fazer-manifestacao-policia -impede.

60. "Mozambique Ex-Rebel Renamo Camp Raided by Police," BBC News, March 8, 2012, www.bbc.com/news/world-africa-17299319.

61. "Cordial Meeting Held with Dhlakama," *Mozambique News Newsletter*, no. 444, Agencia de Informação de Moçambique, April 26, 2012.

62. Joseph Hanlon, *Mozambique News Reports & Clippings*, no. 278, February 9, 2015, www.bit.ly/mozamb. It's worth noting that Dhlakama's return to Maputo to sign the peace agreement in September 2014 (where he subsequently stayed after the election) was his first time in the capital in five years. See Joseph Hanlon, *Mozambique News Reports & Clippings*, no. 272, September 7, 2014, www.bit.ly/mozamb.

63. Joseph Hanlon, *Mozambique News Reports & Clippings*, no. 291, June 26, 2015, www.bit.ly/mozamb.

64. Joseph Hanlon, *Mozambique News Reports & Clippings*, no. 310, February 10, 2016, www.bit.ly/mozamb.

65. Joseph Hanlon, *Mozambique News Reports & Clippings*, no. 299, October 8, 2015, www.bit.ly/mozamb.

66. "Fears Mozambique Trying to Kill Dhlakama: Analyst," Enca.com, July 3, 2016.

67. João Manuel Rocha, "Renamo anuncia morte de deputado na ofensiva do exército de Moçambique contra a sua base," *Público*, October 25, 2013, www.publico.pt/2013/10/25/mundo/noticia/renamo-anuncia-morte-de -deputado-na-ofensiva-do-exercito-contra-a-sua-base-1610333.

68. "Secretário-geral da RENAMO Manuel Bissopo baleado no centro de Moçambique," Deutsche Welle, January 20, 2016, www.dw.com/pt-002 /secretário-geral-da-renamo-manuel-bissopo-baleado-no-centro-de -moçambique/a-18994319.

69. Joseph Hanlon, *Mozambique News Reports & Clippings*, no. 340, October 10, 2016, www.bit.ly/mozamb.

70. Joseph Hanlon, *Mozambique News Reports & Clippings*, no. 351, December 26, 2016, www.bit.ly/mozamb.

71. The one exception, according to President Nyusi, was a skirmish sparked by miscommunication, when each side wasn't aware of where the other's soldiers were.

72. Joseph Hanlon, *Mozambique News Reports & Clippings*, no. 369, April 24, 2017, www.bit.ly/mozamb.

73. In addition to two working groups on decentralization and military issues, made up of Frelimo and Renamo surrogates, there is a third "contact group," made up of foreign ambassadors, well placed to help fund any possible resolution. See Joseph Hanlon, *Mozambique News Reports & Clippings*, no. 362, March 2, 2017, www.bit.ly/mozamb.

74. Joseph Hanlon, *Mozambique News Reports & Clippings*, no. 371, May 2, 2017, www.bit.ly/mozamb; Joseph Hanlon, *Mozambique News Reports & Clippings*, no. 361, February 22, 2017, www.bit.ly/mozamb; Joseph Hanlon, *Mozambique News Reports & Clippings*, no. 358, February 5, 2017, www.bit.ly/mozamb.

3. Branco é Branco—Zambezia

1. Contemporary saying cited in Madeleine Fairbairn, "Indirect Dispossession: Domestic Power Imbalances and Foreign Access to Land in Mozambique," *Development and Change* 44, no. 2 (2013): 335–56.

2. European Research Institute on Cooperative and Small Enterprises, *Identifying Processes and Policies Conducive to Cooperative Development in Africa: Mozambique Country Report* (Trento, Italy: Euricse in partnership with the International Cooperative Research Group, 2017), 2.

3. Ian Rose and João Carrilho, "Building Mozambique's Cadastre: A Delicate Balancing Act" (Annual World Bank Conference on Land and Poverty, Washington, D.C., April 26, 2012).

4. Lei de Terras, no. 19/97, available at http://www.inatur.org.mz/por/content/download/680/4193/file/LEI.TERRAS.pdf.

5. Twelve percent of Mozambique communities have had their land demarcated, according to the World Bank. (Klaus Deininger and Derek Byerlee, "Rising Global Interest in Farmland: Can It Yield Sustainable and Equitable Benefits?," January 10, 2011, https://elibrary.worldbank.org/doi/abs/10.1596/978-0-8213-8591-3.)

6. Cited in Joseph Hanlon, *Mozambique Political Process Bulletin*, no. 48, February 22, 2011.

7. Simon Norfolk and Joseph Hanlon, "Confrontation between Peasant Producers and Investors in Northern Zambézia, Mozambique, in the Context of Profit Pressures on European Investors" (paper prepared for presentation at the Annual World Bank Conference on Land and Poverty, World Bank, Washington, D.C., April 23–26, 2012), www.open.ac.uk /technology/mozambique/sites/www.open.ac.uk.technology.mozambique /files/pics/d137047.pdf.

8. Gemfields, Annual Report, 2015, https://d2lm500aoik26w.cloud-front.net/gemfields/wp-content/uploads/2017/04/13101203/June_2015 _Annual_Report_and_Financial_Statements.pdf.

9. Estacio Valoi, "Blood Rubies of Montepuez," *Foreign Policy*, May 2016.

10. Sayaka Funada Classen, "Análise do discurso e dos antecedentes do programa ProSAVANA em Moçambique—enfoque no papel do Japão" (Tokyo University, 2013).

11. Lídia Cabral, Arilson Favareto, Langton Mukwereza, and Kojo Amanor, "Brazil's Agricultural Politics in Africa: More Food International and the Disputed Meanings of 'Family Farming,'" *World Development* 81 (2016): 47–60.

12. Patrícia Campos Mello, "Moçambique oferece terra à soja brasileira," *Folha de São Paulo*, August 14, 2011, www1.folha.uol.com.br/fsp/mercado /me1408201102.htm.

13. "Interview: Mozambique Offers Brazilian Farmers Land to Plant," Reuters, August 15, 2011, af.reuters.com/article/commoditiesNews/idAFN 1E77E05H20110815.

14. Joseph Hanlon, *Mozambique News Reports & Clippings*, no. 209 (2012), www.bit.ly/mozamb.

15. Joseph Hanlon, *Mozambique News Reports & Clippings*, no. 329 (2016), www.bit.ly/mozamb.

16. Joseph Hanlon, *Understanding Land Investment Deals in Africa: Country Report, Mozambique* (Oakland, CA: Oakland Institute, 2011).

17. Kojo Sebastian Amanor, *Land Governance in Africa: How Historical Context Has Shaped Key Contemporary Issues Relating to Policy on Land* (Rome, Italy: International Land Coalition, 2012), www.landcoalition.org /sites/default/files/documents/resources/FramingtheDebateLandGovernan ceAfrica.pdf.

18. Colin Darch and David Hedges, "Political Rhetoric in the Transition to Mozambican Independence: Samora Machel in Beira, June 1975," *Kronos* 39, no. 1 (2013), www.scielo.org.za/pdf/kronos/v39n1/04.pdf.

19. Samora Machel, "The Beira Speech," *African Yearbook of Rhetoric* 2, no. 3 (2011): 67–83, www.africanrhetoric.org/pdf/Q%20%20%20Machel%20-%20Beira%20English.pdf.

20. Lei de Terras, *Lei* no. 19/97, October 1, 1997.

21. Ian Convery, "Lifescapes and Governance: The Régulo System in Central Mozambique," *Review of African Political Economy* 33, no. 109 (2006): 449–66.

22. Helene Maria Kyed and Lars Buur, "New Sites of Citizenship: Recognition of Traditional Authority and Group-Based Citizenship in Mozambique," *Journal of Southern African Studies* 32, no. 3 (2006): 568.

23. Allen Isaacman, *Cotton Is the Mother of Poverty: Peasant Resistance to Forced Cotton Production in Mozambique, 1938–1961* (Portsmouth, NH: Heinemann, 1995), 588.

24. Ibid.

25. Present-day Niassa Province; the "Niassa" spelling was used in the colonial era.

26. Isaacman, *Cotton Is the Mother of Poverty*. Quote from Eduardo Mondlane, *The Struggle for Mozambique* (London: Zed Press, 1983).

27. Isaacman, *Cotton Is the Mother of Poverty*.

28. Ibid.

29. Ibid.

30. *Mozambique Revolution*, no. 46 (1971), psimg.jstor.org/fsi/img/pdf/t0/10.5555/al.sff.document.numr197101_final.pdf.

31. Norfolk and Hanlon, "Confrontation between Peasant Producers and Investors."

32. Lei de Terras, *Lei* no. 19/97, October 1, 1997.

33. Hanlon, *Understanding Land Investment Deals in Africa*.

34. Norfolk and Hanlon, "Confrontation between Peasant Producers and Investors."

35. World Food Programme, Country Page, Mozambique, www1.wfp.org/countries/mozambique.

36. Joseph Hanlon, *Mozambique Political Process Bulletin*, no. 48, February 22, 2011.

37. Ibid.

38. Hanlon, *Understanding Land Investment Deals in Africa*.

39. See Fairbairn, "Indirect Dispossession."

40. Redação Nampula, "Alerta de cheias na Zambézia," *A Verdade*, January 13, 2015; "A fúria do caudal do rio Molócue destrói o desvio alternativo da ponte em construção," O Portal do Governo da Zambezia, January 19, 2016.

41. Teresa Smart and Joseph Hanlon, *Chickens and Beer: A Recipe for Agricultural Growth in Mozambique*, based on *Galinhas e cervjea: uma receita para o crescimento*, by the same authors (Kapicua: Maputo, 2014).

42. Ibid.

43. Plano Estratégico de Desenvolvimento do Sector Agrário (PEDSA), 2011, quoted in translation in Smart and Hanlon, *Chickens and Beer*.

44. Ibid.

45. Ibid.

46. João Feijó, *Moçambique: 10 anos em reflexão* (Maputo: Justiça Ambiental, 2015), 84.

47. Ibid., 86.

48. Fairbairn, "Indirect Dispossession," 39, 41.

49. Hanlon, *Understanding Land Investment Deals in Africa*.

50. Fairbairn, "Indirect Dispossession."

51. Afonso João Colaço, técnico de Serviços de Geografia e Cadastro, Direcção Distrital de Agricultura e Desenvolvimento Rural de Alto-Molócue, personal communication.

52. International NGOs and advocacy groups like UNAC have tried to step into the breach to fill the massive gaps in education, legal and otherwise, that limit communities' wherewithal to conduct negotiations on their own behalf. Nonprofits have launched capacity-building programs for government officials and pilot projects to formalize community landownership through a more inclusive process. For now, though, those efforts seem to be eclipsed by the basic power imbalances at play in land transactions.

53. Analysis by Centro de Formação Jurídica e Judiciária, cited in Hanlon, *Mozambique Political Process Bulletin*, no. 48 (February 2011), www .open.ac.uk/technology/mozambique/sites/www.open.ac.uk.technology .mozambique/files/pics/d128132.pdf.

54. Nicholas Hess, "Community Need, Government (In)action and External Pressure: A Study of Civil Society and Land Rights in Mozambique" (master's diss., University of Sheffield, 2012).

55. Jessica Milgroom, "Policy Processes of a Land Grab: Enactment, Context and Misalignment in Massingir, Mozambique" (LDPI working paper 34, Land Deal Politics Initiative, 2013).

56. Joseph Hanlon, *Mozambique Political Process Bulletin*, no. 48 (February 2011), www.open.ac.uk/technology/mozambique/sites/www.open.ac .uk.technology.mozambique/files/pics/d128132.pdf.

57. Fairbairn, "Indirect Dispossession," 342.

4. Confessions of a Human Smuggler—Nampula

1. International Organization for Migration (IOM), *In Pursuit of the Southern Dream: Victims of Necessity. Assessment of the Irregular Movement of Men from East Africa and the Horn to South Africa* (Geneva, Switzerland: IOM, 2009), publications.iom.int/books/pursuit-southern-dream-victims -necessity.

2. The lion's share of asylum seekers in South Africa during this period were Zimbabweans who left home in the midst of the country's hyperinflation crisis. Since then, war in Syria has dramatically increased the flow of refugees worldwide, and Germany's backlog has overtaken South Africa's, according to the UNHCR. South Africa was tenth on the list of countries where most new asylum applications were filed in 2015. United Nations High Commissioner for Refugees (UNHCR), *UNHCR Global Appeal 2012–2013: South Africa* (Geneva, Switzerland: UHHCR, 2012–13), 108, www.unhcr .org/4ec230fe16.pdf.

3. Ibid.

4. IRIN, "Horn of Africa Migrants Heading South 'Pushed Backwards,'" August 2, 2011, syndicated by Thomson Reuters at, news.trust.org//item /20110802162900-05ui6.

5. Ibid.

6. UNHCR, *Global Trends: Forced Displacement in 2015* (Geneva, Switzerland: UHHCR, 2016), www.unhcr.org/576408cd7.pdf.

7. Human Rights Watch, *"Welcome to Kenya": Police Abuse of Somali Refugees* (New York: Human Rights Watch, 2010), www.hrw.org/sites/default /files/reports/kenya0610webwcover.pdf.

8. Xan Rice, "Somali Refugee Settlement in Kenya Swells as Row Grows over Empty Camp," *The Guardian*, August 11, 2011, www.theguardian .com/world/2011/aug/11/somali-refugees-kenya-camp-empty.

9. "Kenya Court Quashes Government Order to Close Dadaab," *Al Jazeera*, February 9, 2017, www.aljazeera.com/news/2017/02/kenya-court -quashes-government-order-close-dadaab-170209101027645.html.

10. "Focus on Africa: Somali National Front," BBC News, April 4, 1991, www.bbc.co.uk/programmes/p03mn7tm.

11. "These Are the Biggest Townships in South Africa," *BusinessTech South Africa*, August 14, 2016, businesstech.co.za/news/general/132269/these -are-the-biggest-townships-in-south-africa.

12. M.C. Horton, "Early Muslim Trading Settlements on the East African Coast: New Evidence from Shanga," *Antiquaries Journal* 67, no. 2 (1987): 290–323. DOI: doi.org/10.1017/S0003581500025427; Felix Chami, *The Tanzanian Coast in the First Millennium AD: An Archaeology of the Iron-Working, Farming Communities* (Sweden: Societas Archaeologica Upsaliensis, 1994).

13. "93 estrangeiros ilegais detidos em Nampula," *O País*, January 26, 2010, opais.sapo.mz/index.php/sociedade/45-sociedade/4200-93-estrangeiros -ilegais-detidos-em-nampula.html.

14. Ibid.

15. "Tanzania nega cooperar no repatriamento de imigrantes ilegais," *O País*, February 13, 2010.

16. Anadarko / Environmental Resources Management, *Environmental Impact Assessment (EIA) Report: Liquefied Natural Gas Project*, Areas 1 & 4 Offshore of Rovuma Basin (Environmental Resources Management, February 2014), 9–164, www.mzlng.com/content/documents/MZLNG/EIA /Volume_I/English/Chapter_9-_LNG_Final_EIA_Sept_2014_Eng .pdf.

17. José Raymundo de Palma Velho, *A tomada da bahia de Tungue no parlamento e na imprensa* (La Bécarre Papelaria e Typ, 1887), 10, play.google .com/store/books/details?id=buc7AQAAMAAJ&rdid=book-buc7AQA AMAAJ&rdot=1.

18. "Field Listing: Natural Gas—Consumption," *World Factbook*, CIA, https://www.cia.gov/library/publications/the-world-factbook/fields/print _2250.html.

19. "Tanzania nega cooperar."

20. "Mozambique: North Overwhelmed by Asylum Seekers," IRIN via AllAfrica.com, May 12, 2011. allafrica.com/stories/201105120920.html; "Mozambique: Most Refugees Abandon Refugee Camp," Agência de In-

formação de Moçambique via AllAfrica.com, January 18, 2011, allafrica .com/stories/201101140245.html; "Mozambique: Somali Immigrants Flee Refugee Centre in Nampula Province," Agência de Informação de Moçambique via AllAfrica.com, January 13, 2011, allafrica.com/stories/201101190280 .html.

21. Júlio Paulino, "Cerca de 500 ilegais entram diariamente na província de Nampula," *O Pais*, January 19, 2011. opais.sapo.mz/index.php/sociedade /45-sociedade/11847-cerca-de-500-ilegais-entram-diariamente-na-provin cia-de-nampula.html.

22. "Mozambique: More Somali Migrants Arrested," Agencia de Informação de Moçambique via *Club of Mozambique*, December 8, 2010.

23. "Polícia apreende camião com 108 somalis ilegais na Zambézia," *O país*, December 8, 2010.

24. "Mozambique: Somali Immigrants Flee Refugee Centre."

25. "11 Illegal Migrants Drowned in Northern Mozambique," *Jornal Notícias*, January 8, 2011, via Club of Mozambique, January 10, 2011.

26. "Illegal Immigrants Asphyxiated in a Container," Radio Moçambique via Club of Mozambique, April 2, 2011, www.clubofmozambique .com/solutions1/sectionnews.php?secao=mozambique&id=20908&tipo =one.

27. "51 Somali Migrants Killed in Mozambique Boat Sinking: Police," AFP via Hiiraan Online, www.hiiraan.com/comments2-news-2011-Feb-51 _somali_migrants_killed_in_mozambique_boat_sinking_police.aspx.

28. UNHCR press release, "UNHCR Condemns Shooting of Somali Asylum-Seekers in Mozambique," May 6, 2011; "Nearly Five Somalis Shot Dead in Mozambique Border," Club of Mozambique via Shabelle Media Network, July 28, 2011, www.clubofmozambique.com/solutions1/sectionnews .php?secao=mozambique&id=22440&tipo=one.

29. According to UNHCR, this was an extreme instance in a pattern of beatings and forced expulsions of migrants who entered Mozambique along the Rovuma. Groups of more than one hundred people reportedly had their clothes and cell phones confiscated by the Mozambican police to dissuade them from returning. See remarks by spokesperson Melissa Fleming, "UNHCR Calls on Mozambique Authorities to Stop Deporting Asylum-Seekers," June 24, 2011, www.unhcr.org/cgi-bin/texis/vtx /search?page=search&skip=45&docid=4e0476089&query =Mozambique.

30. "Horn Migrants Beaten, Deported, Imprisoned," IRIN, September 19, 2011, reliefweb.int/report/united-republic-tanzania/horn-migrants -beaten-deported-imprisoned.

31. Inácio Dina, Nampula police spokesman, personal interview, July 29, 2011.

32. "Mozambique: Trafficked Bangladeshis Repatriated," AllAfrica. com, January 20, 2011, allafrica.com/stories/201101210157.html.

33. These are both nicknames for Abdul Aziz.

34. "Mozambique: Hundreds of Asians Deported to Country," Agencia de Informação de Moçambique via Allafrica.com, allafrica.com/stories/201 102070005.html.

35. "Mozambique: Ethiopian Airlines Denies Responsibility for Drugs," Agencia de Informação de Moçambique via Allafrica.com, November 7, 2011, allafrica.com/stories/201111071333.html.

36. I returned to Marratane once more, nearly four months later. The camp was eerily calm. All was as Liban had said it would be: in the previous three months, not a single new arrival from Ethiopia or Somalia had been registered there. Supply tents had vanished. Churches stood vacant. No columns of smoke rose from the transit center. Oxfam Spain had installed a new set of wells and aboveground water tanks to ease the burden of the camp's overpopulation, but Marratane was no longer overpopulated at all. A dozen Ethiopian men lounged beneath a cashew tree with broad smiles fixed on their faces by the sight of outside visitors. They were the only ones of their countrymen left in the camp. "South Africa!" they explained when I asked where the others had gone, raising their eyebrows. No one would say just how. Why hadn't they gone too? They rubbed two fingers together with their thumbs: no money.

In 2016, I saw Liban in an apartment block within sight of the Presidential Palace, in Maputo, and we went for a drive with his girlfriend as he drank Johnnie Walker out of a plastic water bottle. On the phone, he had pleaded with me to help him get a visa to the United States in exchange for an interview. "The woman I love, my life, one Somali girl, she stay in Kansas," he said, lingering on the *s*'s. Mixed migration has continued to flow through Mozambique in spurts, even as the routes out of Africa have shifted, through Libya to Europe, or through Cuba and South America to the United States. In the car, Liban took a phone call, talking loudly in Somali. "That guy is calling from Kenya. Human traffic. I get him money. I don't like that job." I thought you left that job, I said. "How can I leave that job!" Liban retorted. "I have no country. I like to help my people. Somalia. Is it a country? Human traffic, is girl, is children. You are selling them. But if you know where you go, is it a traffic?" he asked, bristling at the suggestion.

Liban returned the radio to full volume and swayed, giddy, to the sounds of Mozambique. He reached into the back seat and took a swig from a fresh one-liter carton of milk. "I'm sick," he said after a few seconds. "I want to enjoy my country. I want to drink milk my country." Liban stepped on the gas, careening into a roundabout and slamming on the brakes. "Don't destroy the car!" his girlfriend protested. "My country is destroyed," Liban said. "What's a car?"

5. Where Have You Hidden the Cholera?—Nampula

1. The first and second epigraphs are from Geoffrey Gill, Sean Burrell, and Jody Brown, "Fear and Frustration—the Liverpool Cholera Riots of 1832," *Lancet* 358, no 9277 (2001).

2. Alejandro Cravioto, Claudio F. Lanata, Daniele S. Lantagne, and G. Balakrish Nair, *Final Report of the Independent Panel of Experts on the Cholera Outbreak in Haiti*. United Nations, May 4, 2011. "Frustration Boils Over in Haiti as Riots Disrupt Efforts to Contain Cholera," interview with Jacqueline Charles, *PBS NewsHour*, November 17, 2010.

3. Cravioto et al., "Final Report on the Cholera Outbreak"; Ivan Watson, "Haitians Unleash Anger over Cholera Epidemic at Peacekeepers," CNN, November 17, 2010.

4. Watson, "Haitians Unleash Anger over Cholera Epidemic at Peace-keepers"; Doctors Without Borders, "Haiti: Demonstration in St. Marc Disrupts Outbreak Response," October 27, 2010.

5. "Unrest 'Must Not Stop Haiti Polls,'" Reuters via *Al Jazeera*, November 19, 2010; "Frustration Boils Over in Haiti."

6. "Unrest 'Must Not Stop Haiti Polls.'"

7. Jonathan Katz, "U.N. Admits Role in Cholera Epidemic in Haiti," *New York Times*, August 17, 2016.

8. Joseph Guyler Delva, "Haiti Urged to Halt Cholera Anti-Voodoo Lynchings," Reuters World News, December 23, 2010.

9. "It's not good to go into details," a technician with Nampula's Department of Water and Sanitation office told me about their cholera prevention work in the field, "but when we go there as the government, they may accept or reject it. Sometimes people have different political positions, and they look at the government as a political party."

10. International Federation of Red Cross Societies, *DREF Operation Final Report*, DREF operation no. MDRMZ003, GLIDE no. TC-2008-000033-MOZ, November 28, 2008; Jean-Luc Martinage, "Mozambique: More than 10,000 Houses Destroyed by Cyclone Jokwe," International Federation of Red Cross and Red Crescent Societies (IFRC), March 12, 2008, www.ifrc.org/es/noticias/noticias/africa/mozambique/mozambique-more-than-10000-houses-destroyed-by-cyclone-jokwe; Joseph Hanlon, "The Panic and Rage of the Poor," *Review of African Political Economy* 119 (March 2009).

11. Liupo has since been designated as its own district; Namige is now the district seat of Mogincual.

12. J. Cliff, "Konzo and Continuing Cyanide Intoxication from Cassava in Mozambique," *Food and Chemical Toxicology* 49 (2001): 631–35.

13. Hanlon, "Panic and Rage of the Poor."

14. Ibid.

15. Administratively speaking, Curuhama is part of the *regulado* of Muanhapo (meaning area under supervision of a traditional chief, or *régulo*), in the city of Quinga.

16. Carlos Serra, *Cólera e catarse* (Maputo, Mozambique: Imprensa Universitaria, Universidade Eduardo Mondlane, 1998, 2002).

17. "Revolta em Nampula contra Cruz Vermelha," *Diário de Notícias*, March 24, 2009.

18. Reports differ as to the identity of the second person killed. Some say it was another Red Cross volunteer; others say it was a *secretario*. See, e.g., "Revolta em Nampula contra Cruz Vermelha" and Hanlon, "Panic and Rage of the Poor."

19. "Ipo" is a kind of grasshopper that Paulo says his father was particularly fond of. The nickname stuck, and since Makua generally take their father's or grandfather's names as their own last names, lived on into the next generation.

20. "Comissão de inquérito da AR responsabiliza Renamo," *O País*, April 29, 2009.

21. "Revolta em Nampula."

22. Wamphula Fax, February 27, 2009, macua.blogs.com/moambique _para_todos/2009/02/activista-da-cvm-morto-no-mogincual.html.

23. Hanlon, "Panic and Rage of the Poor."

24. "Mozambique: Policeman Killed in Cholera Riot," Agencia de Informação de Moçambique via AllAfrica.com, March 4, 2009, allafrica.com /stories/200903040806.html; "Moçambique: Três activistas da Cruz Vermelha mortos, 20 desaparecidos e 10 feridos em Nampula," *Lusa*, March 19, 2009, noticias.sapo.pt/lusa/artigo/9455278.html; "Mozambique: Where Have You Hidden the Cholera?" Agencia de Informação de Moçambique via Allafrica.com, April 9, 2009.

25. "Comissão de inquérito da AR responsabiliza Renamo."

26. "Mozambique: Where Have You Hidden the Cholera?"

27. "Mozambique: Pupils Leave School Because of Violence," Allafrica. com via Agencia de Informação de Moçambique, March 16, 2009.

28. "Mozambique: Mogincual Deaths—Attorney-General Gives Details," Allafrica.com via Agencia de Informação de Moçambique, April 22, 2009.

29. Augusta Eduardo, Book Sambo, Salva Revez,Tarciso Abibo, *Relatório da Liga dos Direitos Humanos: caso Mogincual*, Nampula, March 25, 2009.

30. Ibid.

31. At the closest jail, in Angoche. Ibid.

32. "Mozambique: Mogincual—Frelimo and Renamo Blame Each Other," Agencia de Informação de Moçambique via Allafrica.com, March 27, 2009.

33. Mouzinho de Albuquerque, "Dialogando: Mogincual," *Jornal notícias*, March 18, 2009, comunidademocambicana.blogspot.com/search/label /Mogincual.

34. Eduardo et al., *Relatório da liga dos direitos humanos: caso Mogincual*.

35. Lenny Bernstein, "First-Year Doctors Would Be Allowed to Work 24-Hour Shifts Under New Rules," *Washington Post*, November 4, 2016; Amy Witkoski Stimpfel, Douglas M. Sloane, and Linda H. Aiken, "The Longer the Shifts for Hospital Nurses, the Higher the Levels of Burnout and Patient Dissatisfaction," *Health Affairs* (Millwood) 31, no. 11 (2012): 2501–9, www.ncbi.nlm.nih.gov/pmc/articles/PMC3608421; "Corruption Undermining Health Service," IRIN, November 28, 2012, www .irinnews.org/report/96903/mozambique-corruption-undermining -health-service.

36. World Health Organization (WHO), "Mozambique: WHO Statistical Profile," 2015, www.who.int/gho/countries/moz.pdf ; WHO, *WHO Country Cooperation Strategy 2009–2013: Mozambique* (Brazzaville, Congo: World Health Organization, Regional Office for Africa, 2009), 7, 9.

37. WHO, "Mozambique: WHO Statistical Profile." In 2009, more than one in ten adults in Mozambique was HIV positive. See Carolyn Audet, Kate Groh, Troy D. Moon, Sten H. Vermund, and Mohsin Sidat, "Poor-Quality Health Services and Lack of Programme Support Leads to Low Uptake of HIV Testing in Rural Mozambique," *African Journal of AIDS Research* 11, no. 4 (2012): 327–35; Andrew Auld, Ray Shirashi, A. Couto, F. Mbofana, K. Colborn, C. Alfredo, T.V. Ellerbrock, C. Xavier, and K. Jobarteh, "A Decade of Antiretroviral Therapy Scale-up in Mozambique: Evaluation of Outcome Trends and New Models of Service Delivery Among More Than 300,000 Patients Enrolled During 2004–2013," *Journal of Acquired Immune Deficiency Syndromes* 73, no. 2 (2016): e11–e22, doi: 10.1097/QAI.0000000000001137.

38. UNICEF Mozambique, "Nutrition: Current Situation," www.unicef .org.mz/en/our-work/what-we-do/nutrition.

39. WHO, "Mozambique: WHO Statistical Profile," 2015.

40. Ibid.

41. WHO, *WHO Country Cooperation Strategy*. The United States had one doctor for every 400 people in 2011, according to the World Bank.

42. Ministério de Saúde, *MISAU Plano estratégico do sector da saúde: PESS 2014–2019*, 2014.

43. Ibid.

44. Maria Paula Meneses, "'Quando não há problemas, estamos de boa saúde, sem azar nem nada': para uma concepção emancipatória da saúde e das medicinas," paper presented as part of the proceedings of the conference Moçambique e a Reinvenção Social, Boaventura de Sousa Santos and Teresa Cruz e Silva, eds. Maputo, 2004.

45. Ibid.

46. "Mais de 120 mil curandeiros dos 300 mil existentes não estão registados," *O País*, September 2, 2015.

47. Meneses, "'Quando não há problemas, estamos de boa saúde, sem azar nem nada.'"

48. "Mozambique: Zambezia Residents Apologise for Cholera Riot," Agencia de Informação de Moçambique via Allafrica.com, April 2, 2010.

49. The Catholic priest I stayed with in Liupo, an easygoing, chain-smoking Indonesian man named Marcelo Anggo who runs a mission just outside of town, told a similar story about trying, on occasion, to raise the subject of cholera during church services. "I tell them, cholera is not a person. It doesn't have legs. No one brought that sickness here. It has to do with cleanliness and hygiene," he told me. This is when he gets drowned out with recriminations and disagreement. "No, come on, Father, we know who brought the cholera," and so forth. Anggo thinks his parishioners take it easy on him because he's a priest and said he'd be fearful of being tied up if he were not. In 2010, in Monapo, a small city along the road to Nampula, locals told him that it was forbidden to use the word "cholera": "'You must speak of diarrhea instead,' they said, 'because cholera doesn't exist here.'"

50. Hanlon, "Panic and Rage of the Poor."

51. Serra, *Cólera e catarse*.

52. Ibid. (italics mine).

53. World Health Organization, "Cholera" fact sheet, www.who.int /mediacentre/factsheets/fs107/en.

54. Miguel Aragon, Avertino Barreto, Philippe Tabbard, Jonas Chambule, Clara Santos, and António Noya, "Epidemiologia da cólera em Moçambique no período de 1973–1992," *Revista de saúde pública* 28, no. 5 (1994), dx.doi.org/10.1590/S0034-89101994000500004.

55. Ibid.

56. Richard Evans, "Epidemics and Revolutions: Cholera in Nineteenth-Century Europe," *Past & Present*, no. 120 (1988): 124, http://www.jstor.org /stable/650924.

57. Aragon et al., "Epidemiologia da cólera."

58. Ibid.

59. World Health Organization, "Global Health Observatory Country Views," apps.who.int/gho/data/node.country.

60. Ibid.

61. This, in spite of the fact that since 2008, UNICEF and other organizations working with the government have promoted Community-Led Total Sanitation, which calls for helping communities build traditional latrines. The Departamento de Água e Saneamento does not count the number of traditional latrines constructed through this approach.

62. Iaué has several alternate spellings, most commonly "Hiawe."

63. Eduardo et al., *Relatório da liga dos direitos humanos: caso Mogincual.*

64. Jacqueline Charles, "U.N. Security Council Supports Replacing Haiti Peacekeepers with Smaller Mission," *Miami Herald*, April 11, 2017.

65. Paisley Dodds, "AP Investigation: UN Troops Lured Kids into Haiti Sex Ring," AP News, April 12, 2017; Paisley Dodds, "AP Exclusive: UN Child Sex Ring Left Victims but No Arrests," AP News, April 12, 2017.

66. See, for instance, Eric Jean Baptiste, "L'Heritage de MINUSTAH," *Le nouvelliste*, April 17, 2017; Ann Simmons, "U.N. Peacekeepers Are Leaving after More than Two Decades, but Where Does That Leave Haiti?" *Los Angeles Times*, April 17, 2017.

6. Go Tell the Crocodiles—Tete

1. Shlomo Felberbaum, trans., *Inquiries of Herodotus*, book 2 (Losttrails.com: 2003).

2. Raymond Dart, "The Myth of the Bone-Accumulating Hyena," *American Anthropology* (1956).

3. Community courts are governed by a 1992 law but stand apart from the justice system. For a discussion of the range of practices, makeup, and history of community courts, see Boaventura de Sousa Santos, "The Heterogeneous State and Legal Pluralism in Mozambique," *Law & Society Review* 40, no. 1 (2006): 56–59.

4. Gerald Wood, *The Guinness Book of Animal Facts and Feats* (New York: Sterling, 1983).

5. Gregory Erickson, Paul M. Gignac, Scott J. Steppan, A. Kristopher Lappin, Kent A. Vliet, John D. Brueggen, Brian D. Inouye, David Kledzik, and Grahame J. W. Webb, "Insights into the Ecology and Evolutionary Success of Crocodilians Revealed through Bite-Force and Tooth-Pressure Experimentation," *Plos One* (March 14, 2012).

6. EIA figures on state-by-state consumption for Vermont: U.S. Energy Information Administration, "Consumption & Expenditures," www.eia .gov/state/data.cfm?sid=VT#ConsumptionExpenditures; as of 2013, the most recent year's data available, the World Bank estimated electricity consumption of 435.6 kilowatt-hours per capita for Mozambique, or roughly 11.5 billion kilowatt-hours total. See World Bank, "World Development Indicators," http://data.worldbank.org/data-catalog/world-development -indicators.

7. Watchbands and handbags are actually a major funding source for research on wild crocs: since Nile crocodiles are listed as a threatened species by the International Union for Conservation of Nature, getting a license to hunt them or export their hides first requires a study to document the size of the population. In Tanzania, Fergusson recalls getting survey work only after wildlife managers there realized that there was a good market for extra-large crocodile skins, only available in the wild, and typically used in golf bags.

8. Patrick Aust, "The Ecology, Conservation and Management of Nile Crocodiles Crocodylus niloticus in a Human Dominated Landscape" (doctoral diss., Imperial College London, 2009).

9. Ibid.

10. Ibid.

11. Ibid.

12. Diane Ackerman, "Crocodilians," *New Yorker*, October 10, 1988, 52; Job 41:13–15, 22, 25 (NIV), www.biblegateway.com.

13. Cited in Mwelma C. Musambachime, "The Fate of the Nile Crocodile in African Waterways," *African Affairs* 86, no. 343 (1987): 201.

14. R.C.F. Maugham, *Portuguese East Africa* (London: Murray, 1906), 50.

15. Musambachime, "Fate of the Nile Crocodile."

16. Peter Ashton, "The Demise of the Nile Crocodile (*Crocodylus niloticus*) as a Keystone Species for Aquatic Ecosystem Conservation in South Africa: The Case of the Olifants River," *Aquatic Conservation* 20, no. 5 (2010): 489–93.

17. Ian Games and Jacques Moreau, "The Feeding Ecology of Two Nile Crocodile Populations in the Zambezi Valley," in *Advances in the Ecology of Lake Kariba*, ed. Jacques Moreau (Harare: University of Zimbabwe Publications, 1997).

18. Aust, "Ecology, Conservation and Management of Nile Crocodiles."

19. "There's nowhere in Mozambique," he added, "where it comes even close to that."

20. Ian Games, "The Feeding Ecology of Two Nile Crocodile Populations in the Zambezi Valley" (doctoral diss., University of Zimbabwe, 1990).

21. "Africa's Population Boom: Will It Mean Disaster or Economic and Human Development Gains?" World Bank, October 22, 2015, www.world bank.org/en/region/afr/publication/africas-demographic-transition.

22. Aust, "Ecology, Conservation and Management of Nile Crocodiles."

23. Ken Wilson, "Mozambique's Tchuma Tchato Initiative of Resource Management on the Zambezi: A Community Perspective," *Society & Natural Resources* 10, no. 4 (2008): 409–13.

24. Ministério da Agricultura, Direcção Nacional de Terras e Florestas, *Estudo do impacto do diploma ministerial no. 93/2005 de 4 de Maio sobre os mecanismos que regulam a canalização dos 20% das taxas de exploração florestal e faunística às comunidades*, February 2012.

25. Luis Dos Santos Namanha, "Artisanal Fishing and Community-Based Natural Resources Management: A Case Study of Tchuma Tchato Project in Mozambique" (master's thesis, University of Natal, Pietermaritzburg, 1999).

26. The problem continues today: when a stockpile of rhino horn was burned in 2015, 20 percent of the haul had been confiscated from a police warehouse.

27. Wilson, "Mozambique's Tchuma Tchato Initiative."

28. Anthony Maughan Brown, "Revisiting Community Based Natural Resource Management: A Case Study of the Tchuma Tchato Project in Tete Province, Mozambique" (master's thesis, University of KwaZulu-Natal, 1998).

29. Ibid.

30. Unfortunately, other programs that have followed Tchuma Tchato do not seem to have fared much better. In 2011, a team of researchers from the Ministry of Agriculture spent two months on a nine-thousand-mile trip around the country to evaluate the impact of "the 20%"—fees set aside from logging and hunting operations since 2005, analogous to the 32.5 percent earmarked for communities under Tchuma Tchato. "Although 103,908,364 meticais have been transferred to-date," the authors write—equivalent to roughly $3 million at the time—"there is still a general feeling in the local community that the projects that have been implemented have not had much effect on family and community quality of life." Close to 90 percent of the communities where money had supposedly gone had no proof or documents showing how it might have been spent; two-thirds of planned projects were never completed. In Tete Province, half the money set aside for local communities never made it out of accounts belonging to the provincial government. Even corrupt uses of the 20 percent gave some indication of how badly it was needed: committee members used the 20 percent to buy

themselves bicycles, cell phones, clothes. Some people had a notion of how the program was supposed to work but were never told how often transfers would be made or in what amount. "The people from the district agriculture office came here and they said they wanted people to open bank accounts," said a woman in Gaza who was a member of her local committee—formed expressly to manage spending of the 20 percent. "They came by our houses and we signed papers, and we never heard anything about it again." See Ministério da Agricultura, Direcção Nacional de Terras e Florestas, *Estudo do impacto do diploma ministerial*.

31. Miguel Wilson, personal communication, Zumbo, November 25, 2011; Claudio Masango, personal communication, Tete, December 1, 2011; Oscar Zalimba, personal communication, Tete, November 2, 2011.

32. Tracy Brooks, "A New National Park for Tete," *Zambezi Traveller*, December 7, 2013, www.zambezitraveller.com/cahora-tete/conservation/new-national-park-tete.

33. "New National Park in Mozambique Has No Money," VOA via *Club of Mozambique*, September 29, 2016, clubofmozambique.com/news/new-national-park-mozambique-no-money.

34. Luis Namanha, "Progesso do Programa Tchuma Tchato," 2017. Unpublished report, courtesy Luis Namanha.

35. "Poachers Killed Half Mozambique's Elephants in Five Years," *The Guardian*, May 26, 2015, www.theguardian.com/environment/2015/may/26/poachers-killed-half-mozambiques-elephants-in-five-years.

8. Neighborhood Headquarters—Beira

1. Joseph Hanlon, *Mozambique Political Process Bulletin*, no. 29, December 2003.

2. Ibid.

3. Carter Center, *Observing the 1999 Elections in Mozambique: Final Report* (Atlanta, GA: Democracy Program, Carter Center, 2000).

4. Itumeleng Magetia, "Building Beira: A Municipal Turnaround in Mozambique, 2003–2010" (case study, Initiatives for Successful Societies, Princeton University, 2010).

5. Ibid.

6. See, for instance, "Inventariar depois do assalto," *Savana*, July 16, 2010.

7. Colleen Lowe Morna, "Doing Business in Beira," *Africa Report* 32, no. 4 (1987): 61.

8. Sergio Chichava, "MDM: A New Political Force in Mozambique?" (paper prepared for the conference Election Processes, Liberation Movements and Democratic Change in Africa, Instituto de Estudos Sociais e Económicos [IESE], Maputo, April 8–11, 2010).

9. Portuguese Parliamentary Biography of Jorge Jardim, app.parlamento.pt/PublicacoesOnLine/DeputadosAN_1935-1974/html/pdf/j/jardim_jorge_pereira.pdf.

10. Paul Fauvet, "Roots of Counter-revolution: The Mozambique National Resistance," *Review of African Political Economy*, no. 29 (1984): 108–121, 109.

11. Ibid.

12. Ibid., 110.

13. Chichava, "MDM."

14. Fauvet, "Roots of Counter-revolution," 111.

15. Barnabe Lucas Ncomo, *Uria Simango: um homem, uma causa* (Maputo, Mozambique: Createspace 2012).

16. Ibid.

17. Selected as part of the party's slate, or *bancada*, by leadership. One, Albano Obedias, has since died; "Daviz Simango reestrutura vereações no município da Beira," *O País*, February 26, 2015.

18. "Obedias Simango obrigou comerçantes a declararem em seu favor ao tribunal," *Diário de Moçambique*, November 16, 2011, 2.

19. Joseph Hanlon and Marcelo Mosse, "Mozambique's Elite—Finding Its Way in a Globalized World and Returning to Old Development Models" (working paper 2010/105, United Nations University, World Institute for Development Economics Research, UNU-WIDER, 2010), oro.open.ac.uk/23271/1/wp2010-105%255B1%255D.pdf.

20. Ibid.

21. Marcelo Mosse, "Can Mozambique's New President Lead the Fight against Corruption?" in "Oiling the Wheels of Imperialism," *Review of African Political Economy* 32, nos. 104/105 (2005): 431–36.

22. Ibid.

23. "Mozambique's Valentina Guebuza 'Killed by Husband,'" BBC News, December 15, 2016; See, for example, Joseph Hanlon, *Mozambique News Reports & Clippings*, no. 288, May 11, 2015, www.bit.ly/mozamb.

24. Adriano Nuvunga and José Adalima, "Mozambique Democratic Movement (MDM): An Analysis of a New Opposition Party in Mozambique," *American Review of Politics* 14 (2001): 665–84.

25. Chichava, "MDM"; "Renamo contesta prémios atribuidos a Daviz Simango," *Jornal notícias*, June 19, 2015; Simango has been repeatedly honored by the South-Africa-based organization Professional Management Review-Africa. See also www.pmrafrica.com.

26. Mozambique follows a European-style model of electoral politics, with party leadership choosing candidates to represent the ticket in each election, or, in the case of city council and the national legislature, simply designating a list of people to serve as representatives after the election has been held, according to the party's total share of the vote. Chichava, "MDM."

27. Chichava, "MDM."

28. Magetia, "Building Beira"; Chicava, "MDM."

29. In 2009, MDM was barred from competing in all but four constituencies in the parliamentary elections. The National Elections Commission (CNE) cited inadequate documentation in MDM's candidate lists but didn't disclose any particulars as to why specific candidates had been excluded. "The justifications given by the CNE are not at all convincing," read a statement by a joint delegation from the European Union, the United States, and several other Western governments issued after meetings with the CNE's president and head of state Armando Guebuza. Opposition newspapers denounced a conspiracy by "FRenamo" to keep MDM out of the elections.

30. Lutero now serves as the head of MDM's delegation in parliament.

31. One for Maputo City and two for Maputo Province. For a complete list, see www.mdm.org.mz.

32. Cesaltina Chefalquina, "Governo distrital de Beira accusa municipio de usurpação de poder, após Daviz Simango inaugurar infra-estruturas que não são do CMB," *Diário de Moçambique*, February 8, 2016, 2.

33. Great photos are available at Moçambique Terra Queimada, ambicanos .blogspot.com/2016/02/o-presidente-do-conselho-municipal-da.html.

34. Magetia, "Building Beira."

35. "Mozambique: Beira City Council Defies Ruling on Houses," All Africa.com, December 16, 2004.

36. Edy Ndapona, "Beira: imóveis em litigio entre a Frelimo e o município: Daviz Simango deposita recurso ao tribunal supremo," *Canal de Moçambique*, March 2, 2007.

37. David Morton, "From Racial Discrimination to Class Segregation in Postcolonial Urban Mozambique," *Geographies of Privilege* (2013); James D. Sidaway and Marcus Power, "Sociospatial Transformations in the 'Postsocialist' Periphery: The Case of Maputo, Mozambique," *Environment and Planning A* 27, no. 9 (1995): 1463–91. In addition to rental properties and businesses owned by Mozambicans. See David Morton, "Age of Concrete."

38. "Inventariar depois do assalto," *Savana*, July 16, 2010.

39. Fernando Mbanze, Mediafax, Maputo, January, 3 2007, macua. blogs.com/moambique_para_todos/2007/01/page/5; the penalty of 792,502 meticais, at the December 2006 exchange rate of 25.893544 per dollar, works out to roughly $30,600.

40. Adelino Timoteo, "Munícipes frustram entrega de edifícios municipais ao partido Frelimo," *Canal de Moçambique*, July 13, 2010.

41. Mbanze, Mediafax.

42. Ndapona, "Beira: imóveis em litigio entre a Frelimo e o município."

43. José Chirinza, "Braço de ferro na Beira," *Savana*, July 24, 2010.

44. "Advogado da Frelimo atira culpa ao presidente do tribunal," *O País*, July 23, 2010.

45. Ibid.

46. Paulo Machava, "Guebuza dialoga com Daviz Simango," *Diário de Notícias*, July 30, 2007, macua.blogs.com/moambique_para_todos/2010/08 /guebuza-dialoga-com-daviz-simango.html. Machava edited the *Diário* as well as writing for *Savana* and Rádio Moçambique. In 2015, he was assassinated on a walk near his house at sunrise, in what many saw as retaliation for organizing protests to protect the economist Carlos Castel-Branco from prosecution for an open letter to President Guebuza. Nara Madeira and Michel Santos, "Jornalista moçambicano Paulo Machava assassinado," *Euronews*, August 28, 2015.

47. Eurico Dança, "Daviz Simango manipula e usa munícipes como escudos," *Diário de Moçambique*, July 30, 2010.

48. Ibid.

49. "Dom Jaime defende construção de novas sedes de bairros na Beira," *O país*, August 23, 2010.

50. Eurico Dança, "Tribunal ordena entrega de 14 instalações à Frelimo," *Diário de Moçambique*, November 16, 2010, 2.

51. "Sedes de bairros estão a ser entregues pacificamente," *O País*, November 18, 2010.

52. Eurico Dança, "Davis Simango promete para breve início de construção de novas sedes," *Diário de Moçambique*, November 22, 2010, 2.

53. "Daviz Simango apela união de autarcas beirenses para construção de novas sedes de bairros," *A Verdade*, November 22, 2010.

54. See Manuel dos Santos Mussanema's Facebook profile.

55. Chichava, "MDM."

9. The Selling Life—Maputo

1. William Finnegan, *A Complicated War*, 4.

About the Author

Rowan Moore Gerety is a journalist based in Miami. His writing has appeared in *The Atlantic, Foreign Policy,* the *Miami Herald, Slate,* and *Virginia Quarterly Review,* and he has produced radio stories for NPR and PRI. He studied anthropology at Columbia University and was a Fulbright fellow in Mozambique. This is his first book.